the Firearms Dictionary

R. A. STEINDLER

the Firearms Dictionary

STACKPOLE
BOOKS

THE FIREARMS DICTIONARY
Copyright© 1970 by
THE STACKPOLE COMPANY
Published by
STACKPOLE BOOKS
Cameron and Kelker Streets
Harrisburg, Pa. 17105

Standard Book Number 8117-0614-1
Library of Congress Catalog Card Number 75-107957

PRINTED IN U.S.A.

TO

LUCY

FOREWORD

The concept for THE FIREARMS DICTIONARY goes back to the fall of 1964 when I completed the text of the "Modern ABC of Guns." While writing that book, I found that many gun terms were used differently by various writers, that some terms even had conflicting definitions tacked onto them, that errors and misconceptions had been perpetuated over the years in the gun literature.

This prompted me to set up a file system of the most frequently encountered gun terms and after a few months, I had collected better than 6000 file cards. In the spring of 1965 I began the research that has culminated in THE FIREARMS DICTIONARY.

It soon became obvious that a comprehensive firearms dictionary would be the endeavor of a staff of skilled researchers for several decades. To cover the entire history and development of firearms and firearms terminology, from the day of the Chinese fireworks and Roger Bacon to the latest sporting arms developments, would have required several large tomes. Anyone who has ever become involved with guns as a hobby or sphere of interest must realize quickly that there are countless areas of special interest.

Consider, for a moment, the huge field encompassing self-contained metallic rifle cartridges—there are the European ones in the metric sys-

7

tem, and the British sporting cartridges, and the U.S. cartridges. Add to this the many military variations, the changes in bullet designs, headstamps on military and contract cartridges, developmental cartridges—both sporting and military—and there is one area so vast that an all-inclusive book would be virtually impossible to compile since much of the original source material has been lost or is simply unobtainable. Add to this the historic evolution of the cartridge, the various developments in that area due to changes in the ignition systems, and the men who, in one way or the other, materially contributed either to the firing mechanism or the cartridge.

Similarly, there are the areas of special interest, such as the development of military small arms, the histories of gun companies now long out of business, antique guns, and last but not least, the thousands of men who devoted their lives to firearms research and development. A mere listing of these names alone and delving into the achievements of some of these men, like Dr. Franklin W. Mann or Charles Newton, would require several volumes.

Primarily designed for the shooter, hunter, firearms hobbyist, THE FIREARMS DICTIONARY offers a single source of reference for many of the terms that are either hard to understand or which have never been completely explained in any of the popular texts. THE FIREARMS DICTIONARY differs from the usual dictionary in that it goes beyond the mere defining of a term or word. Wherever possible the textual matter, as well as the photographs and the drawings, further explain the term itself and its relationship with other terms of our gun language.

As our everyday language changes, so does gun terminology. Take a classic example: The crosshairs of a scope are—or rather were—known as reticle. Some gun writers began to call them reticules, but reticules were the little knit bags our grandmothers used to carry. Then Webster's Dictionary suddenly gave us a choice—the crosshairs could be called reticle or reticule.

The British have given us many of their gun terms, yet others are totally foreign to us. If a British friend tells you he is having "a spot of trouble with the kicker," he simply means that the ejector of his gun—and here he means shotgun and most likely a side-by-side—isn't working right.

Whenever possible, three or four sources were consulted before the final definition of a term was written. To help readers broaden their understanding of firearms and firearms terminology, I have added a short bibliography. These are the basic source references I have used in collecting the material contained in this book.

8

How To Use This Book

While it is a simple matter to look up one word or term, the concept of the book is such that it will guide the interested reader to other terms and definitions.

To simplify listings and make possible the use of a specific illustration under one heading, the main category is listed first, thus you will find: BULLET, ARMOR PIERCING, rather than armor piercing bullet under the A's.

Categories In order to give the reader the most comprehensive presentation possible, the subject matter was divided into categories, alphabetically grouped of course. Thus, all actions described are to be found under ACTION, bullets are described in detail under the main heading of BULLET, and so on. In a few cases there have been exceptions, and these were made only because common usage dictates such a listing, or where a term such as Garden Gun would be sought under Garden gun, rather than under the main category, GUN, GARDEN.

Cross references In the text matter, many cross references appear, and these are indicated by *(q.v.)*. This means that the term preceding the *(q.v.)* has a separate listing, and that the cross reference contains material that is germane to the discussion. Thus, under BEDDING, there are the following cross references: Barrel Channel, Free-floating, and Glass-bedding.

Secondary references In many definitions, it was found that other terms were often used which, although of importance, were not deemed to be of primary importance. At the end of such discussions as on BEDDING, there is a secondary reference, which, in this instance, is listed as *"Also see:* Inletting." These secondary references were felt to be important to give the reader the desired understanding of the subject matter, and some cross references (*Also see:*) contain numerous such listings.

Some listings contain phrases or terms which are covered in some detail under a different heading or under a different category. Sometimes these references, such as BEAVERTAIL FOREND, FOREND, SPLINTER FOREND encompass several entries, and references germane to the term under discussion have been set in CAPITAL LETTERS within the text matter, especially when that particular definition was long and only one reference is made to the capitalized phrase or word. For instance, SPLINTER FOREND is referred to BEAVERTAIL FOREND, and in that definition the words SPLINTER FOREND are capitalized to make it easier to locate the term in the text.

Choice of definitions   We glibly talk about proof tests and blue pills. Why these red-painted proofloads were ever called blue pills appears to be a mystery, but to retain accuracy of definition categorization, there is an entry for BLUE PILL which refers the reader to the more accurate term PROOFLOAD. Similarly, we often hear that the BEARING SUR-FACE is not large enough when in actuality we are talking about the bearing surface of a bullet, more accurately known as BULLET BEAR-ING SURFACE.

Definitions omitted   Some years ago I wrote an article which consisted in its entirety of gun terms that have become part and parcel of our every-day language. Such terms as trigger happy, shotgun wedding, flash in the pan, straight shooter, etc., have no place in a firearms dictionary, but they can be found in any of the current dictionaries of American slan-guage.

Tradenames   Every manufacturer and many importers of guns, am-munition, scopes, and related shooting equipment give their products an identifying name which is often protected by a trademark or tradename. Some tradenames have been so popularized that the name itself has be-come representative of any product that incorporates one or more fea-tures of the original product to which the tradename had been applied. In some instances, such as Nosler bullets, the term is limited, that is, only bullets of a certain configuration and made by the Leupold-Nosler concern are considered. However, while the Nosler bullet is best known to handloaders, two commercial ammunition distributors incorporate Nosler bullets into their ammunition.

In some instances, the tradename is zealously—and—jealously pro-tected by the legal holder of the tradename, but in other instances, es-pecially in the area of proprietary cartridges, the name of the company that should follow the caliber designation is often omitted—even by the companies holding these rights.

Some tradenames have been used so widely that many shooters are not aware that the name is protected by law. So for instance, the name of Georg Luger has been tacked on to the description of the German Pistole Parabellum 08, 1908 being the year the gun was accepted by the German army. While the gun is still called by its official name in Germany, and this being sometimes shortened to Parabellum Pistole, the toggle-linkage gun in the U.S. is commonly known as the Luger pistol. However, the name Luger in this conjunction is reserved, by tradename law, for the exclusive use of the concern holding the tradename and may be applied only to those guns made by or for that concern.

10

Thus, tradenames have been incorporated in THE FIREARMS DIC-TIONARY only if the name has become a part of our gun language or when it is so unique and widely used that, as in the case of the Nosler bullets, it has found wide acceptance.

Mathematical Formulas Only those formulas which are of impor-tance for shooters with but a slight interest in ballistics have been included and the ones that have been incorporated, have been reduced to their simplest terms. Some of the ballistics calculations done by many gun buffs require the use of higher mathematics, and lacking that background, they would become meaningless in a volume of this nature.

Tables Conversion tables from the metric system to the inch system, or weight tables, and similar tables and graphs have been omitted since a great many other books contain them and since they would have added nothing of importance to the basic concept and premise on which this book was founded.

Photographs and sketches The graphic presentation of the gun part under discussion was felt to be of sufficient importance to warrant sacri-ficing the relationship of the actual size of the item to scale. Thus, a trap or skeet field is of course much, much bigger than a wheellock, and sim-ilarly, some of the close-up photographs may give the reader the impres-sion that the item under discussion is considerably bigger than it is in actuality. However, several trial and error runs in trying to keep all art work to scale produced some problems and I felt it best to sacrifice actual scale to visual clarity.

R.A. Steindler
Erewhon Farm, Ill.

A

ABERRATION imperfect image of an object when it is viewed through a single lens or a system of lenses. It is due to failure of light rays to pass through a single point in the lens or lenses after refraction. Six aberrations are recognized: chromatic, spherical, coma, astigmatic, curvature of field & distortion.

ABRASION normal & abnormal. Normal bore abrasion is caused by passage of bullets through bore. Scratches or abrasion of bore can also be caused by use of poor cleaning equipment or by firing bullets to which grit & other foreign materials have adhered. This is a mechanical process. *Also see:* Barrel Corrosion; Barrel Erosion; Bore Leading; Fouling.

ACCELERATOR device in automatic & semiautomatic arms to facilitate & increase rearward travel of bolt. It applies leverage at mechanical point of advantage on bolt, promotes faster bolt travel, hence increases rapidity or cyclic rate of fire.

ACCOUTREMENT all equipment carried by a soldier on outside of uniform, but does not include weapons. Belt buckles, canteens, etc.

ACCURACY ability of a firearm to group or place projectiles into a small group or cluster at a specific distance. It decreases as range or angle of trajectory increases. Accuracy of semiautomatic pistols depends on care with which functioning parts are assembled & the smooth functioning of these parts. In a rifle,

A 3 shot group at 100 yards measured only 15/16″ from 340 Weatherby Magnum with 250 gr. Nosler bullets. Size of group, not location, is important when considering accuracy.

it depends on care with which barrel was made, the perfection of the bore, the bedding & stocking of the rifle. Ammunition & shooting conditions also affect accuracy.

ACCURACY BLOCK   small aluminum part especially designed for Remington M740, to prevent barrel stress. It is inserted between forward end of forearm & gas port lug on barrel.

ACHROMATIC LENS   has compound design that refracts colors almost identically & equally, thus does not produce unequal refraction of various colors. Single lenses usually have unequal refraction. Most spotting & rifle scopes have achromatic lenses.

ACP   abbr. for Automatic Colt

Pistol, used in conjunction with caliber designation such as 25 ACP, 32 ACP, 380 ACP, 45 ACP.

ACTION   breech mechanism by which the gun is loaded, fired, & unloaded. Action also contains either extractor or ejector that removes the empty cartridge case once a gun has been fired.

ACTION, AUTOMATIC   fires cartridges or shells as long as the trigger is depressed & cartridges remain in the magazine. Ownership of full automatic arms is illegal, term is often misused when semiautomatic action is meant. Semiautomatic guns fire one round for each time the trigger is pulled until the magazine is empty. *Also see:* Action, Semiautomatic; Automatic Action.

ACTION, AYDT   a German single shot action where breechblock is curved & has an extension that is hinged below & forward of chamber. By lowering trigger guard lever, breechblock moves downward in an arc. These actions are relatively rare, were once widely used in precision Schuetzen rifles.

ACTION, BALLARD   once one of the best single shot actions made in the U.S. & produced by a number of firearms companies. *Also see:* Single Shot.

ACTION BAR FLATS   *see* Flats.

ACTION BAR LOCK   *see* Action Slide Lock.

ACTION BARS   also known as

14

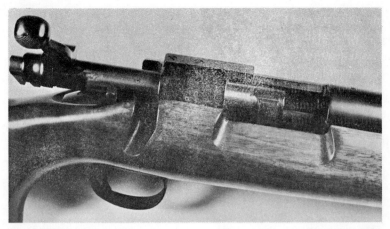

Typical bolt action rifle. Shown is a target grade rifle, but action designs do not vary much from maker to maker.

operating rods, connect forend & breechblock of pump gun, or gas cylinder & breechblock of semiautomatic rifle or shotgun. Depending on design, there may be one or two bars or rods. *Also see:* Action Slide Lock.

ACTION, BLOWBACK   found in automatic & semiautomatic guns where no mechanical locking system is used. When such a gun is fired, the weight of hammer, slide, & other mobile parts, as well as recoil spring, combine to keep action closed. Total weight of parts is greater than bullet weight & projectile begins its travel before breech opens rearward due to residual gas pressure. *Also see:* Action, Semiautomatic.

ACTION, BLOW FORWARD found in automatic & semiautomatic guns. The breech is standing or immobile, but the barrel moves forward with pressure of expanding gases to open the action & eject the fired cartridge case. When ejection is completed, spring returns barrel to orig-

inal position against standing breech. As barrel moves back, gun is reloaded & cocked.

ACTION, BOLT   breech closure is accomplished by moving breechblock or bolt in line with bore. This type of action is the oldest of modern actions. Bolt is operated by means of bolt handle *(q.v.)*. When cocking & feeding of fresh cartridge from magazine or clip is accomplished by merely moving bolt handle rearward, action is of STRAIGHT-PULL design, e.g. Swiss Schmidt-Rubin. If bolt handle is turned to lock or unlock one or more bolt locking lugs *(q.v.)*, it is a TURN-BOLT action. *Also see:* T-Bolt.

ACTION, BOX LOCK   typified by Parker shotgun in the U.S., the Westley Richards in England, is generally considered not to be as strong as the side lock action *(q.v.)*. Developed by Anson & Deeley, the box lock is hammerless, has two disadvantages: hammer pin must be placed directly below knee of action which

15

is its weakest spot & action walls must be thinned out to receive locks. These are inserted from below into large slots in action body, which is then closed with a plate. Greener cross-bolt, when made correctly, overcomes many of the box lock weaknesses.

ACTION, DROPPING BLOCK designed in Germany by Ernst F. Büchel, this type of single shot became the basis for many fine target rifles. Most of these actions are hammerless, often have reversed front trigger which sets rear trigger. *Also see:* Trigger, Set.

ACTION, FALLING BLOCK either extracts or ejects fired case. These actions are rugged due to solid breechblock that travels up & down in the rear of the chamber. When block is in locked position, cartridge in chamber is locked in place by solid steel. Typical are the English Farquharson, Winchester, Stevens, Ballard & Sharps Borchardt actions.

ACTION, FARQUHARSON probably the strongest single shot action, it is also the best known British single shot action. A number of different designs were manufactured, complete guns in good to excellent condition are highly desirable collector's specimens. The action is often used, in conjunction with a new barrel & new stock, to make up varmint rifles which are usually based on rimmed cases such as the 30-30, the British 303. Many of the original guns were made up for match use, others were chambered for big game cartridges, since the strength of the action is capable of withstanding the higher chamber pressures, and therefore the back thrust of the more powerful cartridges.

ACTION, FLOBERT ROLLING BLOCK one of the earliest single shot designs, was first made for parlor cartridges & 22 Shorts. By drawing hammer to rear, the pivoting breechblock is drawn back, the

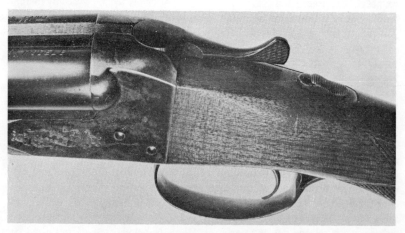

U.S. made box lock gun in 20 ga. with single non-selective trigger.

A side-by-side 12 ga. shotgun with hinged frame action and double triggers.

breech is then exposed for loading. The firing pin may be on the hammer, in which case the block is pierced to allow pin to make contact with head of cartridge. Or the firing pin may go through the block, being activated by falling hammer. Guns using this action are usually chambered for cartridges which develop fairly low gas pressure levels, such as the 4 mm, the 177, the 22's & the 6 mm's.

ACTION, GUEDES-CASTRO DROPPING BLOCK adopted in 1885 by Portugal as military action. Some references indicate that Guedes should be spelled Geddes. Rifles were made in Austria, were chambered for the 8mm cartridge.

ACTION, HAENEL-AYDT ARC BLOCK relatively rare single shot, made by Haenel of Suhl, Germany. It is characterized by one or two levers at the side of the action

for cartridge extraction & take-down. The same dropping block system, but with internal cartridge extraction, was also used by Udo Anschütz.

ACTION, HINGED FRAME uses a standing breech, is found on firearms with one or more barrels. Barrels are hinged to breech so that, when action is opened, the jointed barrels swing up or down, or pivot sideways for loading & unloading. Opening of action is usually accomplished by lever atop breech, although other systems may be used. *Also see:* Action, Top-break; Action, Under-lever; Top-lever.

ACTION, LEVER once used in rifles & shotguns, lever action rifles are still popular, but shotguns using this system are now collector's items. There is an increased use of the system in single shot rifles as well as rifle/shotgun combination guns.

17

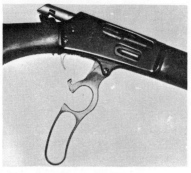
Lever action rifle.

Breech closure is accomplished by a lever linked to breechblock so that operating lever back & forth opens & closes the action. Lever is usually located underneath receiver or frame, forms the trigger guard, & extends to the rear to the pistol grip or the wrist of the stock (*see* Stock, Small of the). Guns with this type of action usually do not have separate safeties, but hammer is placed on safety notch *(q.v.)*.

ACTION, LOCKED BREECH so named because breechblock is locked to barrel & recoil unlocks the

system after bullet has left the barrel. Toggle of the Luger (Pistole Parabellum) semiautomatic pistol is typical of this action. *Also see:* Toggle Joint; Pistole Parabellum.

ACTION, MARTINI named after the Swiss inventor who improved the Peabody single shot action by substituting the outside hammer with a concealed spiral spring striker or firing pin. This action was widely used, is based on breechblock that moves down to permit insertion or extraction of cartridge. Block moves up when lever is moved to the rear, & block movement is entirely within receiver or breech frame. When block is in firing position, it is one of the strongest single shot actions.

ACTION, MAUSER an improvement of Dreyse's needle gun, is considered the major firearms design improvement for rifles using the bolt action system. Change consisted of camming the action by raising & lowering bolt handle. Peter Paul Mauser's work has been the basis of most currently produced bolt action

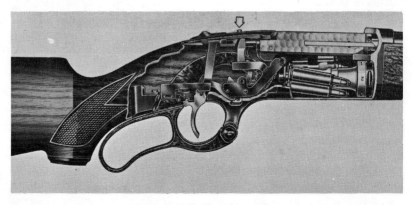
Savage Model 99 with rotating magazine.

guns. He also invented the system of cocking the gun on opening of bolt, which leads to easier operation because of greater leverage produced. Cocking on opening eases work of closing bolt on dirty or poorly sized cases, an important military consideration. Basic Mauser design is in world-wide use today.

ACTION PARTS OF DOUBLE SHOTGUN *see* Shotgun, Double.

ACTION PORT is a cut or opening in the action of a semiautomatic,

The operating handle seated in the breech bolt closes the action port when bolt is in closed and locked position.

lever action or pump gun which allows single feeding of cartridges, as well as ejection of fired cases.

ACTION, PUMP also known as SLIDE or TROMBONE, a type of action found in long guns (rifles & shotguns) where the shooter moves the forend back to eject a fired case, & forward to chamber a fresh round. The forward movement also cocks the gun, making it ready to fire. Prevalent in shotguns & 22 rimfire rifles, the action is also used for a centerfire rifle.

ACTION, RECOIL OPERATED *see* Action, Semiautomatic.

ACTION, RETARDED BLOW-BACK blowback action *(q.v.)*

where rearward motion is slowed down by mechanical means to permit bullet to leave the barrel before action opens fully.

ACTION, RISING BLOCK usually employed with 22 caliber guns or the light German, or metric *(q.v.),* calibers, is a single shot action that has not seen extensive use lately except in the Belgian Flobert-Warnant guns. Two arms of the breechblock, extending forward along the barrel, are elevated when the hammer is cocked. These arms pivot on barrel pins, & as the breechblock is raised, the extractor is activated. Some of the German guns using this system have the firing pin in the breechblock.

ACTION, ROLLING BLOCK single shot action, designed in the U.S. and widely used in early Remington arms. Also known as the REMINGTON-RIDER action, the breechblock, actuated by a lever, rotates

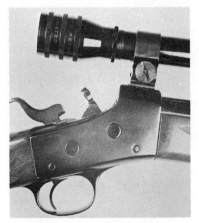

This Remington Rolling Block action was equipped with new barrel and stock. Note high scope base which is needed so that there is access to hammer and rolling block.

down and back from the chamber. Firing pin is contained in block, is activated by hammer fall.

ACTION, SEMIAUTOMATIC also known as AUTOLOADING or SELF-LOADING & incorrectly as "auto" or "automatic." A rifle, shotgun or pistol that is loaded manually for the first round. Upon pulling the trigger, the gun fires, ejects the fired case, cocks the firing mechanism & feeds a fresh round from the magazine. The trigger must be released between shots, must be activated for each round fired until the magazine is empty. There are 3 basic semiauto actions: recoil operated, blowback, & gas operated.

RECOIL OPERATED: Typical of short recoil operated guns is the 45 ACP pistol, the Walther P38, the Mauser pistols, the Luger (see Pistole Parabellum). Long recoil operated actions, such as many semiautomatic shotguns, have barrel & bolt recoil backwards fully, with both parts locked solidly, compressing the springs of both parts. The bolt is caught by a hook. As the barrel moves forward, it separates itself from the bolt which holds the case. When barrel is nearly fully forward, it releases the hook that holds the bolt which, in its forward movement, chambers another round from the magazine.

BLOWBACK: see Action, Blowback.

GAS OPERATED: Gases from burning powder are siphoned off, activating a gas piston below the barrel. The piston rod exerts force on the action rod or bar which is linked to bolt & counter recoil spring. The rod

unlocks the bolt & moves it back, extracting & ejecting the fired case. Simultaneously, action is cocked again, & counter recoil springs move bolt, rod & piston forward. Bolt strips fresh cartridge from magazine, chambers it, & force locks bolt again.

ACTION, SHARPS best known of the American single shot actions, was made in many models; saw military service during Civil War. A falling block action, it was later incorporated, with modifications, into the famed Sharps Borchardt rifle.

ACTION, SIDE LOCK British design, forms the basis for the best side-by-side shotguns & rifles. In the BAR-ACTION side lock, the mainspring is located forward of the ac-

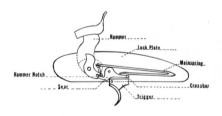

tion, but if mainspring is located to the rear of the action, the design is known as the BACK-ACTION side lock. British double rifles are usually made with the inherently stronger back-action side lock. Side lock guns are often made with detachable locks or firing mechanisms.

ACTION, SINGLE SHOT when self-contained cartridges (see Cartridge, Self-contained) became popular, single shot actions were designed that allowed easy extraction of the fired case & insertion of a fresh cartridge. Rifles built on these single shot actions established an enviable record for accuracy, & numerous American & European arms designers developed such actions. Many of the single shot actions are highly desirable, & a number of original factory rifles qualify as collectors' specimens. These actions vary in several design features, often bear the name of the inventor or company that produced them. *See:* Action, Aydt; Action, Ballard; Action, Rolling Block, etc. *Also see:* Single Shot.

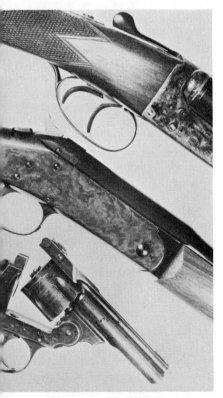

Gun at top is a side-by-side 20 ga. shotgun; in the center, a single barrel rifle; at the bottom, a revolver. All have top-break actions.

ACTION, SLIDE   *see* Action, Pump.

ACTION SLIDE LOCK   or bar lock, is a device that locks the slide or bar of a pump gun in the forward position when the gun is cocked, so that the action is closed when gun fires. If gun is to be opened without firing, slide lock must be operated manually.

ACTION, TOP-BREAK   most frequently encountered in side-by-side, O/U, & single shot shotguns, double rifles, combination guns such as drillings *(q.v.)*, & inexpensive single shot rifles. System was also used in revolvers, notably those where barrel & cylinder were mounted on a hinged frame. Revolvers of this kind are often known as TIP-UP guns. Hinged frame firearms use a standing breech with one or more barrels so hinged to receiver that, when action is opened by means of top-lever *(q.v.)*, barrel or barrels swing down for extraction or loading.

ACTION, TRAP DOOR   a single shot that opens by pivoting breechblock up & forward. Best known trap door rifle was that designed by E.S. Allin of Springfield Armory.

ACTION, TRIGGER PLATE   *see* Trigger Plate.

ACTION, TROMBONE   *see* Action, Pump.

ACTION, UNDER-LEVER   another means of opening & closing hinged frame or top-break actions

21

Old side-by-side top-break with underlever
opening system. Lever fits below trigger guard,
swings to right to permit opening of gun.

(q.v.). Lever is usually located below
or in trigger guard.

ADAPTER   a device used for training purposes that permits firing of a
firearm with ammunition usually of
smaller caliber than gun is chambered
for.

ADAPTER, GRIP   *see* Grip
Adapter.

AFGHAN STOCK   *see* Stock,
Afghan.

AIR RESISTANCE   one of the
two forces which affect the flight of a
projectile (bullet or shot). a 152 gr.
30-06 bullet with a muzzle velocity of
2700 fps meets almost 1 1/4 lb. air
resistance. The other force acting on
a projectile is gravity *(q.v.)*.

AIR SPACE   the space not taken
up by either powder charge or bullet
base in a loaded cartridge case.

AIR SPIRAL   the turbulence created by an unbalanced bullet in flight
as it meets air resistance *(q.v.)*.

ALL GAUGE   also known as ALL

BORE. In skeet *(q.v.)*, an event open
to guns 12 gauge & smaller.

ALTITUDE & EFFECT ON ZERO
gun zeroed at low elevation will not
place bullets materially off-zero if
fired at high elevation. Effect of
altitude can, therefore, be ignored.

AMERICAN PRIMER   *see* Primer, Boxer.

AMMUNITION   today is self-
contained within a cartridge case. In
shotshells this case is known as HULL
or CASE, may be of paper or plastic.
Metallic ammunition, often termed
AMMO, describes rifle & handgun
ammunition in metallic cases, usually
brass. Brass shotshells were popular
at one time, can still be obtained, but
must be handloaded. Ignition of
ammunition is by means of a primer
(q.v.). Atop the primer is the powder
charge which is ignited by the primer
explosion. As the smokeless propellant powder burns, the combustion
gases under pressure force the projectile out of the case or hull & into
the barrel.

ANGLE OF DEPARTURE   the
vertical angle formed between the line
of bore *(q.v.)* when the gun is pointed
at the target & the line of bore the
moment the bullet leaves the muzzle.

ANGLE OF ELEVATION   the
vertical angle formed between the line
of sight to the target & the axis of the
bore. To obtain approximate angle of
elevation of a given cartridge at a
given distance, first compute total
drop of the bullet at that distance by

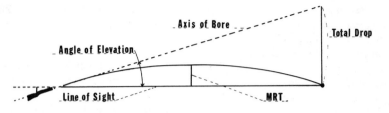

Angle of Elevation.

multiplying the midrange trajectory by 4. Angle of elevation is then expressed in minutes of angle, based on drop of 1″ for each 100 yds. approximately. For example, a total drop of 6″ at 200 yds. is equal to an angle of 3 minutes (*see* Minute of Angle), based on MRT *(q.v.)* of 1.5″.

ANNEAL   to heat metal, specifically brass cartridge cases, to a low heat level, then cool quickly. Annealing makes brass more ductile. Manufacturers anneal cases several times during manufacture, while handloaders use process during forming of obsolete or hard to get cartridge cases.

ANNULAR RIM   *see* Cartridge, Crispin.

ANSON-DEELEY LOCK   lock system used widely on the better box lock side-by-side shotguns. Deeley also designed a special ejector for this action which often is erroneously called the Anson-Deeley ejector.

ANVIL   *see* Primer.

APERTURE SIGHTS   *see* Sight, Aperture.

ARMORY   place for storing mili-

tary small arms; sometimes designates governmental facilities for manufacturing arms & ballistics research, such as Springfield Armory.

ARQUEBUS   *see* Harquebus.

ARSENAL   same meaning as armory *(q.v.)*, also designates such installations as Frankford & Picatinny Arsenals.

ASSEMBLY   any group of parts functioning together & often interlocking with each other, such as trigger assembly, bolt assembly, magazine assembly.

AUTOLOADING   *see* Action, Semiautomatic.

AUTOMATIC ACTION   similar

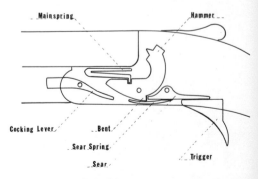

Anson-Deeley lock system.

23

in design to the semiautomatic action, except that the arm continues to load, lock & fire so long as there are cartridges in the magazine & so long as the trigger remains continually depressed. Fully automatic machine guns & rifles are capable of sustained AUTOMATIC FIRE with a high cyclic rate, that is the number of shots fired during a given time interval, usually a minute.

AUTOMATIC REVOLVER   is a gun oddity. The British Webley-Fosberry automatic revolver is the best known example of this design. Gun fires like a semiautomatic pistol, has configuration of a revolver. Union Arms Co., of Toledo, Ohio, also made such a gun around 1904.

AUTOMATIC SAFETY   *see* Safety, Automatic.

AUXILIARY BARREL or TUBE, *see* Barrel Insert, Subcaliber Barrel.

AUXILIARY CARTRIDGE   *see* Cartridge, Auxiliary.

AXIS OF BORE   an imaginary straight line through the center of the bore of a gun.

AXIS PIN   sometimes called CENTER PIN, aligns cylinder of revolver in the frame of the gun.

AYDT ACTION   *see* Action, Aydt. *Also see:* Single Shot.

B

BACK-ACTION   *see* Action, Side lock.

BACKLASH   undesirable continued rearward movement of the trigger after the firing pin or hammer has been released. Term is also applied to sight adjustment screw that fails to move the sight the proper distance in the desired direction.

BACKSTRAP   that part of the revolver or pistol frame that is exposed at the rear of the grip.

BACK THRUST   force exerted by gases under pressure in a cartridge case when powder burns. The back thrust of the case head against breechblock or bolt face is considerable. In the 30-06 cartridge with a

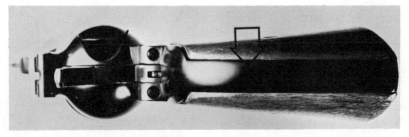

Arrow points to backstrap of a single action 357 Magnum.

pressure level of 50,000 psi, back thrust is 8,674 lb.

BALANCE in a rifle or shotgun is the center of gravity where the gun can be made to balance. Good balance is highly desirable in a hunting gun.

BALL or bullet. Now used in military circles primarily, word refers back to the days when only round balls, cast from lead, were used. Ball ammunition is jacketed, military ammunition.

BALL, FRANGIBLE bullet that breaks up readily when it hits a target or backstop without inflicting damage to the target.

BALL, HARD usually a fully jacketed bullet, but term is sometimes misused when reference is made to a very hard cast lead bullet. The Colt 45 pistol for competition has the feeding ramp milled for hard ball ammunition, soft ball cartridges will fail to function through a "hard ball" gun.

BALL, PATCHED metal jacketed, full metal jacketed (FMJ), or cased bullet.

BALLARD ACTION *see* Action, Ballard. *Also see:* Single Shot.

BALLISTIC COEFFICIENT reflects the bullet's ability to overcome air resistance *(q.v.)*. Mathematically, it is the ratio of the sectional density *(q.v.)* of the bullet to its coefficient of form *(q.v.)*.

26

BALLISTICS the science of a projectile in motion. This includes range, trajectory, velocity, penetration, killing & knock-down power, etc.

BALLISTICS, EXTERNAL or EXTERIOR concerns the projectile's flight after it leaves the muzzle.

BALLISTICS, INTERNAL or INTERIOR considers everything that occurs to projectile & cartridge case or shell from the moment the firing pin hits the primer. Barrel shape, weight, twist, number of lands & grooves, barrel length; cartridge case properties; burning properties of powder; projectile weight, length, & shape; pressure of gases—all these factors affect internal ballistics.

BALLISTITE *see* Powder, Ballistite.

BALL POWDER *see* Powder, Ball.

BAR part of a gun frame that extends below the barrel or barrels in a top-break gun. The bar has cutouts for the barrel lugs, contains hinge pin & lock parts, often houses

Typical bar of side-by-side English shotgun.

the gun's bolting mechanism. In some gun designs, the bar also contains a major part of the ejector system.

BAR-ACTION *see* Action, Side Lock.

BARLEYCORN SIGHT *see* Sight, Barleycorn.

BAR LOCK *see* Action Slide Lock.

BARREL the steel tube of a rifle, shotgun, handgun or air gun through which a projectile travels towards its target. A barrel may be rifled (*see* Rifling) as for rifles, handguns & some airguns, or its interior surface may be smooth as in shotguns & airguns not designed for competitive shooting. The projectile travels the length of the barrel from breech to muzzle & then begins its free travel toward the target.

BARREL ARRANGEMENTS are standardized to some degree. The side-by-side & O/U shotguns, as well as combination rifle/shotgun arrangements are frequently seen. The German drillings have two shotgun barrels with one rifle barrel centered below. Double rifles, as used on dangerous African game, have the two rifled barrels side-by-side. Double guns, either rifled or smoothbored, make possible a very fast second shot, while the various combination guns *(q.v.)* give the hunter the instant choice between shotgun & rifle.

BARREL BAND a metal band, either fixed or adjustable, around the forend of a gun that holds the barrel to the stock.

BARREL BLANK a barrel that is bored & rifled, but not chambered or threaded for an action.

BARREL CHANNEL is the groove in the forend part of a stock *(q.v.)* that has been hollowed out or inletted so that it will contain & support a part of the barrel. The wood in the barrel channel should be sealed so that moisture cannot enter it, thus warping the stock & thereby affecting accuracy of the gun.

BARREL, CONTOURED often used in lightweight sporter rifles to give gun pleasing lines, also helps to reduce barrel weight. Thus, barrels are tapered to various degrees, may be made round on the bottom, hexagonal on top. Barrels for rifles are generally & loosely classified as

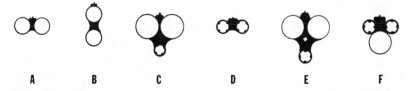

A   B   C   D   E   F

Barrel arrangements. A: Side-by-side shotgun (Doppelflinte) B: Over and under shotgun (Bock-doppelflinte); C: Side-by-side shotgun with rifle barrel below (Drilling); D: Side-by-side rifle (Doppelbüchse); E: Side-by-side shotgun with two rifle barrels below (Vierling); F: Side-by-side rifle with shotgun barrel below (Doppelbüchsdrilling).

sporter barrels, varmint barrels & benchrest barrels, the latter not tapered or contoured in any way & much heavier than varmint barrels.

BARREL CORROSION   is due either to rust, or to the chemical action of primer & powder residues that have collected in the barrel. Even with modern, non-corrosive primers, barrel corrosion can occur.

BARREL, DAMASCUS   made by twisting together strips of unlike metals, then welding them together over a mandrel. These barrels are not safe with modern ammunition, were made during & prior to the last century for shotguns exclusively.

BARRELED ACTION   most commonly used in connection with rifles. A rifle consists of three main parts: stock, action, barrel. In making a custom rifle, an action of some kind is fitted with a suitable barrel, the barreled action is then stocked. Some manufacturers sell barreled actions; fitting of barrel to action & checking headspace are jobs for a gunsmith.

BARREL EROSION   is the gradual wearing out of bore due to projectile friction & hot powder gases.

BARREL EXTENSION   in some semiautomatic shotguns, serves to lock breech against gas pressure. Also encountered in some box lock guns of British origin.

BARREL, FLUTED   barrel with narrow, longitudinal grooves. Of German & Swiss origin, fluting is

used mostly in rifled target arms to give barrels greater stiffness without over-stepping weight limitations. Also encountered in some military rifles, notably Winchester's 224 automatic.

BARREL INSERT   usually a rifled tube, often of smaller caliber, that is placed into a larger barrel, to allow the firing of light recoil am-

Top, barrel insert converts 12 ga. shotgun into single shot 30-30 rifle. Insert below, made in Germany, converts 12 ga. shotgun into single shot 22 LR gun.

munition for practice. However, at least one manufacturer offers insert barrels for shotguns that allow shooting high power, centerfire rifle ammunition. Inserts for handguns, notably semiautomatic pistols, are also popular. Accuracy of barrel inserts is often quite good. *Also see:* Subcaliber Barrel.

BARREL, INTERCHANGEABLE dates back to the early 1500's. Now widely used in shotguns where shooter can purchase more than one barrel for his gun, can change barrels to suit shooting conditions. Usually, interchangeable barrels are in the same caliber or gauge, but some 12 ga. shotgun frames can be fitted with 20 ga. barrels. Another system is that used in the Mauser 66 rifle. With this rifle, shooter can change barrels to fire 30-06, 270 & even 243 through three different barrels. However, cartridges must have the same basic head diameter *(q.v.)* or measurements.

BARREL, LAMINATED   on a shotgun dates that gun to the days of Damascus & twist barrels. Not suitable for modern shells, laminated barrels can only withstand pressures of black powder loads.

BARREL LEADING   *see* Bore Leading.

BARREL LINER   is inserted into some barrels, especially those on machine guns, to prevent rapid wear of barrel due to heat & friction. Modern military small arms with high cyclic rate of fire tend to wear out barrels quickly, hence special steel liners are often used. *Also see:* Barrel Relining.

BARREL LUG   in addition to the usual recoil lug, a barrel lug is used to prevent splitting of stock in heavy recoil rifles. Barrel lug should be an inherent part of barrel, not merely soldered on, since such method of fastening barrel lug could affect accuracy.

BARREL OBSTRUCTION   if not cleared before next round is fired, can bulge or ring barrel, even burst it. Mud & snow are most frequent obstructions, with cleaning patches next, & 20 ga. shell in 12 ga. shotgun barrel another major source of trouble.

BARREL RELINING   done to restore a worn-out or shot-out barrel to usefulness & to avoid complete barrel replacement. Relining sometimes requires reaming out of original barrel, then inserting liner chambered for the same caliber or larger caliber, providing rifle action can handle the new cartridge.

BARREL, SETTING BACK   is a gunsmithing operation which is done for various reasons. Barrel is removed from action, a small portion of shank is cut off, then barrel is rethreaded. If needed the extractor cut is lengthened, barrel is then screwed back into action, & headspace *(q.v.)* is checked.

BARREL SHANK   the chambered end of the barrel that fits into the receiver or action.

BARREL STEP   or steps are most frequently seen on military rifles such as the Japanese Arisaka. One or more such steps are used to reduce barrel diameter from area

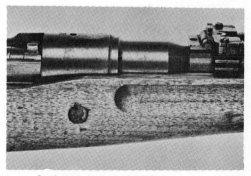

Barrel step on Japanese Arisaka rifle.

where barrel fits into receiver to muzzle. Such a step-down taper has been found to aid accuracy, but step-down tapering has never become popular in U.S.

BARREL STRIKING   the term used when a rough-turned barrel is hand filed, especially a shotgun barrel.

BARREL THREADS   at breech end allow screwing barrel into action. Most threads are right hand, European as well as some Oriental barrels have metric threads.

BARREL TIME   the interval it takes from the moment a projectile leaves the case neck to the moment it emerges from the muzzle.

BARREL VENT   small hole in the receiver ring of a rifle, near the chamber, that allows excessive powder gas pressure to escape.

BARREL VIBRATION   *also see:* Barrel Whip. The firing of a cartridge, bullet jump *(q.v.),* as well as travel of the bullet down the barrel to the muzzle, set up barrel vibrations. This can be divided into barrel whip & a true vibration. Vibration & whip are of major concern to riflemen since these motions affect accuracy. If vibration is uniform from shot to shot, accuracy won't be affected.

BARREL WEAR   a normal mechanical process. *Also see:* Abrasion; Barrel Erosion.

BARREL WEIGHT   *see* Stabilizer.

BARREL WHIP   that part of barrel vibration that occurs at the muzzle as the bullet leaves the barrel. High velocity bullets from very light, tapered barrels produce sufficient barrel whip to ruin accuracy. Heavy untapered barrels, such as those on target rifles, are not prone to barrel whip.

BAR SHOT   *see* Chain Shot.

BASES   *see* Scope Bases.

BATTERY CUP   *see* Primer, Battery Cup.

BAYONET LUG or STUD   on military rifles permits fastening of bayonet. This stud is an integral part of front barrel band, is usually ground or sawed off when such a rifle is sporterized.

BB   can refer either to the size shot found in a shotgun shell, or to the pellet used in various spring and air guns. BB shot has a diameter of .181″, while pellet guns are chambered for .177″ or .22″ pellets.

BB CAP   the oldest (1845) self-contained cartridge, consisting of an enlarged primer & a tiny bullet. The Bulleted Breech Cap had its origin in France, where it was made for the Flobert rifles which were designed for parlor or salon shooting. This type of target shooting is still popular in Europe, but not practiced in the U.S. Currently, no U.S. BB Caps are produced, only British and European makes are available. Despite its small size, the BB Cap can kill small pests, can also be used to sight in rimfire guns at short ranges.

BEAD or BEAD SIGHT   usually found on shotguns, which come with one or two such sighting devices. To make front bead more visible, it is often brass, ivory, or painted red. If two beads are provided, they must be aligned with target & shooter's eye when trigger is pulled.

BEARING BAND   *see* Driving Band.

BEARING SURFACE   see Bullet Bearing Surface.

BEAVERTAIL FOREND   the wide, hand-filling forward part of the stock, usually found on a shotgun, occasionally on a rifle. This type of forend is predominant on U.S. side-by-side shotguns, while Continental guns come with narrow, slender forends, often called SPLINTER FORENDS. *Also see:* Forend.

BEDDING   fitting of the lower half of rifle barrel in the barrel channel *(q.v.)*. Tight bedding, that is, a close fit between metal & wood is highly desirable, but free-floating *(q.v.)* barrels are encountered in competition rifles. Glassbedding *(q.v.)* is often employed to obtain a perfect fit in barrel channel. *Also see:* Inletting.

BEDDING TENSION   *see* Forend Tension.

BELL MOUTH   the flared muzzle of a blunderbuss. The round or oval bell shape was thought to give better shot distribution.

BELLY GUN   a short-barreled revolver, sometimes also called a SNUB-NOSED revolver, often carried concealed inside the trouser band, with or without a holster.

BELT or BELTED   *see* Case, Belted.

BENCHREST   a portable or permanently installed bench or table primarily used by riflemen for accuracy shooting, sighting-in, as well as for competitive shooting. Shooter is seated, supports both elbows on bench. Gun's forend is supported by means of a rest or sand bag, rear end of gun may or may not be supported. *Also see:* Rest.

BENCHREST TARGET   the specially designed target sanctioned for

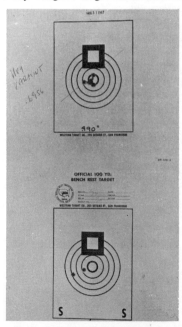

Target used in competitive benchrest shooting under NBRSA rules. Upper target is the scoring one, lower is the sighter target.

NBRSA matches by the National Bench Rest Shooters Association.

BEND   *see* English Gun Terms.

BENT   notch, usually in the hammer, that holds sear or trigger under tension of the mainspring until it is released by pulling the trigger.

BERDAN PRIMER   *see* Primer, Berdan.

BERENGER PELLET   probably the first (1824) patented percussion priming system.

BEST or BEST GRADE   British usage, indicating highest quality in a gun that, more often than not, has been custom made.

BICYCLE RIFLE   sometimes also called POCKET RIFLE, is basically a single shot handgun with long barrel & removable skeleton stock. BUGGY RIFLE is of similar design, but muzzle-loading.

BIG BORE   as used by British gunmakers, indicates a rifle caliber larger than .450. In U.S., term designates a rifle with a bore diameter greater than .30 caliber, but is also used to differentiate between small-bore or rimfire ammunition or shooting vs. big bore or centerfire ammunition or shooting.

BIPOD   a two-legged support that can either be attached to the forend of a rifle or carried by the shooter. In use, the bipod serves to steady the firearm for greater accuracy. Main

users are varmint hunters shooting from prone position & the military.

BIRD SHOT   *see* Shot.

BIRD'S HEAD GRIP   grip of a handgun, usually a revolver, that comes to a point in front so that its shape resembles a bird's head.

BITES   cuts or slots in the rear face of the lumps (*see* Lump) in a top-break shotgun. The bolt, in side-by-side shotguns, locks the action & barrels by sliding into the bites of the lumps.

BLACK POWDER   *see* Powder, Black.

BLADE SIGHT   *see* Sight, Front.

BLANK   *see* Stock Blank.

BLANK CARTRIDGE   *see* Cartridge, Blank.

BLIND BOX MAGAZINE   *see* Magazine, Blind Box.

BLISH PRINCIPLE   a design incorporated into the two forward bolt locking lugs which employed helical grooves to lock the bolt. Thought to act by adhesion on the lock during peak pressure period, it was later found to be a hesitation system of doubtful value.

BLOWBACK   *see* Action, Blowback.

BLOW FORWARD   *see* Action, Blow Forward.

BLOW, LIGHT   insufficient firing pin blow that fails to ignite the
primer in a cartridge case.

BLOWN PATTERN   *see* Pattern, Blown.

BLOWN PRIMER   *see* Primer,
Blown.

BLUE PILL   *see* Proofload.

BLUING   the chemical process of
artificial oxidation (rusting) applied
to gun parts (action, bolt handle,
barrel, sights, swivels, etc.) so that
metal attains a dark blue or nearly
black appearance, prevents rusting &
reduces light reflection. In factories
& gunshops, bluing is done by the
HOT bath method. Meticulous cleaning of metal parts & special BLUING
SALTS are needed, plus special bluing
tanks. COLD BLUING can be done at
home with special kits. TOUCH-UP
BLUING solutions to repair minor
scratches & defects are used by pro-
fessionals & amateurs. Military arms
are PARKERIZED *(q.v.)*.

BLUNDERBUSS   wheel-lock or
flintlock smoothbore with bell mouth
& round or oval barrel. Origin is
probably Dutch. Blunderbuss was
used as close range defense gun.

BOATTAIL BULLET   *see* Bullet,
Boattail.

BOBBER or BOBBING TARGET
remote controlled silhouette target
that is presented to the shooter for a
limited time, then turns sideways or
disappears into the target pit.

BOLT   the breechblock or breech
bolt that seals breech end of barrel,
locking the shell or cartridge in chamber. Hollow bolt houses firing pin &
firing pin spring. Extractor on bolt
face removes unfired cartridge or
empty case from chamber. Locking
lugs on bolt body cam into matching
cuts inside receiver to lock action
while gun is being fired. Bolt, as in
top-break shotgun, *see* Lock.

BOLT ACTION   *see* Action, Bolt.

BOLT, ALTERED   angle of bolt
handle to bolt cylinder must often be
changed on military actions so that
sporterized rifle can be equipped with
scope. Angle of military bolt inter-
feres with scope mounting, safety is
also changed in many such sporterizing jobs. Alteration is done either by
replacing military bolt handle or by
bending old one in bolt bending jig.

BOLT BODY   also known as Bolt
Cylinder *(q.v.)*.

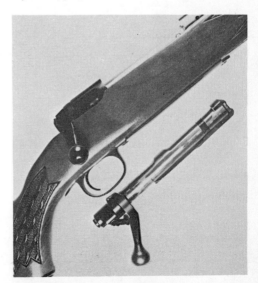

Above, bolt in rifle has been turned down by
means of the bolt handle, gun is locked and
cocked. Below, typical bolt with extractor near
bolt face.

BOLT CYLINDER   in a one piece bolt is the entire bolt body with extractor on bolt head, locking lugs, bolt handle, & containing firing pin & firing pin spring (or mainspring).

BOLT FACE   forward end of bolt which rests against base of cartridge or shell when latter is chambered, bolt is locked & gun ready to fire.

BOLT HANDLE   a protrusion from rear part of bolt body or bolt sleeve, topped by bolt knob, that allows manual operation of bolt.

BOLT HEAD GUIDE   groove milled into inside of receiver in which one of the bolt locking lugs travels as bolt is moved back & forth.

BOLT KNOB   the spherical, often knurled, end of the bolt handle. To

Bolt from Mauser M98 at left, and recessed bolt face of modern magnum rifle.

reduce weight, bolt knob is frequently hollowed out.

BOLT LIFT   the required amount of upward movement of the bolt handle, from the turned down position, until the bolt is unlocked & can be moved to the rear.

BOLT LOCKING LUG or LUGS projections on the bolt that cam into corresponding cuts in the action. When bolt is locked into its most forward position by means of this mechanical system, the gun can be fired. Locking lugs can be located toward the forward end of the bolt (front locking), or toward the rear of the bolt (rear locking). Locking lugs must close the bolt securely, so that bolt can withstand back thrust *(q.v.)*.

BOLT RACEWAY   also called BOLT RAILS or guides. Grooves milled inside receiver to accomodate bolt locking lugs. *Also see:* Bolt Head Guide.

BOLT, RECESSED   the bolt face, in some of the newer bolt action ri-

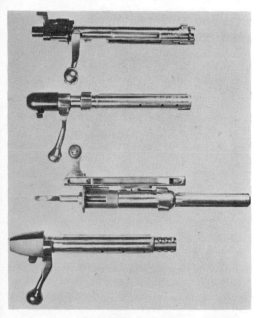

Top to bottom: Bolt from German M98 rifle; Schultz & Larsen rear locking bolt. Note position of bolt locking lugs on these bolts. Third bolt is from Swiss Schmidt-Rubin service rifle; last is from a Weatherby rifle. Contrast the locking lugs of the top two bolts and the two bottom ones.

fles, has a rim of steel around it. This encases head of cartridge, thus supporting case better in chamber, offering greater margin of safety in case excessive chamber pressure occurs for some reason.

BOLT RELEASE   to remove bolt from action, lift bolt handle up, move bolt to rear until rearward movement is halted by bolt stop *(q.v.)*. Bolt release designs vary, but when release lever is activated, bolt can then be pulled from action completely.

BOLT RETAINING CATCH   *see* Bolt Stop.

BOLT SLEEVE   this component of the bolt is fastened, by means of threads or lugs, to the rear of the bolt in many bolt action rifles. A multi-purpose part, it closes rear of bolt, guides cocking piece & firing pin, holds firing pin spring, often contains safety. In at least one rifle (Krag), it also holds the extractor.

BOLT STOP   a retractable metal hook that stops rearward travel of bolt.

BOLT TRAVEL or THROW   can be either long or short, describes distance bolt has to travel from most forward position until stopped by bolt stop *(q.v.)*.

BORE   inside of a barrel, also the diameter of the barrel as measured across the lands of a rifled barrel.

BORE CAST   casting of the bore

made with a special alloy (Cerrosafe) that has a low melting point. The cast can be used to measure bore diameter, width of lands, etc. A CHAMBER CAST *(q.v.)* is made similarly, gives accurate means of measuring case dimensions.

BORE DIAMETER   is usually measured from land to land, some-

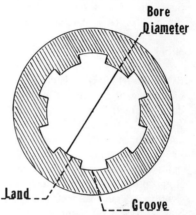

times from groove to groove. In U.S. & British guns, this measure is in decimals of one inch, in European countries in millimeters, e.g. .243 or 6 mm.

BORE LEADING   soft lead bullets leave a deposit in the barrel. The harder the bullet alloy, the less leading. Leading must be removed to maintain gun's accuracy.

BORE PITTING   was unavoidable second stage after rusting, when corrosive primers were only ones available. Now rusting and pitting of bores is troublesome only in humid climates.

BORE PLATING   especially

35

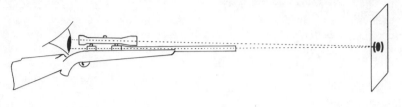

Bore sighting.

chrome plating, makes it somewhat easier to remove leading. Use of chromed bores in humid countries has been claimed to prevent rusting, pitting of bores.

BORE SIGHTING   is the process of aligning rifle sights and bore on a distant target. Can be done readily with bolt action rifles by removing bolt, centering distant target in bore visually, then adjusting sights so that sights align with target. A bore sighter is an optical device that allows pre-sighting of gun without removing bolt. *Also see:* Collimator.

BORE SLUGGING   forcing a soft piece of lead through bore. Since the lead will show lands & grooves, slugging is often used to determine bore diameter *(q.v.)*. *Also see:* Bore Cast.

BOTTLENECK   *see* Case, Bottleneck.

BOXER PRIMER   *see* Primer, Boxer.

BOX LOCK   *see* Action, Box Lock.

BOX RIB   *see* Rib, Solid.

BRAKE   *see* Muzzle Brake.

BRASS   or metallic cartridge case for rifle & pistol, not necessarily made of that metal, e.g. steel "brass" for 45 ACP during WWII. Brass shotshells were once popular.

BRASS, SEASON CRACKING OF splits & cracks appearing in old brass cartridge cases, often due to age or

Season cracking of brass case.

chemical reactions between brass & powder.

BRAZING   joining of metals by means of copper filings, with borax being used as a flux.

BREAK ACTION *see* Action, Top-Break.

BREECH the rear end of barrel where cartridge is inserted into chamber. Term is also used to describe chamber, receiver, breech part of a firearm, mostly on long guns.

BREECHBLOCK solid metal block that closes & locks breech of barrel. *See:* Action, Bolt; Action, Dropping Block; etc. *Also see:* Bolt.

BREECH BOLT *see* Action, Bolt; Bolt; Breechblock.

BREECH LOADER or LOADING any firearm into which a cartridge or shell is inserted from the rear, directly into the chamber. Term differentiates breech loaders from those arms loaded from muzzle.

BREECH LOCK the mechanism that locks the breechblock *(q.v.)* into position. *Also see:* Bolt Locking Lugs.

BREECH PLUG threaded plug

that seals breech of muzzle-loading gun gas-tight.

BREECH PRESSURE thrust or force of the expanding powder gases in the chamber of the gun. Properly called chamber pressure rather than breech pressure. Measured in pounds per square inch or PSI. *Also see:* Back Thrust; Pressure, Chamber.

BREECH-SEATED before self-contained metallic ammunition was invented, the bullet & then the powder charge were inserted in breech separately, the powder being contained in paper or cloth packets.

BREECH, SLIDING solid breechblock, instead of traveling up or down, moves back & forth, as in French Darne shotgun.

BREECH, STANDING solid part of receiver or breechblock, the breech face, that in top-break actions supports cartridge head when action is closed.

BRIDGE MOUNT a one piece

1873 Trapdoor Springfield 45-70.

mount for attaching a telescopic sight to a bolt action rifle. Bridge mount does not interfere with loading port of rifle.

BRIDGING OF SHOT   *see* Shot, Bridging of.

BRIDLE   a plate inside certain shotgun locks that holds tumblers & pins in proper relation to each other.

BRIGHTNESS, RELATIVE   term used in describing optical qualities of telescopic sights.

BRINELL HARDNESS SCALE a method of comparative hardness rating of steel. Like all such tests, this one only shows surface hardness which may or may not be the same as the hardness of the deeper layers of steel. Usually actions are tested for hardness. *Also see:* Rockwell Hardness Scale.

BRISANCE   the ability of an explosive to detonate & shatter. Increased brisance indicates greater demolition power. The priming compounds in all primers are brisant, with magnum primers having the greater degree of explosive power. *Also see:* Primer.

BROACH   a cutting tool with several cutting edges that, when forced into the bore of a barrel, removes metal, each edge a little more than the preceding one. Broaching is used to make rifled barrels, system cuts all grooves simultaneously.

BROWN BESS   muzzle-loading

flintlock smoothbore musket used by British Services from 1730's to 1830's. Gun weighs over 11 lb., barrel length is 3 ft. 6 in., bore diameter .75 in.

BROWNING   chemically induced rusting process for barrels & actions. Browning was fore-runner of today's bluing.

BRUSH LOAD   special shotshell load designed for dense brush hunting, loaded with #8 shot. Shell delivers maximum pattern at close range. Also known as SPREADER LOAD or SHELL.

BT   *see* Bullet, Boattail.

BUCKHORN SIGHT   *see* Sight, Buckhorn.

BUCKSHOT   *see* Shot.

BUFFER   any part of an action that absorbs recoil.

BUGGY RIFLE   *see* Bicycle Rifle.

BULGED BARREL   *see* Barrel Obstruction.

BULLET   a non-spherical projectile designed to be fired through the rifled barrel of a gun. A bullet can be cast from soft lead or a mixture of lead & other metals. Rifle & pistol bullets are often jacketed, have a lead core. Bullet tip is often shaped to overcome air resistance, jacket may or may not cover entire bullet tip.

Three .375" bullets: Left to right, a cast pure lead bullet, spitzer bullet with exposed lead tip, and a full metal jacketed bullet with cannelure.

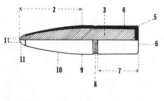

1, Meplat. 2, Head Height. 3, Core. 4, Jacket. 5, Heel. 6, Base. 7, Bearing Surface. 8, Cannelure. 9, Shoulder. 10, Ogive. 11, Point.
Bullet Nomenclature

BULLET, ARMOR PIERCING abbr. AP, military bullet with a steel core capable of going through steel & armor plate. Tests on armor plate have shown that small, lightweight bullets with high velocity have greater penetration than heavier, slower bullets.

BULLET BEARING SURFACE that portion of bullet's radius that is in contact with bore surface as it moves along barrel & which accepts impression of the bore's rifling. The marks on the bullet are sometimes spoken of as ENGRAVING.

BULLET, BOATTAIL base of

bullet is tapered to reduce air drag. This type of bullet design first saw use by military forces, was later adopted for sporting use, especially

long range target shooting. Also known as TAPER HEEL bullet, with the heel being the edge of the base of the bullet.

BULLET, BRENNEKE a German bullet that is designed for limited expansion. Several types of these bullets are made. The company making these bullets also manufactures a special, rifled shotgun slug of the same name.

BULLET, CAPPED also known as METAL POINT BULLET. Made for military handgun ammunition, capped bullet is a standard lead alloy bullet with jacket, but its nose is covered or capped with a piece of metal to prevent expansion in accordance with the Geneva Convention.

BULLET CASTING making bullets at home by casting in a mold or mould. Moulds are sold for many calibers, bullet designs & weights. Can be cast from pure lead, lead mixtures. Impure metals are often

Many styles, shapes, and sizes of cast bullets can be made by the handloader. Dark bands are grease grooves.

used, but bullets cast from these are not as accurate as those cast from pure lead or alloys. Bullets have lubricating or grease groove, must be sized & lubed, or lubricated, before loading them.

BULLET CORE   sporting bullets have lead core or center. A part or the entire core may be covered by bullet jacket. Military bullets for special purposes have special cores, such as armor piercing, incendiary, etc.

BULLET DESIGN & SHAPES

are governed by the ultimate use of the bullet, e.g. target shooting, varmint hunting, big game hunting. Bullet weight depends on barrel twist (*q.v.*), caliber of rifle & therefore bullet diameter (*q.v.*), & proposed use. Type of jacket metal, as well as jacket thickness, is also determined by bullet's use, anticipated velocities. Thus, during developmental stages of the 17 caliber bullets, many of them disintegrated in flight when thin bullet jackets were unable to hold together at velocities of around 4000 fps. For thick skinned game such as cape buffalo & elephant, the bullet jacket thickness is increased, the nose or forward portion of the bullet is encased in one or more layers of jacket metal (*see* Bullet, Solid). The amount of lead exposed at bullet tip, bullet ogive (*q.v.*), & ballistic coefficient (*q.v.*) also play an important role in bullet design. Varmint bullets are designed to blow up on contact & internal as well as external construction of these bullets prevents ricochets. For long

Left to right: 85 gr. .243″ BTHP, and .257″ 117 gr. BT; .308″ for the 30-30 170 gr. flat nose and 150 gr. .270″, both cannelured; 180 gr. .308″ and 285 gr. bullet for the 375 in semi-spitzer design; 240 gr. 44 flatnose and a 458 500 gr. FMJ bullet.

range target shooting where bullet flight is affected by wind, bullet design & shape for accuracy & wind

Bullet making machine, courtesy Speer, Inc.

bucking are more important than ability of bullet to expand or mushroom (*see* Bullet, Mushroom). Bullets are manufactured by swaging (*q.v.*) or cold-forming of bullet core (*q.v.*). A circle or disc is stamped from a sheet of jacket metal which is then formed into a cup. Cup and core are swaged together until desired bullet weight, shape are achieved. Military bullets, particularly special purpose bullets such as armor piercing, tracer, etc. are not recommended for sporting use; solid military bullets without exposed lead tips are not legal for hunting in most states.

BULLET DIAMETER is expressed in decimals of an inch in the U.S. & England, in millimeters (mm) in Europe. However, bullets for the 270 Winchester cartridge have a diameter of .277; those for rifles with a .308 bore, such as the 30-06 or the 300 Weatherby Magnum, have a diameter of .308-.3085. Use of metric designation, such as 6 mm, is becoming popular & the metric designation is often used interchangeably with the U.S. designation, e.g. 6 mm or 243. Factory bullets for the 38 Special cartridge usually have a diameter of .358, but lead bullets, cast by handloaders, are made oversized, are then sized to the proper diameter. Jacketed rifle bullets fit bore tightly, lead bullets for handguns are over-size, that is slightly bigger than actual bore diameter. A bullet must seal the bore completely to prevent gas escape around its sides. *Also see:* Bullet Upset.

BULLET DROP begins as soon as the bullet leaves the barrel. The effect of gravity combined with air resistance (*q.v.*) reduces velocity (*q.v.*) & bullet drop must be taken

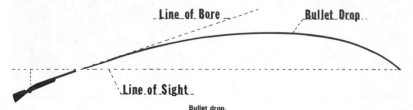

Bullet drop.

into account when sighting-in a rifle or handgun. *Also see*: Line of Bore; Line of Sight; Midrange Trajectory.

BULLET, DUMDUM   an open point, expanding bullet first manufactured at the British Arsenal at Dumdum, India. Some sources state that these were service bullets hollow-pointed, others claim that cross-cuts in the jacket produced the extensive tissue damage caused by these bullets. Term is now obsolete, but laymen often call any expanding projectile a Dumdum bullet.

BULLET ENERGY   *see* Energy, Bullet.

BULLET ENGRAVING   impressions of the rifling left on the outside of the bullet after it has been fired. Sometimes incorrectly called striae or striata.

BULLET EXPANSION, CONTROLLED   occurs when, upon penetrating the body of a game animal, the bullet diameter increases to 2-2 1/2 times its original diameter without material weight loss.

BULLET, FLAT-NOSED   used in cartridges designed for rifles with tubular magazines. The pointed or spitzer bullet can, when such a magazine is filled with live rounds & the gun is fired, set off the primer in the cartridge ahead of it due to recoil. Flat-nosed bullets are generally better adapted for close range use, are said to be better suited for brush shooting than the spitzer bullets.

BULLET, GALLERY   refers to a special 22 Short RF bullet that splatters or disintegrates when hitting backstop of an indoor range or gallery. These bullets are not made from lead, but from powdered iron & a special binding agent. At one time, gallery bullets consisted of 90 per cent lead dust, 9 per cent zinc dust, with oil as the binding agent, were

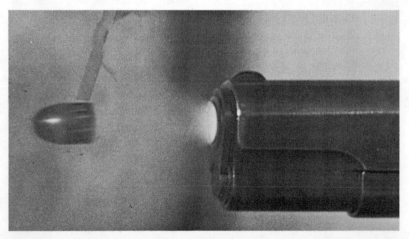

A bullet from a 45 ACP clearly shows the rifling marks or bullet engraving. Photo courtesy *Shooting Times* magazine.

formed under tremendous pressure in a press, disintegrated when making contact with any hard surface.

BULLET, GAS-CHECK lead bullet to which a small copper cup is applied at the base. When lead bullets are fired at greater than normal velocities, the powder gases formed by the larger powder charges create excessive heat which, when making contact with the base of the plain lead bullet, melts the base. The gas-check prevents this, gives the bullet also a somewhat flatter trajectory since the bullet base is not deformed. In order to apply gas-check, bullet base as cast must be slightly smaller than the regular cast lead bullet for the same caliber.

BULLET, GEHRLICH named after the German inventor H. Gehrlich, who claimed ultra-high velocities for some of his rifles & ammo. The Gehrlich barrel using this bullet had three tapered sections, where bore as well as groove diameter decreased from chamber to muzzle (0.35"-0.25" at muzzle). The bullet has two skirts or fins which close the bore perfectly. As the bullet comes to the first bore

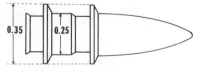

Gehrlich Bullet - caliber .35 - .25

reduction step, fins fold under; when the bullet reaches 0.25" groove at muzzle, the bullet has become one solid bullet with a higher than average velocity. U.S. Army trials failed

to substantiate Gehrlich's velocity claims, experiments were abandoned.

BULLET, H-MANTEL a hollow point partitioned big game bullet manufactured in Germany. Created for effective big game performance, its design has been copied widely. The D-MANTEL bullet has no internal partition, but its jacket is double thickness around the base & halfway up the bullet, from there thins out to single thickness. Upon expansion, the thicker jacket at lower half of bullet holds it together well, permits weight retention, thus offers greater weight to rear of projectile. This, in turn, creates greater driving mass behind opened front portion of bullet, thus greater shocking power.

BULLET, HOLLOW POINT abbr. HP. A bullet design feature,

the cavity in the bullet tip permits a faster, more complete bullet expansion. HP bullets are now widely used for small game & varmint hunting.

BULLET IMPACT the force or

43

power exerted by a moving projectile when hitting a target. *Also see:* Knock-down Effect.

BULLET, INCENDIARY   a military bullet with a hollow rear part that contains incendiary material which burns fiercely when ignited by impact. U.S. rounds carry light blue marking on tip, cartridges loaded in this manner should not be used in hunting fields or anywhere where fire danger exists.

BULLET, INSIDE LUBRICATED a lead bullet in which the LUBRICATION or GREASE GROOVES are covered by the cartridge case when the bullet is seated properly & the case mouth has been crimped. Typical of this type of bullet is the 38 Spl. wadcutter round.

BULLET JACKET   metal covering of a bullet. Most frequently used is gilding metal, but steel, copper, brass are also used.

BULLET JUMP   distance a bullet travels before engaging the lands of the barrel. Worn throats are major cause for bullet jump in rifles. In revolvers, bullet jump is the distance the bullet travels after leaving case mouth & cylinder before engaging lands in barrel.

BULLET LUBRICATION   is essential when cast or swaged lead or lead alloy bullets are fired through rifled barrels. Lubrication with grease or wax-grease mixtures reduces barrel friction, bore leading *(q.v.)*, keyholing *(q.v.)*. After casting, the BUL-

LET LUBRICANT is forced into the bullet LUBRICATION GROOVES, either mechanically by means of a special tool, or by standing bullets in a pan filled with liquefied bullet lubricant. When this has hardened, bullets can be removed, bullet lubrication grooves will have been filled with lubricant.

BULLET MOULD or MOLD   a metal block with one or more cavities for casting bullets of a specific weight & configuration. Bullet

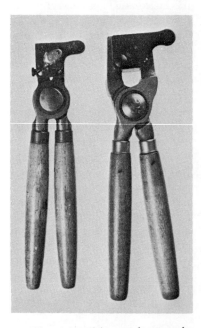

moulds are precision made, must be treated accordingly. GANG MOULDS for casting 4, 6, or 8 bullets simultaneously are often used by commercial casters. If a perfect mould casts less than perfect bullets, mould may have to be VENTED, that is fine grooves are made into the block.

Care must be taken so that mould will close properly. Some moulds contain an adjustable pin that makes possible the casting of hollow point bullets.

BULLET, MUSHROOM bullet that expands to the shape of a mushroom on or immediately after bullet impact.

BULLET, NATIONAL MATCH usually a boattail bullet, made especially for competitive big bore shooting events. Not available except at the National Matches, Camp Perry, Ohio, and only as loaded ammunition issued to competitors in the match.

BULLET, NEWTON also known as WIRE POINT bullet, was the invention of Charles Newton, a rifle designer & maker. A piece of copper wire about 0.5" long was placed into the center of the bullet core, and the jacket was then swaged to the usual spitzer point. The wire gave the bullet tip stiffness, prevented accidental battering of the tip in the magazine due to recoil, or when the cartridge was fed from the magazine into the chamber. The .30 caliber, 170 gr. Newton bullets were copper-jacketed. *Also see:* Bullet, Sabre-Tip.

BULLET, NOSLER a partition bullet, somewhat similar in construction to the German H-Mantel bullet (*see* Bullet, H-Mantel). Made in the U.S. primarily for handloaders, Norma as well as Weatherby offer factory loaded cartridges with Nosler bullets.

BULLET OGIVE the radius of the curve of the bullet tip.

BULLET, OPEN POINT EXPANDING abbr. OPE, designates a hollow point bullet of U.S. manufacture.

BULLET, OUTSIDE LUBRICATED as typified by the 22 LR rimfire cartridge, differs from the inside lubricated bullet in that the grease filled lubrication groove of the 22 RF bullet is seated so that the groove is not covered by the cartridge case or case mouth.

BULLET, PAPER-PATCHED cast from pure lead or lead alloys to exact bore diameter, this type of bullet did not have a cannelure *(q.v.)* or lubrication groove. The bearing surface as well as the base of the bullet were protected with a layer of paper. This prevented fouling *(q.v.)*. Now obsolete, these bullets were factory loaded for the large black powder cases, were especially popular with target shooters. The paper patch at the base increased bullet diameter to groove diameter. Rifling did not engrave on bullet (*see* Bullet Engraving), patch dropped away at muzzle.

BULLET, PATCHED *see* Ball, Patched.

BULLET PENETRATION the specific distance a given bullet will traverse through a specific substance. The standard of comparison is a penetration box, with 7/8" thick pine baffles, set one inch apart. Com-

Bullet penetration box.

parison is made between bullets by firing at first baffle from a given distance, then comparing depth of penetration to numbered baffles. Bullet penetration decreases as bullet sheds velocity. Bullet energy is a mathematical function of bullet velocity & bullet weight, is closely linked to penetration. As terminal ballistics decrease, so does bullet's ability to penetrate.

BULLET, PLASTIC   used for indoor practice, primarily handgun shooting, these bullets are loaded into special plastic cartridge cases. Most of these plastic bullets have as the only propellant source the explosive power of the primer. Lack

of penetration, low noise level, plus low cost, are outstanding features of these practice bullets.

BULLET PULL   is that force with which the bullet is held in case neck. The harder the bullet pull, the greater the pressure needed to push the bullet out of case mouth. Velocity is usually higher when bullet pull is hard or strong.

BULLET PULLER   device used by handloaders to remove a bullet from a cartridge case without harming either the bullet or the case. Two types are widely used: inertia & collet pullers. Inertia bullet pullers can be used for many different types of cali-

46

bers & cartridges, are used without a loading press. However, no attempt should be made to remove a bullet from a rimfire cartridge with an inertia puller! Collet pullers require the use of different size collet & shellholders, as well as the use of a loading press.

BULLET RAMP   *see* Feeding Guide.

BULLET RECOVERY   is done for three reasons: (1) to check expansion, (2) to inspect the engraving of an unexpanded bullet, (3) forensic. Expansion & bullet performance can be checked by recovering the fired bullet from a game or varmint kill, or by firing the bullet into such substances as blocks of modeling clay, wet telephone directories of suitable thickness, wet sand, etc. Unexpanded bullet recovery is accomplished by shooting into water or into a box containing finely sifted hardwood sawdust that has been soaked with oil. Forensic bullet recovery is undertaken so that bullet from scene of crime can be compared with bullet test-fired from gun assumed to have been used in the crime.

BULLET, ROTATION SPEED OF *see* Speed of Rotation.

BULLET, SABRE-TIP   a spitzer bullet, made in Canada by C-I-L, that has a nylon tip rather than a lead tip. Nylon tip is locked in bullet core, prevents bullet tip damage or mutilation of unfired rounds in magazine or while being fed into chamber from magazine. Nylon tip also appears to

contribute to destructive effect of bullet on tissues.

BULLET SIZING   is an essential step in bullet casting. As newly cast bullet comes from mould, it is slightly oversized. Sizing to proper diameter & lubricating bullet is accomplished by forcing the bullet through a lubricator-sizer tool.

BULLET SLIPPAGE   occurs when a bullet, on entering the rifling, drives ahead without engraving or taking on the rifling. This occurs most frequently with cast bullets in handloads which are near maximum, or when especially soft bullets are driven at excessive velocities.

BULLET, SOFT POINT   abbr. SP, a bullet design in which a part of the core of the bullet is exposed at the bullet's tip or point. The rest of the bullet is encased in jacket metal.

BULLET, SOLID or FULL JACKETED or FULL METAL JACKETED   abbr. FMJ, sometimes also called FULL PATCH BULLET. A bullet in which the core is entirely encased in the jacket, excepting a small circular area at the base. According to the Geneva Convention, all military bullets are fully jacketed, and FMJ's are also widely used in Africa on heavy game.

BULLET, SPENT   is a bullet that was not stopped or deflected during its flight & which had lost all of its terminal velocity when the force of gravity brought it to the ground.

BULLET SPIN or ROTATION is the spinning movement given to the bullet as it passes through a rifled bore. Bullet spin or gyrational rotation gives the bullet greater accuracy, aids in stablizing the flight of the bullet.

BULLET SPINNER a device that enables the user to determine the eccentricity, or the lack of it, in a bullet. In use, the base & tip of the bullet are held in place in such a fashion that the bullet can be rotated around its axis manually. A super-sensitive feeler is then brought into contact with the bearing surface of the bullet. The feeler is linked to a direct reading dial micrometer. As the bullet is rotated, the dial shows eccentricity in .001 or .0001 of an inch. Bullets with too much eccentricity are discarded as not suitable for precision bench-rest shooting.

BULLET, SPITZER a bullet that has a pointed tip or nose. This type of bullet usually has an ogive (*see* Bullet Ogive) radius of seven or more calibers.

BULLET SPLASH the scattering of bullet metals when the bullet hits a solid or hard backstop, such as steel plate.

BULLET STABILIZATION occurs when a bullet that has the correct gyrational rotation, thanks to suitable twist & velocity. A stabilized bullet has very little or no tumbling or yaw *(q.v.).* Some experimental evidence seems to indicate that even the best of the stabilized bullets have some slight amount of yaw & tumbling. But some experimenters feel that the motion recorded on high speed film is nothing more than the actual bullet spin.

Concentricity of bullet is measured by means of a bullet spinner; is especially important in bullets used in rifle matches.

BULLET, STEEL JACKETED jacket made of mild steel & copper or tin plated. Plating acts as rust preventive. These bullets are war-time military production when copper for jacket metal is scarce. Use a magnet to detect steel jacketed bullets.

BULLET STRIPPING occurs when a soft bullet fails to follow pitch of the rifling, goes straight through the barrel with the outer surfaces of the jacket being stripped of engraving.

BULLET, SWAGED (1) a bullet, jacketed or unjacketed, that is formed in a swaging die. In a jacketed bullet, the core is seated in the jacket through pressure, the jacket is then formed, with excess lead being extruded through a bleed hole in the die. Swaging is a form of cold working *(q.v.)*. Wadcutters are commercially produced by swaging rather than by casting, the grease grooves being factory-lubricated. Home bullet swaging is again becoming popular & most benchrest shooters swage their own super-accurate bullets. (2) When a slightly over-sized bullet is fired through a tight bore or a barrel of smaller diameter than suitable for the bullet, the recovered bullet is often referred to as having been swaged.

BULLET TIPPING occurs when a bullet with an imperfect base is being fired. The uneven base permits escape of powder gases, thus tipping the bullet to one side or the other as it leaves the muzzle. This results in poor accuracy.

BULLET, TRACER bullet that contains, in its base, a mixture that delivers a bright flame or light when the cartridge containing such a bullet is fired. Tracer ammunition is dangerous, has only military use.

BULLET TRAP mechanical device employed on some target ranges to stop small caliber bullets. Commercial traps are often equipped so that bullet metals can be recovered. Home-made traps usually consist of wooden boxes containing various bullet stopping materials such as barnyard lime.

BULLET, TRUNCATED term once used to describe a flat-nosed bullet.

BULLET UPSET occurs when an under-sized bullet, due to the sudden force exerted by the peaking gas pressure on its base, expands to fill the bore or rifling grooves. The better the upset, the better the gas seal in the bore. Soft bullets made from pure lead upset more readily than jacketed bullets.

BULLET WABBLE or WOBBLE is induced when a bullet is not properly made or has been damaged. In bullet wabble, the nose of the bullet departs from its straight path. Wabble can be discovered by shooting through several targets spaced some distance apart; wabble will show up in the form of out-of-round holes.

BULLET, WADCUTTER cylindrical handgun bullet with a sharp shoulder usually cast for use in 38

The wadcutter bullet, a cast lead bullet for the 38 Special match load usually weighs around 148 gr., contains three grease or lubrication grooves and is seated in the manner shown at right.

Spl. handgun, & used for target shooting. Bullet cuts clean round hole into target, makes hits easy to score. *Also see:* Bullet Lubrication; Grease Groove.

BULLET, WAX made from paraffin as well as wax mixtures commercially prepared especially for short range indoor target shooting in revolvers. Wax bullet loads do not use a powder charge, only a primer, & cartridge cases often have enlarged flash holes to prevent backing out of primer, thus freezing cylinder movement. Frequent cleaning to remove wax from bore is essential when wax bullets are used.

BULLET, WILLIAMS is falsely known as "poison" bullet. This two piece bullet was designed by E. J. Williams in 1861 to aid in cleaning bore of .58 caliber muzzle-loading rifles in the U.S. services. It has been

said that this method of removing fouling was quite successful.

BULLET, WOODEN frangible bullets of this kind are military in origin, are designed to be loaded into various types of practice rounds.

BULLET, WOTKYNS-MORSE also known as the 8S bullet to describe its point, has a long, soft point, was made only in .22 caliber.

BULL GUN an extra heavy gun with heavy barrel, used primarily for target shooting, sometimes for varmint hunting.

BULL PUP a shortened bolt action rifle where action & barrel are of standard length, but are set back in the stock so that the action is located in the rear part of the stock. This, in essence, shortens the gun length by the distance from butt to trigger guard. Bull pups are custom made, have never been offered commercially.

BULLSEYE (1) center of a target; (2) a tradename for a smokeless propellant powder, widely used by reloaders for handgun ammunition.

BUMP upper edge of the heel of the buttstock.

BURNING RATE *see* Powder Burning Rate.

BÜCHEL DROPPING BLOCK *see* Action, Dropping Block. *Also see:* Single Shot.

BUSHING is often used in fire-arms to give two adjoining parts a tighter fit or a bearing surface; for

Barrel bushing on 45 ACP.

example, the barrel bushing in the 45 ACP semiautomatic pistol.

BUTT in revolvers, the bottom part of the grips or stocks; sometimes used to describe the shape of the butt, such as round or square butt. In long guns, the rear end of the stock, often indicating buttstock. *Also see:* Grip; Stock.

BUTTCAP metal cap on some handguns that covers the butt.

BUTTPLATE a plate, either plastic or steel, sometimes hard rubber, that is fastened to the butt of the stock on long guns. In target guns, sometimes made of aluminum. *Also see:* Recoil Pad; Stock.

BUTTPLATE, SKELETON a metal buttplate in which the center has been cut out, thus exposing the wood of the butt. The wood is often ornately checkered, & this type of buttplate is usually seen on custom guns.

BUTTSTOCK the part of the stock of a long gun that extends from the receiver area to the butt or most rearward part of the stock. *Also see:* Stock.

BUTTERKNIFE BOLT HANDLE a distinctive design or shape given to

the bolt handles of the Austrian Mannlicher-Schoenauer rifles.

BUTTON RIFLING one method of rifling a barrel. Button rifling is currently used by several U.S. gun & barrel makers. *Also see:* Rifling.

BUTTS *see* Target Butts.

C

CALIBER the bore diameter of a rifled barrel, usually measured from land to land. In U.S. & England, this measurement is given in decimals of an inch; in Europe, caliber is given in millimeters or mm. Caliber is also used sometimes to designate bullet diameter.

CALIBER DESIGNATIONS in the U.S. as well as in countries using the metric system, describe a cartridge, although some caliber designations are somewhat confusing. The 338 Winchester has a bore diameter of .338″; the 22/250 has a bore diameter of .22″, but designation also indicates that the case of this cartridge is based on the 250 case, also known as 250/3000 or the 250 Savage. This was the first .25 caliber cartridge with an 87 gr. bullet to attain a muzzle velocity of 3000 fps. In U.S. black powder cartridges, designations usually show bore diameter, weight of powder charge, plus bullet weight; thus, the 45-70-500 has a bore diameter of .45″, contains a powder charge of 70 gr. & a 500 gr. bullet. However, this caliber is frequently referred to as 45-70, with the bullet weight being left off. The 38 Spl. & the 357 Magnum have the same diameter: .357″. Metric designations in millimeters indicate bore diameter & cartridge case length. The 7x57 Mauser has a bore diameter of 7 mm, with a case 57 mm. long. The term CALIBER DESIGNATION is often used interchangeably with CARTRIDGE DESIGNATION when cartridges are discussed. While the interchangeability is technically incorrect, common usuage has made it permissible.

Also see: Cartridge Designation, Metric; Cartridge Designation, U.S. & British.

CALLING A SHOT   the ability of an experienced shooter to predict where his bullet will hit. Prediction is based on sight picture at the moment of firing.

CAM   an eccentrically pivoting & sloping part that, by sliding contact with another part, gives either motion or a locking action to the second part.

CAMLOCK   a type of lock found in certain breechloaders, such as the 1873 Springfield.

CANISTER   a cannon round consisting of a cylindrical metal can filled with metal scraps, giving a shrapnel-like effect.

CANNELURE   sometimes called a CRIMPING GROOVE; also used incor-

rectly to mean grease groove. A cannelure is a groove around the circumference of a bullet or cartridge case.

On bullets, the cannelure can serve as expansion groove of an expanding HP bullet, as crimping groove, or as means of lessening bullet resistance to rifling. Around the base of a cartridge case, a cannelure acts as extractor groove for rimless or semi-rimmed cases.

CANNON LOCK   is probably the earliest means used to produce ignition. Fire was applied directly to the powder charge through a touch hole located in the rear of the barrel.

CANT   the tilting of a rifle or handgun to one side or the other as gun is being fired. Canting will place bullet in the direction of the cant & somewhat lower than normal. While canting is not considered good shooting form, some shooters have learned to compensate for it, placing bullets exactly where desired despite considerable canting.

CAP   *see* Percussion Cap.

CAP AND BALL   phrase used to indicate that a firearm is loaded with a lead ball, a loose charge of black powder, with ignition being supplied by a cap.

CAP CHAMBER   *see* English Gun Terms.

CAP FLASH   the residue plus the hot gases which are the end result of the explosion produced when a firing pin hits a primer, thereby igniting the priming mixture.

CAPLOCK   one system of ignition

used in muzzle-loading guns. In this type of system, a percussion cap *(q.v.)* is placed over the nipple *(q.v.)* which transmits the flame of the percussion cap to the powder charge when the cap is struck by the hammer of the gun.

CAPPED BULLET   *see* Bullet, Capped.

CAPS, BB and CB   *see* BB Cap; CB Cap.

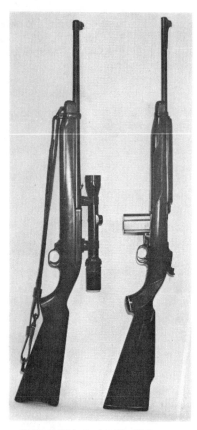

Carbine at left is chambered for 44 Magnum, the one at right is a sporterized military carbine but chambered for a wildcat cartridge.

CARBINE   a short, lightweight rifle with a barrel that usually measures less than 22″. Originally designed for military use, the carbine has been found increasing acceptance among hunters. Numerous U.S. as well as foreign gunmakers offer carbines in various calibers for brush & mountain hunting. In German, Karabiner means carbine.

CARTOUCHE   French for cartridge, often erroneously used to mean paper cartridge, cartridge box, or a case holding cannon balls.

CARTRIDGE   self-contained rifle or handgun ammunition, consisting of a metallic cartridge case (copper, brass, aluminum, etc.) which contains a primer, the powder charge & the bullet or projectile. CASELESS ROUNDS, sometimes incorrectly called caseless cartridges, have been claimed to be the "cartridges of the future." Shotshells are not considered as cartridges, although the definition theoretically includes shotshells. *Also see:* Case.

CARTRIDGE, AUXILIARY   a specially made case that resembles a cartridge case but that holds an entire pistol or rifle cartridge which is not designed for the gun in which the auxiliary cartridge is to be used. However, the diameter of the bullet on the inserted cartridge & the bore diameter of the gun in which the auxiliary cartridge is used must be the same, since the bullet takes on the rifling of the barrel. The auxiliary cartridge is equipped with a separate firing pin which, when struck by the

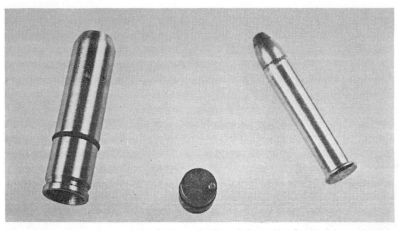

This auxiliary cartridge converts a centerfire rifle into one that fires a rimfire cartridge. Cartridge is inserted into body of auxiliary cartridge, then plug in center is seated in base of auxiliary cartridge.

firing pin of the gun, transmits its force to the primer of the cartridge seated in the auxiliary cartridge. A number of these auxiliary cartridges were offered, but their use has declined in the past years. Their primary purpose was to enable a hunter to shoot small game or pests with his large caliber rifle; in many instances, the inserted cartridge was a pistol round which was relatively inexpensive. Typical of the auxiliary cartridges offered in 1936 is the one for the 250/3000 which allowed the use of 25 ACP ammunition. *Also see:* Subcaliber Barrel.

CARTRIDGE, BIG BORE   used to describe any cartridge or caliber over .30″, while in England the big bores start with a caliber of .450″ or bigger. In recent years, the term has also come to mean any caliber over .22″.

CARTRIDGE, BLANK   military cartridge that contains a special

propellant powder, but no bullet. Powder is held in the case by means of a cardboard wad. Blanks are also used occasionally in signalling and in dog training.

CARTRIDGE, CASELESS   *see* Caseless Round.

CARTRIDGE, CENTERFIRE abbr. CF, formerly also called Central Fire. In the CF cartridge, the primer is seated in the primer pocket *(q.v.)* located in the center of the case head *(q.v.)*. In the center of the primer pocket is the flash hole *(q.v.)* that permits entry of the explosive force of the priming compound into the powder charge within the loaded cartridge.

CARTRIDGE CLIP   *see* Clip.

CARTRIDGE COOK-OFF   occurs mainly in rapidly firing military weapons, such as machine guns. As the barrel heats & retains the heat,

55

barrel temperature rises to such an extent that the heat may eventually fire the cartridge in the chamber. It has been claimed that cook-off also may occur in the tropics where high temperatures heat the gun steel so much that it may fire the chambered round. It has been proved repeatedly that maximum handloads brought on safari often develop excessive pressures because of the higher atmospheric temperatures.

CARTRIDGE, CRISPIN rare Civil War cartridges, invented by Capt. Silas Crispin & distinguished by an annular rim or ring that projected from the body of the cartridge case & contained the fulminate, or priming compound.

CARTRIDGE, CUPFIRE or CUP PRIMED one of the many attempts to develop an ignition system similar to that of Rollin White/Smith & Wesson, without violating that company's patents.

CARTRIDGE DESIGNATION, METRIC indicates bullet diameter & cartridge case length, e.g.: 7x57, where bullet diameter is 7 mm, case is 57 mm long. Sometimes a letter is added to the metric designation. An "R" indicates a rimmed case (*see* Case, Rimmed), military cartridges have a "J" added, such as the 8x57J. If the letter "S" appears in conjunction with the caliber designation, the round carries the longer spitzer bullet. In the 8 mm's of military persuasion as well as in a lot of the older German custom hunting rifles, the "S" indicates the use of a .323 bullet

in contrast to the 8x57J Model 88 that carries a .318 bullet. Some of the European calibers have been widely accepted by U.S. shooters & hunters. As a consequence, common usage & gun writers have, in some instances, altered the name of the cartridge somewhat. For instance, the 6.5 Swede is the 6.5x55, the 8 mm (also known as the 8 mm Mauser) is the 8x57, while the 8 mm M-S is properly called the 8x56 Mannlicher-Schoenauer.

CARTRIDGE DESIGNATION, U.S. & BRITISH is somewhat more complicated than the metric system. Modern U.S. & British cartridge designations indicate inside diameter of barrel, the measure being taken either from land to land (bore diameter) or from groove to groove (groove diameter), e.g.: 222, 243, 338, 455 etc. To that designation may be added the proprietary name of the cartridge such as 222 Remington, 455 Colt. However, the 455 Colt is not the same as the 455 Webley Revolver or the 455 Webley Automatic, but it is the same cartridge as the 455 Enfield Mk-1. Similarly, the British have no less than four different 500 caliber rifle cartridges: the 500 No.2 Express also known as the 577/500, the 500 Nitro Express 3", the 500 Nitro Black Powder Express, and the 500 Rimless Jeffrey, that latter designation indicating case design & inventor or maker. In the U.S., the caliber designation may be followed by either the inventor's name, such as 257 Roberts, or by a descriptive term, such as the 220 Swift. The term Magnum is often attached to a caliber, such as the 350 Remington Magnum, or the 375 H & H (Holland & Holland) Magnum. Wildcat cartridges often have double or triple designations, such as the 6 mm/303 Brit. Imp., or the 228/6.5x55. The 6 mm shows that the case used in the cartridge is the old 303 British military case, but that Imp. or Improved, also indicates that case shape has been altered somewhat. The 228 wildcat is based on the Swedish service cartridge case, the 6.5x55. Nearly everyone is familiar with the 30-06 cartridge, often simply called the '06. Here the 30 indicates bore diameter, while the '06 shows that 1906 was the year the U.S. Army adopted the cartridge as the official service round. The older U.S. black powder cartridges carry two designations, occasionally three, and often have other descriptive names tacked on. The 44-40 indicates that the bullet diameter is .44″, the 40 indicates the weight of the black powder charge. If a third number is added, that number indicates bullet weight in grains. The name of the inventor, or the name of the cartridge, or both are sometimes seen, e.g. 44-95 Peabody "What Cheer." In addition, the case length & configuration are also sometimes indicated, such as the 45-120 3 1/4″ Straight Sharps. In the past few years, a number of cartridges introduced in the U.S. carry metric designations. This trend began with the military usage of the designation 7.62 Nato which, in sporting caliber designations, is known as the 308 Winchester. The 223 for the M16 is designated as the 5.56 mm round. Remington offers the 6 mm Reming-

ton as well as the 6.5 mm Remington Magnum, a necked-down version of the 350 Remington Magnum, a belted case holding a .35 caliber bullet. The same company also offers the 7 mm Magnum, properly called the 7 mm Remington Magnum.

Other designations are sometimes confusing. One long-time favorite was the 250 Savage, also known as the 250/3000. A ballistic milestone was reached when the original 87 gr. bullet attained the magic 3000 fps velocity, hence the 3000. There are three factory 300 Magnums, but cartridges are not interchangeable (the 300 Weatherby Magnum, the 300 Winchester Magnum, and the 300 H&H Magnum), and all are

Left to right: 7 mm Remington Magnum round made by Federal Cartridge Co., a Remington-Peters round in 257 Roberts, a 220 Swift round with the old REM-UMC headstamp, and a current production Remington-Peters 6 mm Remington round.

based on a belted case (*see* Case, Belted). The 308 Norma Magnum is another .30 caliber Magnum with ballistics similar to those of the Weatherby & the Winchester rounds.

Other designations frequently encountered are: ACP for Automatic Colt Pistol, CF for centerfire, RF for rimfire, RFM or WRFM for rimfire Magnum or Winchester rimfire Magnum. Markings at the base of a cartridge case are referred to as the headstamp *(q.v.)*.

CARTRIDGE, DUMMY cartridge case without powder charge, a deactivated or fired primer, plus either a standard bullet as is found

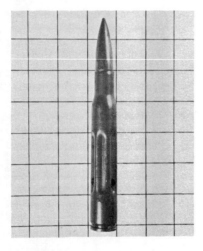

in a live round, or a bullet-shaped material, often wood. Some military dummy rounds contain various inert materials to give the dummy round the weight of the live round.

CARTRIDGE, EXPRESS a British term that originated around 1885 with several of the British ammo makers. In order to obtain greater velocities from the large cases for big game hunting, they loaded heavier charges of black powder behind lighter-than-usual bullets. These loads were originally called "Express Train" cartridges, but usage soon abbreviated this to Express cartridge.

CARTRIDGE, GRENADE military blank cartridge, that is a round without bullet, often with a special propellant, that can be fired in a standard service rifle to launch grenades; aboard ship, these grenade cartridges are often used to shoot lines to another ship or to launch flares.

CARTRIDGE, GUARD reduced charge service cartridge issued to guards on military installations or guarding prisoners. Cases have flutes or grooves for ready identification. Guard cartridges are now obsolete.

CARTRIDGE, HIGH INTENSITY is an indefinite description. At one time, the term was applied to any cartridge with a muzzle velocity (*see* Velocity) greater than 2500 fps.

CARTRIDGE, HIGH POWER term once used to describe any cartridge with a muzzle velocity (*see* Velocity) between 1925 and 2500 fps. High power is now often used to differentiate between a centerfire round & a rimfire round.

CARTRIDGE INDICATOR device that indicates whether or not the chamber of a gun contains a cartridge. Usually a small lever or pin, the cartridge indicator is an aid to the shooter, can often be seen as well as felt. In some semiautomatic pistols, the ejector projects from the slide, thus serving as cartridge indicator. When the cartridge indicator is in the shape of a pin, then it is called a SIGNAL PIN.

CARTRIDGE INTERCHANGEA-BILITY often makes it possible to fire a gun, either rifle or pistol, with ammunition using metric designations.

RIFLE CARTRIGES

22 Hornet	5.6x35R
22 Savage	5.6x52R
25 Remington	6.5x52
25-35 Winchester	6.5x52R
7 mm Mauser	7x57
30-30 Winchester	7.62x51R
7.62 Russian	7.63x53R
308 Winchester	7.62 Nato
30-06	7.62x63
8 mm Mannlicher-Schoenauer	8x56
8 mm Mauser	8x57

PISTOL CARTRIDGES

25 Auto. or ACP	6.35 mm Browning
30 Luger	7.65 mm Parabellum
30 Mauser	7.63 mm Mauser
32 Auto. or ACP	7.65 mm Browning
38 Automatic	9 mm Browning
380 Automatic	9 mm Browning Short (*kurz* or *corto*)
9 mm Luger	9 mm Parabellum

CARTRIDGE LENGTH the total length of the cartridge, from the base of the case to the tip of the bul-

let. Particularly important when conversion from one caliber to another is considered, since some cartridges, being of nearly identical length, can function through an action & magazine of a given length; e.g. a 270 Winchester cartridge will function through an action of 30-06 length, similarly, the 30-06 magazine will accomodate the 270 cartridge.

CARTRIDGE, LIP-FIRE a now obsolete type of rimfire cartridge.

CARTRIDGE, LOW POWER term once used to designate any cartridge that developed less than 1850 fps at the muzzle.

CARTRIDGE, LUBRICATED, INSIDE or OUTSIDE a term actually applicable only to the bullet, it is widely used in describing metallic cartridges. The outside lubricated bullets were the first of the self-contained metallic cartridge developments. Cartridge cases were straight-walled, and bullet bearing surfaces *(q.v.)* were lubricated by means of shallow lubricating grooves (*see* Bullet Lubrication). The heel or base of the bullet was slightly narrowed so that the bullet would fit into the case mouth, the latter being crimped onto the bullet. The only outside lubricated cartridge in use today is the 22 Long Rifle rimfire round. The carrying of outside lubricated cartridges was not satisfactory.

Inside lubricated cartridges, such as the 38 Special wadcutter load, have the bullets seated deeper into the case, thus the lubrication grooves, with the lubricant, are wholly contained within the cartridge case.

CARTRIDGE, MAGNUM merely designates, at least in the U.S., that the cartridge is a big, powerful one. British gunmakers & shooters use the term magnum to describe a cartridge that develops a muzzle velocity (*see* Velocity) over 2500 fps.

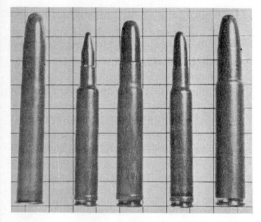

Magnum cartridges come in all shapes and sizes. The one at the left is rimmed, the three center ones are in belted cases, far right is a wildcat magnum without belt.

CARTRIDGE, METALLIC any self-contained cartridge in which the cartridge case is made of metal, mainly brass. However, shotshell cases are also sometimes made of various metals, with brass being most frequently used.

CARTRIDGE, MORTAR IGNITION used by the military, is actually a modified shotshell. The shell lacks the projectile (shot), contains an extra large powder charge, as much as 120 gr. of a loose double-base powder. Mortar ignition cartridges were developed during & after WWI, although manufacture of them apparently continued, the last being the Red Shell of 1935 for the 81 mm

mortar round. The M3 12 gauge shotshell was manufactured by Winchester, bore the headstamp 81 mm M3.

CARTRIDGE, PINFIRE the first wholly self-contained metallic cartridge with its own ignition system & an expanding case that acted as breech seal. In the pinfire cartridge, the "primer" is contained within the head of the case & is not ignited directly by the firing pin or hammer. Most pinfire cartridges contain, as

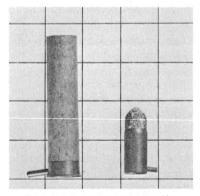

At left, an unfired pinfire shotshell as sold at one time for home-loading the shells; at right, a pinfire revolver cartridge.

primer, a percussion cap with fulminate of mercury. In the cap is lodged a small metal pin that extends through the side wall of the case. When the hammer strikes the pin, the pin is driven into the cap, setting off the fulminate, thus igniting the powder charge.

CARTRIDGE, PROPRIETARY cartridge which was developed by one of the arms or ammunition companies, e.g., the 340 Weatherby, the

6 mm Remington, the 243 Winchester.

CARTRIDGE, RIMFIRE abbr. RF, is a self-contained metallic cartridge where the priming compound is contained in the rim of the cartridge case. Firing of the cartridge is accomplished by having the firing pin *(q.v.)* hit the edge of the rim, thus detonating the priming compound. This in turn ignites the powder charge in the case. Only the various 22's are in actual use today, although some years ago some of the older RF cartridges, such as the 32 RF, were produced.

CARTRIDGE, ROOK *see* Rook Rifle.

CARTRIDGE, SELF-CON-TAINED a cartridge or shotshell that contains the primer *(q.v.),* the propellant powder charge & the projectile, either bullet or shot.

CARTRIDGE, SELF-LUBRICAT-ING better called self-lubricating bullet, was designed to overcome the drawbacks of the outside lubricated bullet, as well as those lubricated inside *(see* Cartridge, Lubricated). According to a contemporary Smith & Wesson catalog, the self-lubricat-ing bullet gave "the highest degree of accuracy, with practically no fouling..." As the powder burned & gases expanded, the plunger in the base of the bullet was driven forward, thereby forcing the lubricant contained in the bullet cavity out through small ducts. Since the plunger in the base of the bullet sealed the ducts fully, there was no loss of pressure. The lubricant coated the rifling just ahead of the bullet bearing surfaces *(q.v.).* The drawing shows the lubricant being forced out of the bullet somewhat like toothpaste being forcefully squeezed out of a tube.

CARTRIDGE, SMALLBORE at one time designated, in the U.S., any cartridge under .30 caliber. In England, the term was used to describe any cartridge under .450 caliber. Now used almost exclusively, in the U.S., to describe 22 rimfire ammunition.

CARTRIDGE, TEATFIRE was patented by D. Williamson in 1864. Designed to circumvent the Smith & Wesson patent, the teatfire cartridges were made with the priming compound—fulminate—contained in either a round or a flat teat. Now collector's items, they were offered in two calibers, for the 32 & the 45

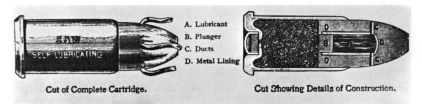

A. Lubricant
B. Plunger
C. Ducts
D. Metal Lining

Cut of Complete Cartridge.   Cut Showing Details of Construction.

Actually a misnomer, since it was the bullet that was to be lubricated, not the cartridge. This drawing first published in an old Smith & Wesson catalog.

revolvers made by the National Arms Co. of Brooklyn, N.Y.

CARTRIDGE, WILDCAT one not manufactured by any ammunition concern. Wildcat cartridges must be handloaded, are based on changes made in standard cases: not only shape & length, but usually caliber as well. Sometimes the changes include reducing case head diameter, removing the belt, & otherwise altering the case.

CASE properly called the cartridge case. The term case has, through usage, come to mean the me-

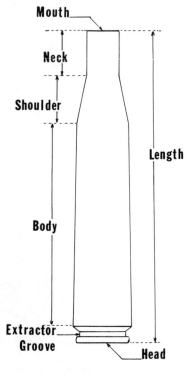

Case nomenclature.

tallic container that holds the powder charge, primer & projectile for a rifle or handgun cartridge. A fired shotshell case is usually called a HULL *(q.v.),* or if loaded, a SHELL *(see* Shotshell). Among the types or shapes of metallic cases are: Balloonhead, belted, bottleneck, rebated-rimless, rimmed, rimless, and semi-rimmed.

CASE, BALLOONHEAD early type of copper cartridge case. Term is often used interchangeably with FOLDED HEAD case. Not very strong, these cases did not withstand high pressure, are now restricted to black powder & low pressure loads. Early folded head cases give the appearance of being rimfire cases, but crimp above head serves to hold internal primer.

CASE, BELTED originated by Holland & Holland, famed British gunmakers, in 1912, the belted case was designed for Magnum cartridges. The case headspaces *(q.v.)* on the belt; actually a sort of reinforcing band, the belt makes this kind of case the strongest type possible.

CASE, BOTTLENECK is representative of the majority of cases in use today. The case body has a larger diameter than the case neck *(see* illustration, Case nomenclature). In relation to its length, the bottleneck case has a greater powder capacity than the straight or tapered case. Since the powder column inside the bottleneck case is shorter, this case usually permits better ignition of the charge.

CASE CAPACITY is an important consideration in handloading metallic cartridge cases. Although outside dimensions of cases are rigidly controlled, case wall thickness & internal dimensions often vary greatly from manufacturer to manufacturer & there are even some variations in production lots. As case wall thickness increases, internal volumetric capacity decreases & loading density *(q.v.)* is altered. Variations in case capacity affect velocity *(q.v.)*, pressure *(q.v.)*, & accuracy *(q.v.)*. Case capacity is measured by filling case, with fired primer in the primer pocket, with water to the top of the case mouth, then accurately weighing the amount of water. Making a comparison of the amount of water contained in several cases gives an indication of case capacity variations. Instead of water, many handloaders use Ball C, Lot #2 ball powder for convenience.

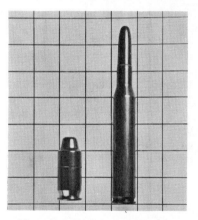

Left to right: Belted 375 round, bottleneck 22 Jet, rimmed 30-30, a rimless 30-06, and a semi-rimmed 225 Winchester.

The cartridge at left is the 45 ACP, the one at right is a 270 Winchester; note differences in extractor groove.

CASE EXTRACTOR GROOVE groove above the head of the case that permits the extractor to grip the case for removal from the chamber (*see* Extraction, Primary).

CASE FIREFORMING a process by which a slightly under-size case is fired, usually with a special fireforming charge, in an enlarged or "improved" chamber. Fireforming of cases is usually essential in making up cases for wildcat calibers (*see* Cartridge, Wildcat). Fireforming expands the case, can alter shoulder shape, usually improves powder capacity of the case being fireformed.

CASEHARDENING a method of hardening steel & iron while imparting to it color as well as surface figure. Metal is heated by means of animal charcoal to 800-900° C, then plunged into cold water.

CASE HEAD the lower end of the cartridge case that holds the primer in the primer pocket in centerfire cartridges. In rimfire cartridges, the priming compound is contained in the rim of the head. The case head also carries the headstamp *(q.v.)*, and above the head may be a case extractor groove *(q.v.)*, depending on the case head form *(q.v.)*. *Also see:* Illustration showing Case nomenclature.

CASE HEAD EXPANSION is a certain sign of excessive chamber pressure *(see* Pressure, Chamber). As a cartridge is fired, the powder gases force the case to expand in all directions within the chamber. If pressures are within normal limits, & in factory loads they always are, extraction of the fired case should be easy. If extraction is difficult, excessive pressures have probably expanded the case head. Handloaders, when developing loads, check case expansion by measuring case diameter with a micrometer before & after firing. Case head expansion of 0.002″ is considered to be the first sign of excessive pressure.

CASE HEAD FORMS a term denoting case head design, e.g. Belted; Rebated-Rimless; Rimmed; Rimless; Semi-Rimmed. First cases were of the balloonhead or FOLDED HEAD design, were made from copper, had little more strength than the then-current rimfire rounds. Col. Hiram Berdan *(see* Primer, Berdan) developed the drawn SOLID HEAD brass case as we know it today. Now cases are made by punching a round disc out of a strip of brass, then the disc is formed into a cup. As the cup undergoes further shaping, the brass is annealed to prevent excessive metal hardening. The processes of shaping & annealing are repeated until the final case shape, form, & case head form are obtained.

CASE HEAD SEPARATION a condition that occurs either from excessive pressure or excessive cold working of brass cartridge cases. Case head separation can be total or partial. In the former, the case body

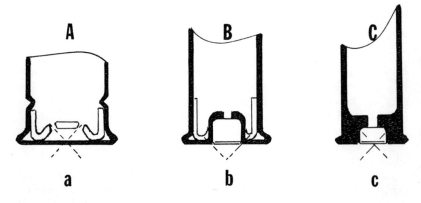

A. Balloonhead. Note crimp above head to hold internal primer. (a) two flash holes to permit entry of primer flash from priming compound located in center of base. B. Folded head with Boxer primer. (b) reinforcing band in base to strengthen case head. C. Modern solid head (c) solid head or web above primer pocket.

Complete separation at left, partial at right. Courtesy *Shooting Times* magazine.

may stick in the chamber, with the head of the case being extracted fully. A partial separation permits the removal of the entire, though damaged, case from the chamber of the gun. *Also see:* Incipient Rupture.

CASE, LAMINATED the appearance of spots on the cartridge case that indicate that the metal has separated due to the inclusion of foreign matter.

CASE LENGTH total length of the cartridge case from the head of the case to the case mouth. Expressed in decimals of inches in modern U.S. cartridges, in fractions for black powder cartridges, & in millimeters in the metric cartridges. All modern U.S. cases are made to SAAMI (Sporting Arms & Ammunition Manufacturers Institute) specifications. *Also see*: Cartridge Designation, Metric; Cartridge Designation, U.S. & British.

CASE LENGTH GAGE device

that permits the handloader to determine visually if a certain case is overly long or short. This is not a measuring, but a comparison device, the gage having been made to predetermined specifications. *Also see:* Case Stretching; Case Trimming.

CASELESS ROUND or CARTRIDGE development that dates back to the early part of WWII when German ammunition makers tried to produce a cartridge that didn't require the use of a relatively expensive cartridge case. In the true caseless rounds, the propellant is combined with a priming compound in a mix that can be shaped into a cylin-

At left, a 22 RF Long Rifle round; center, a 22 Short; at right, the Daisy-Heddon 22 V/L caseless round. Propellant is affixed to base of bullet.

drical form & then dried. The bullet, with a nipple or teat at the base, is pressed onto the charge, the entire round is then fast-dried. Caseless ammo is of military importance, but is now also offered as a 22 round by one U.S. manufacturer (Daisy-Heddon). One ill-fated development of a semi-caseless round was the Dardick Tround. This cartridge had a triangular plastic case that contained a

65

primer, propellant powder charge
& bullet.

CASE LIFE expressed in the
number of firings, refers to the number of times a cartridge case or shotshell hull can be loaded & fired before
becoming useless. Brass cartridge
cases, expanding & shrinking somewhat during firing, are being worked,
that is the brass undergoes internal
structural changes. In reloading the
case, it must be sized back to its
original dimensions so that it once
again will fit the chamber. The more
brass is worked, the more brittle or
hard it becomes & much-worked
brass becomes fatigued to the stage
of case head separation *(q.v.)*. In
making brass cartridge cases (*see*
Case Head Forms), brass is annealed
to combat hardness due to working
of metal. Minimal resizing during
reloading operations increases case
life, which can also be prolonged
by suitable annealing. Paper shotshell hulls usually shows first signs
of wear at the case mouth where the
paper frays. Case life can then be
extended by trimming frayed part
of hull, but this requires adjustment
of wad column height. Incipient
case head rupture also occurs in
shotshells. Plastic shotshells generally have a longer case life than
paper hulls.

CASE MOUTH open end of the
case neck where the bullet is inserted.
It is the case mouth that is crimped
onto the bullet so that rough handling or recoil in the firearm won't
dislodge the bullet from the cartridge. *Also see:* Illustration showing
Case nomenclature.

CASE MOUTH CHAMFERING
done inside & outside the case mouth
with a special tool, gives the case
mouth a bevel that permits easy
entry of the bullet into the case
mouth. Chamfering also removes
any burrs that could damage a cast
lead bullet during bullet seating.

CASE NECK is that portion of
the cartridge case that extends from
the shoulder forward, terminating in
the case mouth *(q.v.)*. It is also that
part of the cartridge case that has
the smallest diameter. Not all cartridge cases have a case neck or
shoulder. *Also see:* Illustration showing Case nomenclature. The case
neck often is the place where excessive cold working of the brass first
becomes apparent. Fine hairline
cracks & splits (*see* Neck Splitting)
often make the case unserviceable
(*see* Case Life), but reloaders often
salvage such cases by annealing the
necks. *Also see:* Anneal; Neck Annealing.

CASE, REBATED-RIMLESS
rimless case *(q.v.)* with a head diameter that is smaller than the diameter
of the case body.

CASE, RIMLESS has a head diameter the same as the case body.
To make extraction of the case from
the chamber possible, an extractor
groove (*see* Case Extractor Groove)
around the case head is formed as
the case is being made. Most of the
current rifle cases are of the rimless
type.

CASE, RIMMED as typified by
the 30-30 case, was one of the first

successful solid case heads. Rimmed cases have a case head of larger diameter than their body diameter. Many of the single shot rifles are chambered for rimmed cases since the rim permits easy extraction or removal of the case from the chamber.

CASE RUPTURE   loosely describes any split that has occurred in a fired cartridge case. The term case rupture is most often used to describe longitudinal ruptures or cracks in the case body itself. *Also see*: Case Head Separation; Case Neck; Incipient Rupture.

CASE, SEMI-RIMMED   has an extractor groove like a rimless case, but a head that is of slightly larger diameter than the case body. However, a few semi-rimmed cases have a rim diameter that is slightly smaller than the body diameter.

CASE SHOULDER   is that part of the bottleneck cartridge case that connects the case body with the case neck *(q.v.)*. *Also see:* Illustration showing Case nomenclature. The angle or slope of the shoulder is measured in degrees. Many wildcat cartridges, especially those designated Imp. or Improved, have been altered only as far as the angle of the shoulder is concerned to give the case a greater powder capacity, thus making possible higher velocities. This change of shoulder angle is accomplished by first altering the chamber of the rifle so that the shoulder will have the desired slope, then firing standard cartridges of the appropriate caliber in the chamber, thus

Incipient case head rupture at left; center: Rupture due to excessive cold working of brass; at right and barely visible, a case mouth fissure at pointer due to too frequent reloading and cold working of case mouth.

fireforming the brass to the new dimensions. *Also see:* Cartridge, Wildcat; Case Fireforming.

CASE STRETCHING   a normal process which occurs during the firing of a cartridge. However, excessive stretching, that is lengthening of the case beyond the normal case length *(q.v.)*, occurs with some calibers. Case stretching can be due to excessive powder charges in handloaded rounds, but it can also be encountered when especially soft brass was used in making the cartridge case. Handloaders carefully check for case stretching, & if this occurs, the length of the case neck *(q.v.)* is reduced until the case length once again meets the specifications for that particular caliber. *Also see:* Case Trimming; Case Length Gage.

67

CASE TAPER slope from the case head to the base of the case shoulder. Not all cases have a taper, shoulder or case neck, & those are called straight-sided, straight-walled, or straight cases. *Also see:* Illustration showing Case nomenclature.

CASE TRIMMING reduction of an overly long cartridge case. Case trimming is usually accomplished by

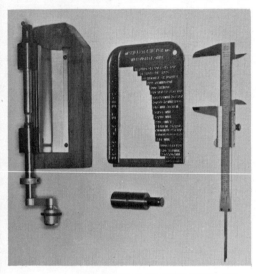

Case trimmer at left permits reducing case length after setting of trimming cutter stop. Center, top, a case length gage suitable for numerous calibers, below a case length gage for one caliber. At the right, a vernier caliper.

means of a case trimmer, but the same results can be obtained by means of a hacksaw & file. Case length is measured with a case-length gage *(q.v.)* to verify suitable over-all case length.

CASTING refers to making lead bullets, or lead balls for muzzle-loading arms. The basic bullet casting metal is lead. Various amounts of

antimony are added to give the bullet the desired degree of hardness. Bullet casters often use other sources of lead, such as wheel weights. Basic equipment for bullet casting includes a melting pot, a suitable mold, a

Bullet casting equipment.

mechanical press to size bullets to correct diameter & lubricate them. Lead pots can be gas operated or electric; molds come in single, double, & multiple cavity models for nearly all calibers & bullet configurations; lubricator-sizers are designed so that the suitable sizing & lubricating die can easily be installed in the press. Cast bullets or balls are used exclusively in black powder guns; cast bullets, especially 38 Special wadcutters & bullets for competitive shooting with the 45 ACP, are widely used by handgunners; cast bullets for rifles were at one time a necessity during the black powder era, were still used for reduced & small game loads when the smokeless powders were introduced. The use of cast bullets in rifles has been declining during the last decade since bullet makers now offer light bullets in many of the calibers for short range practice shooting & small game hunting or pest control. *Also see:* Bullet Lubrication.

CAST-OFF   is that distance which a butt plate is offset to the right of the line of sight for a right-handed shooter. Cast-off is especially important in shotgun stocks. *Also see:* Stock.

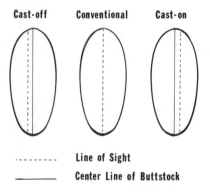

Cast-off   Conventional   Cast-on

- - - - - - -   Line of Sight

─────────   Center Line of Buttstock

CAST-ON   the same as cast-off *(q.v.),* except that the butt plate is offset to the left of the line of sight for the left-handed shooter. *Also see:* Stock.

CB CAP   or Conical Bullet Cap, is a 22 rimfire round with a 29 gr. bullet, presently not manufactured in the U.S. *Also see:* BB Cap.

CCC,   *see* Controlled Combustion Chamber or Chambrage.

CENTERFIRE   *see* Cartridge, Centerfire.

CENTRAL FIRE   *see* Cartridge, Centerfire.

CF   abbr. for Centerfire, *see* Cartridge, Centerfire.

CHAIN SHOT   used in cannon as well as in shoulder guns, consisted of two balls linked by a short length of chain or wire. Inaccurate, military use of the chain shot was abandoned except in naval engagements when chain shot was used to destroy the rigging & sails of enemy ships. When the two balls were connected by an iron bar, the projectile was called BAR SHOT.

CHAMBER   rear part of the barrel that has been reamed out so that it will contain a cartridge. When the

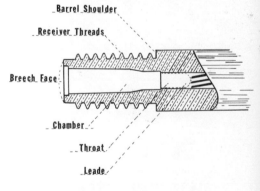

breech is closed, the cartridge is supported in the chamber & the chamber must align the primer with the firing pin, the bullet with the bore.

CHAMBER, AUXILIARY   sometimes referred to as supplemental chamber, the auxiliary chamber is the same as the auxiliary cartridge. *See* Cartridge, Auxiliary.

CHAMBER CAST   when properly made, can determine the exact configuration or dimensions of a chamber & therefore also of the cartridge. A chamber cast can also be used to determine precise bore measurements. In making a chamber cast, the bore & chamber are first cleaned thoroughly, the bore is then plugged tightly with cleaning patches. Bore as well as chamber can be oiled lightly with a fine oil or can be left

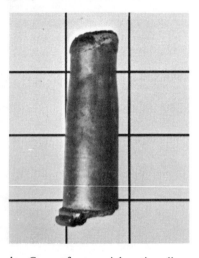

dry. Cerrosafe, a special casting alloy, is then melted & poured into the chamber & bore. The Cerrosafe, after solidifying, shrinks somewhat, but expands to its original size about an hour after the casting. From the cast, it is possible to make precise chamber or bore measurements. A SULFUR CAST is sometimes used, but this method is somewhat messy. In making such a cast, plug the bore with a cork, then mix by volume 10 parts of sulfur & one part of powdered graphite. Before casting, clean the bore & chamber, then cover with a light film of oil. Melt the sulfur-graphite mixture, pour into chamber

& bore, permit to cool. Oiling helps in releasing the cast from the chamber. In making casts, use enough casting material to prevent voids, use a tightly packed cleaning rod from the muzzle to remove the cast from the chamber.

CHAMBER, FLOATING patented device which allows the use of relatively low powered 22 rimfire ammunition in certain guns. The floating chamber increases recoil, so that the gun thus equipped can be used as a training gun for target shooting. The now-scarce Colt Ace has the external appearance of the Model 1911 45 ACP service gun, & even the weight of the Ace is very near that of the bigger caliber pistol. Firing 22 rimfire ammunition in the Ace produces a recoil very similar to the 45. This permits practice shooting at low cost with a gun of the same general heft, weight, & recoil of the service match gun.

CHAMBER, FLUTED system of ridges, or flutes, evenly spaced, in the forward part of the chamber of several foreign assault rifles. Best known rifle with such a chamber is the Cetme, a delayed blowback action gun. As the bolt head starts its rearward travel, gas pressure in the chamber is still high, thus extraction is hampered. Powder gases entering the flutes forestall case sticking to the chamber walls & case expands somewhat into the flutes, thus aiding extraction. The Sig as well as some Russian automatic rifles also have fluted chambers.

CHAMBER LEADE that slightly conical part of the bore just forward of the chamber itself that is cut with a finishing chamber reamer. This enlarges that part of the bore so that the bullet, with a greater-than-bore diameter, can fit into the bore. *Also see:* Chamber Throat.

CHAMBER PRESSURE *see* Pressure, Chamber.

CHAMBER THROAT also called THROAT, is that area in the barrel that is directly forward of the chamber & that tapers to bore diameter.

CHAMFERING *see* Case Mouth Chamfering.

CHARGE *see* Powder Charge.

CHECKERING a collective term describing the patterns of parallel lines & figures, such as oak leaves or fleurs-de-lis, carved into the wood of the forend & in the area of the pistol grip on a gun stock. Checkering gives a better gripping surface than uncheckered wood & is also widely used for ornamental value. *Also see:* Stippling.

CHECKERING CRADLE wooden frame that allows free rotation of a stock during checkering.

CHECKERING, ENGLISH a type of checkering in which the diamonds created by the carving of the parallel lines are square. This is accomplished by running the lines at right angles to each other. The tops of the diamond are often flat, & this type of checkering is found primarily on old English guns.

CHECKERING, HAND the art of carving or checkering by hand in contrast to machine or impressed checkering. *Also see:* Checkering, Impressed; Checkering, Machine.

CHECKERING, IMPRESSED die stamping process used on many U.S. guns that, when applied to wood, gives a reverse type checkering effect. Impressed checkering is as serviceable as hand checkering, but lacks artistic or esthetic appeal, is also less costly to apply.

CHECKERING, LAYING OUT the process of tracing the proposed hand checkering on a stock, complete with all the special carvings to be incorporated in the checkering.

CHECKERING LINE COUNT the greater the number of lines per inch in any checkering, the finer the pattern will be. The average is 20 or 24 lines per inch, extra fine checkering will run 32 lines per inch.

CHECKERING MACHINE device with several sharp cutting wheels, arranged in parallel fashion, that is widely used to carve straight-line checkering. It can be used to cut border lines, but not to carve fleurs-de-lis & other figures.

CHECKERING, MACHINE straight-line carving of gun stocks done with a checkering machine

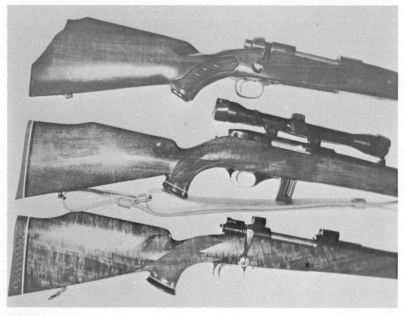

Impressed checkering at top; center, French or skipline checkering; bottom, fine-line checkering with 30 lines to the inch.

(q.v.). Use of a checkering machine does not preclude laying out of the pattern, nor does it prevent checkering runovers *(q.v.).*

CHECKERING, RE-CUTTING OF is undertaken to point up worn or broken checkering, also to correct errors that were made in earlier checkering. Re-cutting often includes addition of decorative checkering to make repairs, as well as to improve the appearance of the stock.

CHECKERING RUNOVERS occur either when the bordering tool goes beyond the intersecting bordering line, or when the checkering tool is moved too fast & crosses the bordering line. The best way to avoid this kind of runover is to use a pull type cutting tool to finish bringing lines out to the border cut. For large area checkering, a push type cutter is used. By stopping short of the border line & finishing the job with the pull cutter, runovers of this kind can be prevented.

CHECKERING, SKIPLINE also known as FRENCH CHECKERING. By skipping or omitting a number of lines during checkering, a pattern is formed that includes large as well as small diamonds. Of French origin, skipline checkering is found on many imported guns, is now also popular on better grade factory guns made in the U.S.

CHECKERING TOOLS can

72

either be power driven (*see* Checkering Machine) or hand tools. The latter are essentially files, although they are used as cutting tools. The design of the cutting head governs the eventual pattern produced. There are spacer, edger, skipline, bordering, deepening, etc., cutters & tools.

CHEEKPIECE a raised & carved portion of the buttstock against which the shooter rests his cheek while aiming & shooting. A cheekpiece can be added to a stock & this may be either a piece of specially shaped wood or a fitted pad. *Also see:* Stock; Stock, California.

Dark stock shows cheekpiece that is incorporated into stock design; below, a cheekpiece that can be attached and shaped after stock has been finished.

CHERRY a fluted cutting tool, the shape of a bullet, used to cut the bullet cavity of a bullet casting mold.

CHOKE the constriction of the muzzle of a shotgun barrel which

controls the spread of the shot pellets. The degree of choke is measured by the percentage of pellets delivered into a 30 inch circle at a range of 40 yards. *Also see:* Pattern. A FULL CHOKE barrel delivers about 65-70 per cent of the pellets into that circle; an IMPROVED-MODIFIED CHOKE, 55-65 per cent; MODIFIED, 45-55 per cent; IMPROVED-CYLINDER, 35-45 per cent; CYLINDER CHOKES usually deliver between 25-35 per cent of the shot into the circle. SKEET CHOKES are bored between cylinder & improved-cylinder. European gunmakers give degree of choke in fractions. Cylinder & full are called the same; improved-modified is termed 3/4 choke; modified is 1/2 choke; improved-cylinder is called 1/4 choke. Cylinder choke has no constriction. Percentage of choke varies from gunmaker to gunmaker, also from barrel to barrel.

CHOKE, ADJUSTABLE or VARIABLE mechanical device fitted to the muzzle of a shotgun barrel that

allows the shooter to vary or change the amount of choke or barrel constriction. Some of these variable choke devices offer a complete range of chokes within the device, others furnish suitable choked tubes which are changed when change of choke becomes desirable or essential. Some

U.S. shotguns come equipped with a choke device, but most adjustable chokes are custom-installed after purchase of the shotgun.

CHOKE, JUG   an enlargement polished out of the inside of a shotgun barrel, about one inch behind the muzzle. This allows the shot charge to spread slightly while passing the enlarged area & charge is then constricted again as it passes through to the muzzle. If the barrel or barrels on a shotgun have to be cut off for some reason, & therefore the original choke removed, jug choking is a partial remedy. However, it is a tedious gunsmithing job, & on single-barrel guns the installation of an adjustable choke (*see* Choke, Adjustable) gives more satisfactory results. Since these devices cannot be installed on side-by-side or over/under guns, jug choking is the only solution.

CHOKE MARKINGS   are often abbreviated, with European gunmakers using stars (*) to denote amount of choke in a barrel.

Full Choke	F	*
Improved-Modified	IM	**
Modified	M	***
Improved-Cylinder	IC	****
Cylinder	C	CL

CHOKE, SKEET   shotgun choking between cylinder & improved-cylinder. In its origins, skeet *(q.v.)* was meant to reproduce game shooting conditions. Since the claybirds are shot at fairly close ranges, an open choke is indicated. However, most true cylinder chokes deliver an uneven shot pattern, hence the addi-

tion of a slight amount of choke has been found to be ideal for skeet shooting. *Also see:* Choke; Pattern.

CHOKE, SWAGED   one of the methods used by firearms makers to produce a choke in a shotgun barrel. The barrel is first inside reamed to cylinder choke, then the muzzle is swaged to produce the desired choke inside the barrel.

CHOKE, VARIABLE   *see* Choke, Adjustable.

CHOPPER LUMP TUBES   a system of joining two barrels & simultaneously forming the lumps, used by English gunmakers for the best grade side-by-side shotguns. After rough boring two barrels, they are brazed together. At the breech end of each barrel has been forged a lump *(q.v.)* & when the barrels are joined, so are the lumps. These lumps are filed by hand until they fit the action.

CHRONOGRAPH   an instrument, operated either from a battery or directly from electric current, that usually measures only elapsed time. The reading obtained is then interpolated to give the velocity of a projectile. Some highly refined chronographs actually measure velocity, the interpolation of time of flight being accomplished by sophisticated electronic circuits. In practice, the first or start screen is set up a given distance from the gun muzzle. Care must be taken to see that muzzle blast does not trigger the screen, thus starting the electronic counting mechanism of the chronograph prematurely, &

giving false readings. The second or stop screen is set in line & to the rear of the first screen, the distance between the screens being measured precisely. As the bullet either breaks the printed & electrically conductive start screen or breaks the light barrier of the first or start photoelectric screen, the chronograph begins to count elapsed time in milliseconds.

Avtron chronograph and Avtron photoelectric screen.

As the bullet goes through the second screen, the electric circuit is closed & the chronograph stops counting. Elapsed time is then easily interpolated, by means of tables, into velocity expressed in feet per second. *Also see:* Velocity.

Chronographs had their origin in the BALLISTIC PENDULUM. Velocities were calculated from the bullet's striking energy. Although nearly obsolete, the pendulum still finds use today in measuring recoil *(q.v.)*. The later Boulenge chronograph was the basis for many other chronograph developments.

CLAW MOUNTS *see* Scope Bases.

CLAYBIRD or CLAY PIGEON a fragile disc originally made of clay which, when thrown from a trap *(q.v.)*, serves as an aerial target for shotgunners, in trap & skeet as well as in informal shooting sessions. When several shot pellets hit the claybird, it shatters. Size & weight of claybirds are regulated for the claybird sports (trap & skeet, *q.v.*). Trap & skeet shooters often call claybirds simply birds, clays, or targets.

CLEANING an essential part of gun care. Even the modern smokeless powders leave residues in the barrel as well as in parts of the action. Dirt, dust & other foreign matter must be removed from action parts to assure functioning of any gun. Whenever possible, barrels should be cleaned from the chamber only & special care must be taken not to damage the rifling *(q.v.)*.

Cleaning equipment needed includes cleaning rods of the proper diameter for each caliber or gauge, cleaning brushes that fit the threaded tip of the cleaning rod. Rods usually come with one or more tips, such as jag or slotted tip. Patches are made from a soft material such as flannel. A powder solvent & a good quality gun oil are also essential. A silicone wiping cloth is especially helpful in caring for gunstocks & in preventing finger marks on the blued steel of guns. Prolonged gun storage requires special care, especially in humid climates.

CLICK   an arbitrary audible & tangible unit of measure employed in the adjustment knobs of receiver sights & telescopic sights. As the adjustment screw is moved a specific number of clicks in one or the other direction, so is the sighting system moved, thus moving the bullet's point of impact on the target. Many of these sights are adjusted so that the movement of an adjusting knob one click moves the point of bullet impact one inch at 100 yards. In some modern scopes, the click is not audible, & graduations are used to indicate in which direction & how many "clicks" a sight adjusting knob is being turned. *Also see:* Sighting-In.

CLIP   a detachable sheet metal frame or box containing a spring & a cartridge follower or platform. In many rifles, all semiautomatic pistols & in bolt action shotguns, the clip, sometimes called cartridge clip or magazine *(q.v.),* serves as ammunition storage area.

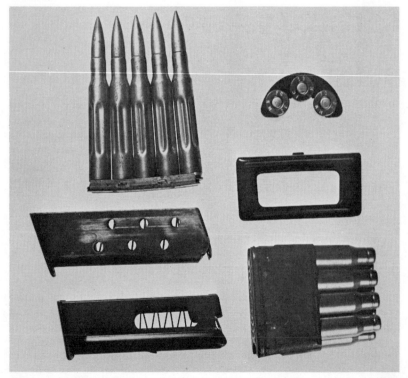

A half-moon clip is at upper right, the two clips at lower left are for two different 22 RF guns, the others are military clips.

CLIP, EN BLOC   type of clip introduced in the 1880's with the Mannlicher straight-pull rifle. Without the en bloc clip, magazines of rifles like the Pederson or the Garand won't function. No sporting rifles utilize this system.

CLIP GUIDES   are slots machined into the receiver, barrel extension or other part of the action that engage the en bloc or the stripper clip. *Also see:* Clip, Stripper.

CLIP, HALF-MOON   3 shot clip that permits the use of the rimless 45 ACP cartridge in the 1917 U. S. service revolver. Two of these half-moon clips are required to load the cylinder. The rounded notches in the clip fit the case extractor grooves *(q.v.),* thus facilitate loading as well as unloading or removal of the fired cases.

CLIP, STRIPPER   a cartridge carrying clip used in some military rifles. When engaged in the guides of the magazine, the cartridges in the stripper clip are pushed out of the clip into the magazine. In some instances, the empty clip is removed manually, in others the clip is ejected as the bolt closes. Also known as CHARGER CLIP, especially in England. *Also see:* English Gun Terms.

CLOCK SYSTEM   the face of an imaginary clock is often used to describe wind direction on the range, or group location on the target. Thus, the wind can come from 3 o'clock, or a number of shots may form a group at 11 o'clock. The clock system is

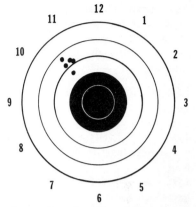

also used to describe a sight picture the moment trigger pull is completed. The pistol shooter, for example, talks about a 6 o'clock hold *(q.v.).*

COCK   originally described the lock that held the flint in flintlock arms. Common usage of "to cock" has come to mean the drawing back of the hammer or firing pin against the force of the mainspring.

COCK, FULL   when at full cock, the trigger system has engaged the hammer or firing pin against the force of the mainspring. When the trigger is pulled, it releases the hammer or firing pin, & the force of the mainspring drives the hammer or firing pin forward until hammer or firing pin forcefully contact the primer or, in the case of a black powder gun, the percussion cap.

COCK, HALF   a notch in the sear & hammer that forestalls accidental hammer fall, which would fire the gun. When on half cock, the hammer is disengaged from the trigger mechanism, hence the gun is safe while

77

the hammer is in this position. In some revolvers, placing the hammer in the half cock position allows rotating the cylinder for loading or unloading.

COCKING DOG *see* Cocking Lever.

COCKING INDICATOR same as Cartridge Indicator *(q.v.)*.

COCKING LEVER sometimes also called COCKING DOG. Two small levers in double barrel, box lock action shotguns (*see* Action, Box Lock), the cocking levers are activated by rods in the forend as the gun is opened or broken. The cocking levers are pushed down on their forward ends by the cocking rods, the rear ends making an upward move, thus pushing the hammers or tumblers into full cock position. There they are held by the sears. Pulling the trigger disengages the sear from the hammer notch, making it possible for the hammer or tumbler to fall.

COCKING ON CLOSING or ON DOWNWARD or FORWARD STROKE a nearly obsolete cocking system where the firing pin spring in bolt action rifles was cocked as a cartridge was being chambered, as in the 1917 Enfield. *Also see:* Cocking On Opening.

COCKING ON OPENING or ON UPWARD STROKE introduced by German arms designer Peter Paul Mauser in the German Model 1898, revolutionized bolt action rifles. Cocking on opening makes manipulation of the bolt easier & all modern bolt actions utilize this system of cocking.

COCKING PIECE a small part of

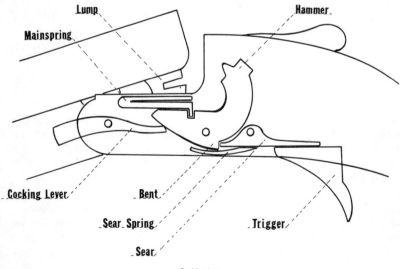

Cocking lever.

the firing mechanism in some guns that is attached to the rear end of the firing pin or striker. Some guns have a knob or spur attached to the cocking piece to make manual cocking possible.

COCKING ROD   a part of the cocking mechanism of box lock shotguns. Cocking rods act on the cocking levers *(q.v.)*.

COCKING STUD   small lug or projection underneath the cocking piece *(q.v.)*. The cocking stud cams the sear or trigger, depending on the design of the action, holding the firing pin in the cocked position.

COCKING, UPSTROKE   *see* Cocking On Opening.

COEFFICIENT OF EXPANSION either linear, volumetric, or both, is based on thermal changes & is of experimental importance in interior ballistics when brass expansion, case life & design are considered.

COEFFICIENT OF FORM   a mathematical index describing the shape of the bullet point or ogive (*see* Bullet Ogive).

COIL SPRING   *see* Spring, Helical.

COLD WORKING   describes the shaping, drawing, SWAGING, or otherwise forming any metal at room temperature. Cold working changes the molecular configuration of metal & excessive cold working will eventually affect the useful life of the part being worked. *Also see:* Case Life; Bullet, Swaged.

COLLIMATOR   an optical system that permits approximate sighting-in of a rifle without firing a shot. A spud of the correct caliber is inserted into the muzzle of the rifle while the gun is held in a vise firmly. With the iron, receiver, or telescopic sight in place, looking through the sight & into the collimator grid makes it possible to adjust the sight so that the first bullet fired will print in or near the bullseye.

COLOR   CASEHARDENING same basic process as casehardening *(q.v.)*, but the water in the quenching bath is agitated to form air bubbles. These air bubbles produce the finely mottled effect characteristic of this decorative finish.

Collimator.

COMB upper part or edge of the buttstock. Properly slanted, it guides the shooter's eye to line of aim. Comb height is often increased on stocks designed for rifles to be fired exclusively with telescopic sights. Comb width, on custom stocks, is governed by wide or narrow face of shooter. Since the shooter's cheek rests on the comb, the comb shape & drop can increase or decrease the recoil transmitted to the shooter's cheek as well as, to some extent, to the shoulder. *Also see:* Cheekpiece; Stock.

COMBINATION GUNS are European in origin. Still popular there, especially in Germany & Austria, the best known of these guns is the DRILLING, a side-by-side shotgun with a rifle barrel located below & between the two shotgun barrels. The German VIERLING features two side-by-side shotgun barrels, between & below them is a small bore rifle barrel often in 22 Long Rifle, & below that a rifle barrel in a caliber suitable for medium & big game. *Also see:* Vierlingspatrone; Drilling.

A number of barrel arrangements have been used in combination guns. The primary purpose of these guns is duality of use in the field; the shotgun barrel or barrels are loaded with shells suitable for feathered or furred game, while the rifle barrel, usually chambered for a rimmed cartridge for ease of extraction, is adequate for medium game such as deer. Traditional in Germany & Austria is the Schonzeit combination gun. SCHONZEIT is the season closed to hunting, except for varmints, & these small caliber rifles are often found with one or two shotgun barrels. Moreover, because the guns have the same general configuration & heft, as well as action, as the regular drilling, these guns are widely used for competition shooting open to hunters & hunting guns only.

Many of the imported combination guns designed specifically for the U.S. market are known as turkey guns. The shotgun barrel is usually below the rifle barrel which may be chambered for 22 rimfire, 22 rimfire Magnum, 222 Remington, or for the rimmed 30-30. The shotgun barrel is usually 20 gauge since this is the smallest gauge that can be used ef-

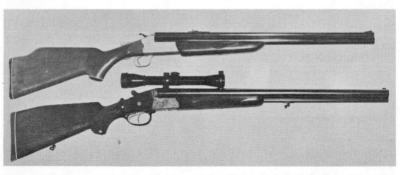

Above, U. S. made Savage M24 chambered for 22 LR and 20 ga. 3″ shell. Below, Krieghoff drilling with two 12 ga. barrels and 30-06 barrel below the smoothbore barrels.

fectively with shotgun slugs as well as with shot loads. Turkey can be hunted with either rifle or shotgun. Depending on range, hunting conditions & bird distribution, the instant choice of shotgun or rifle is considered to make the combination gun the ideal turkey gun.

COMBUSTION   act or process of burning. Ignition of the substance to be burned depends on several factors, including the size of the particles to be burned, their temperature before ignition, their burning speed, the amount of oxygen present, & several other variables. In firearms, combustion is concerned primarily with the burning of the powder charge contained in a cartridge or shotshell.

Oxygen is essential for the burning process, and burning is actually an oxidation of matter. If matter oxidizes slowly & that matter is iron, the process is known as rusting. If combustion is rapid, the process is described as explosion. Heat as well as light is liberated during the burning process. When the rapid combustion of matter takes place in a confined space, such as in a cartridge case, the volume of the gases of combustion increases, & therefore pressure increases. These gases are being heated by the burning, & pressure is further increased. In essence, this is the chemical process that occurs when a cartridge is fired. *Also see:* Powder Burning Rate; Temperature of Ignition.

COMPENSATOR, CUTTS   a patented combination of muzzle brake *(q.v.)* & variable choke (*see* Choke, Adjustable). Installed on a shotgun, the easily interchanged tubes permit the shooter to control the amount of choke *(q.v.)*. The Cutts Compensator, without the choke tubes, has in the past been installed on rapidly firing small arms to reduce recoil. In such cases, it functions as a muzzle brake only.

COMPONENTS   or handloading components, a collective term used to describe the various items contained in shotshell or cartridge. This includes the hull or case, the primer, the powder, the shot or bullet, the various wads used in shotshells, gas checks, etc.

COMPOUND LENS   a system of two or more lenses of simple design & with a common axis. The surfaces of the lenses may or may not make contact with the adjacent lens.

CONE   *see* Nipple.

CONE, FORCING   *see* Forcing Cone.

CONTROLLED COMBUSTION CHAMBER or CHAMBRAGE abbr. CCC, a method of increasing velocities without the attendant increased pressures, while at the same time reducing throat erosion. This was accomplished by reducing case wall taper, sharpening the case shoulder, thus increasing case capacity. The change in chamber shape was combined with careful free-boring (*see* Free-Bore). The result was not only higher velocities, but also less heating of the barrel. CCC had only a relatively short period of popularity, is now virtually unknown in its original form.

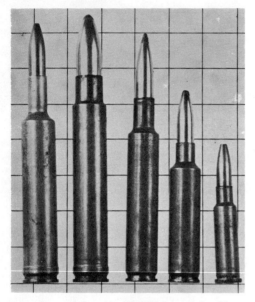

Left to right: 300 H&H case necked to 25, a 375, a 270, a 250-3000, and a 218 Bee, all with CCC case designs. Courtesy L. Corcoran, Hollywood Gun Shop.

CONVERSION as applied to rifles, is the limited rebuilding of military rifles for sporting use. Shotguns & handguns are seldom converted to sporting guns. Conversions usually entail the following changes: altering the military stock & discarding the wooden hand guard; removing military sights & installing new sporting sights if so desired; altering the shape of the bolt handle so that a scope can be mounted (in this case, the action must be drilled & tapped for installation of scope bases); tuning of the trigger to eliminate the military two stage pull or installing a

commercial trigger, often an adjustable one. *Also see:* Sporterizing. The term conversion is also applied, & probably more correctly so, to the act of converting a rifle from one caliber to another, larger one. When the 308 Norma Magnum was introduced, many rifles chambered for the 30-06 were converted to handle the larger, more potent Magnum round. Similarly, rifles that have seen extensive use & show signs of wear in the chamber throat *(q.v.)*, as well as in the rifling, are often converted to a larger caliber. Such changes can sometimes be accomplished by barrel relining *(q.v.)* or setting back of the barrel (*see* Barrel, Setting Back).

COOK-OFF *see* Cartridge Cook-Off.

CORDITE a type of propellant, made in cord-like form, prevalent in obsolete British rifle cartridges. It consists of 37 parts gun cotton, 58 parts nitroglycerin, 5 parts mineral jelly.

CORE *see* Bullet Core.

CORROSION *see* Barrel Corrosion.

CRANE or YOKE, on revolvers with a swing-out cylinder, the part on which the forward end of the cylinder *(q.v.)* & the ejector rod *(q.v.)* are mounted. The crane is fastened to the revolver frame in such a manner that it can pivot freely once the cylinder release latch *(q.v.)* is opened. The crane is the weakest part of a revolver,

is often damaged or bent by carelessly slamming the cylinder back into the frame.

CREEP   *see* Trigger Creep.

CRIMP   a turning-in of the case mouth to effect a closure or to prevent the bullet from slipping out of the case mouth. Some metallic cartridges, that is cartridges for handguns & rifles, are crimped to hold the bullet securely in the case mouth. Rough handling, especially of military cartridges, & severe recoil can loosen a bullet in the case mouth, hence the crimping. Shotshells are also crimped. Here the upper circumference of the case mouth is turned in under pressure, thus sealing the case to prevent shot from spilling out of the shell. The ROLL CRIMP was used when over-shot wads were used to close shells. The PIE CRIMP is now prevalent. Other crimps are the STAR or FOLDED CRIMP, & the ROSE CRIMP which was used to close metallic shotshells.

CRIMPED PRIMER   a method of locking the primer into the primer pocket of the cartridge case. Crimped primers are usually found in military rounds & removal of the fired primer from the primer pocket may require a special technique plus swaging of the primer pocket, after primer removal, to enlarge it so that a new primer can be seated.

CRIMPING GROOVE   *see* Cannelure.

CROSS-BOLT   as used in top-break shotguns, is a transverse bar or rod that locks the standing breech & barrels. Designed by W.W. Greener, it is often referred to as the GREENER CROSS-BOLT. In rifles, especially those developing hefty recoil, a cross-bolt is sometimes used, the cross-bolt being placed through the recoil shoulder. Cross-bolts of this kind help to prevent stock splitting due to set-back of barrel & action during recoil.

CROSS-BOLT SAFETY   *see* Safety, Cross-bolt.

Left to right: **44 Magnum, 444 Marlin, new plastic crimped shotshell, and a now obsolete roll crimp.**

CROSSHAIRS   *see* Reticle.

CROSS-SHOOTING   *see* Regulating Barrels.

CROWN or CROWNING   *see* Muzzle Crowning.

CRUSHER GAGE   a system used to determine chamber pressure. (*see* Pressure, Chamber). As the propellant powder charge in a cartridge burns, the resultant gases are under pressure. The brass of the cartridge case expands, & as pressure increases, the bullet is dislodged from the case mouth, is propelled into & through the barrel. The gas pressure, measured in pounds-per-square-inch or psi, must be kept within limits, & since all guns are made to withstand a certain maximum pressure, determination of psi is important.

The crusher gage is one of several systems used to determine chamber pressure. Used with a special pressure barrel *(q.v.)*, the crusher gage uses a copper cylinder of precise dimensions. The crusher is placed into a special device & into a vertical hole of the barrel that connects directly to the barrel chamber. After the cartridge is fired, the crusher is removed & measured. The pressure crushes or shortens the crusher, and from tarage tables *(q.v.)* the pressure can be interpolated from the new length of the copper crusher. In recent years, experiments in well-equipped ballistics laboratories seem to throw some doubt on the validity of the crusher gage system. Another method used to determine psi is the strain gage system *(q.v.)*.

CUPRONICKEL   copper-nickel alloy that, some years ago, was used extensively as bullet jacket metal. Its fouling tendencies, however, led to the discontinuation of its use in making bullet jackets.

CUT-OFF   sometimes referred to as magazine cut-off. A device built into the receiver of some rifles & shotguns that prevents a round from being fed from the magazine into the chamber of the gun. With the cut-off holding the ammunition in the magazine, it is therefore possible to fire single rounds through the gun. This enables a hunter to employ a rifle cartridge with a different bullet type or weight, or in the case of a shotgun such as the 5 shot Browning autoloader, to use a shell loaded with a different shot size without having to empty the magazine of its original shells.

Gas check and crusher have been seated, and piston of crusher gage system is about to be set in place.

CUTTS   *see* Compensator, Cutts.

CYCLIC RATE OF FIRE   expressed as rounds per minute, indicates the rapidity with which a military small arm, such as a submachine or machine gun, can be fired.

CYLINDER   a rotating cartridge container in a revolver. The cartridges are held in the chambers & the cylinder turns, either to the left or to the right depending on the gunmaker's design, as the hammer is cocked. *Also see:* Cylinder Indexing; Cylinder Rotation; Cylinder Stop.

CYLINDER INDEXING   the mechanical process of lining up a chamber of the cylinder with the barrel on the forward end of the cylinder & the firing pin at the rear. If parts of the functioning or rotating system of a revolver are worn, the cylinder won't index properly, is then said to be "out of timing" or "the timing is off."

CYLINDER RELEASE LATCH sometimes called the cylinder latch, a device on the left side & to the rear

of the cylinder that permits the swinging-out of the cylinder from a revolver's frame.

CYLINDER ROTATION   can be either to the right or to the left. Each pull of the trigger rotates the cylinder, by means of the hand *(q.v.),* so that another chamber is indexed.

CYLINDER STOP   a small spring-activated stud that is linked to the trigger group. Its upper part engages the cylinder stop notches in turn to align each chamber with the barrel & firing pin.

CYLINDER STOP NOTCH   one of the machined grooves in the rear of the cylinder that is engaged by the cylinder stop *(q.v.).*

CYLINDER, SWING-OUT   a term sometimes used to describe a double action revolver where the cylinder is swung out from the gun frame by releasing the cylinder release latch *(q.v.).* This permits the cylinder to pivot by means of the crane. *(q.v.).*

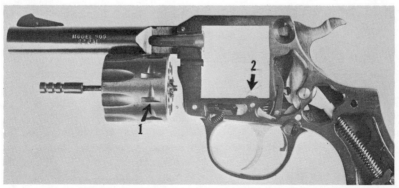

Cylinder stop notch (1) is engaged by cylinder stop (2) so that cylinder indexes properly.

D

DA   abbr. for double action.

DAMASCENE   the decorating of metal with another metal, either by inlaying or attaching in some fashion. Damascene is often confused with Damaskeening or engine turning *(q.v.)*

DAMASCUS STEEL   *see* Barrel, Damascus.

DARDICK GUN   *see* Trounds. *Also see:* Caseless Round.

DARNE   a French shotgun of unique, sliding breech design.

DECAPPING   *see* Handloading.

DEEP-HOLE DRILLING   a modern method of barrel drilling.

DEFINITION   as used in optics, describes the clarity & quality of the image as seen through a telescopic sight or any other system of lenses. Definition depends on the optical correction of the lens system & its aberrations.

DEFLECTION   usually refers only to bullets, although shot can also be deflected. Deflection can be caused by a variety of conditions, wind deflection *(q.v.)* being the primary concern. Under some hunting conditions where the bullet must penetrate brush, deflection due to the projectile hitting branches & other obstacles is of an unpredictable type. Bullets so deflected may keyhole, blow up, or expand prematurely. Bullet flight characteristics may be affected to such an extent that a deer-sized target is missed completely.

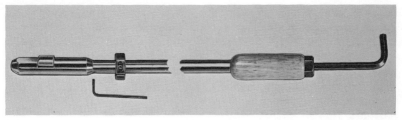

Dent raiser. Courtesy Bob Brownell, Brownell's, Inc.

DENSITY OF LOADING *see* Loading Density.

DENT REMOVER or RAISER tool used by gunsmiths to remove dents in shotgun barrels. These barrels are thin-walled, are relatively easily pushed in or dented. By forcing the dent remover through the damaged portion of the barrel, many such barrels can be salvaged.

DERINGER a small percussion pocket pistol originally made by Henry Deringer, a Philadelphia gunmaker, working there in 1825. The pistols found immediate acceptance, were very popular in the late 1800's, were copied widely by most of the gunmakers of the period. These copies are not Deringers, as so often claimed falsely, but are differentiated from the original Deringer pistol by naming them derringers *(q.v.)*.

DERRINGERS small pocket pistols based on the original design of Henry Deringer. The double "r" & non-capitalization are used to describe these pistols made by Remington, Colt, & others.

DETENT usually spring-operated, is a catch, pawl, or other small part that holds or retains another

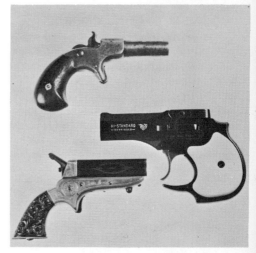

Three derringers.

part that is movable. Typical of a detent is a bolt stop *(q.v.)* in a bolt action rifle.

DIE, LOADING or HANDLOADING cylindrical shaping tool with

Loading dies.

inside dimensions similar or identical to the cartridge case for which it is used; dies are used to size cases, seat bullets, reshape cases. Special dies, such as SWAGING DIES, are used to form bullets; dies to effect closures on shotshells are referred to as CRIMPING DIES. *Also see:* Bullet, Swaged; Cold Working; Crimp.

DIE, LOADING, CARBIDE　　specially hardened dies are used widely for reloading revolver & pistol ammunition. Carbide loading dies can be used without case lubrication. *Also see:* Handloading.

DIE, LOADING, PISTOL　　a complete set of loading dies for any of the popular pistol calibers usually consists of three separate dies: the

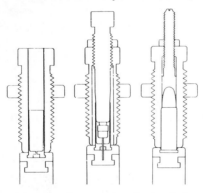

sizing die, the expander die that bells the case mouth, & the bullet seating die. Some handloading tool manufacturers offer four-die pistol sets, the fourth die being a special case mouth crimping die. *Also see:* Crimp.

DIE, LOADING, RIFLE　　a complete set of loading dies for any of the standard rifle calibers usually consists

of two dies: the sizing-decapping die, & the bullet seating die. Three-die sets are sometimes offered, as well as special case forming dies & case length trimming dies.

DIE, LOADING, TUNGSTEN like the carbide loading dies, specially hardened so that they won't scratch cases & will size cases without lubrication. *Also see:* Handloading.

DIE, SWAGING　　*see* Swage.

DISASSEMBLY　　taking-down or stripping of a gun in a methodical fashion to clean, service, or study the functioning of that gun. In disassembling, it is important to understand the interaction of the moving parts of a gun so that when reassembling it, all parts go together easily & without forcing.

DISCONNECTOR　　a device in a semiautomatic gun that prevents the continued firing of the gun while the trigger remains depressed. The disconnector holds the gun at full cock as long as the trigger is held back.

DISPERSION, HORIZONTAL also called horizontal spread, is the maximum distance between the bullet hole on the extreme right & that on the extreme left in a group *(q.v.)*.

DISPERSION, VERTICAL　　also called vertical spread, is the maximum distance between the bullet hole at the extreme top & that at the extreme bottom in a group *(q.v.)*.

D-MANTEL　　*see* Bullet, H-Mantel.

DOG   an old name for the sear *(q.v.)*, also the trigger on old double barreled guns.

DOLL'S HEAD or DOLL'S HEAD EXTENSION   the enlarged protrusion at the rear of the top rib of some double barreled shotguns as well as some combination guns. A recess is cut into the standing breech of the action to accomodate the doll's head. Some shotgun makers even cross-bolted the doll's head. The use of the doll's head for locking the breech is no longer popular since, to be effective, it has to be hand-fitted.

DOT   *see* Reticle.

DOUBLE   a two barrel gun where the barrels are aligned side-by-side. Although over/under shotguns are actually also double guns, usage limits the term to side-by-side guns. Double guns are usually smoothbored, but double rifles, for dangerous game, are sometimes encountered in the U.S.; are fairly common in England, Europe, Africa, as well as in India.

DOUBLE ACTION   *see* Revolver, Double Action; Pistol, Double Action.

DOUBLE-BASE POWDER   *see* Powder, Double-base.

DOUBLES   throwing of, & shooting at, two clay pigeons at the same time. Doubles are thrown in trap *(q.v.)* as well as in skeet *(q.v.)*.

DOUBLE SET TRIGGER   *see* Trigger, Double Set.

DOUBLE TRIGGER   *see* Trigger, Double.

DOUBLING   term with two meanings: (1) accidental & involuntary discharge of both barrels of a double rifle or shotgun. This can be caused by wear & tear of the hammer notches & the two hooks of the trigger. Doubling can also be due to slippage of the second hammer while the gun recoils from the first shot. Inertia weights are used in some shotgun actions to prevent accidental pulling of the trigger while the gun is recoiling. (2) the downing of two birds with two shots out of a flight or group of birds. Sometimes, but this is rare, the killing of two birds with a single shot.

DOVETAIL   a flaring machined slot that is also slightly tapered toward one end. Cut into the upper sur-

face of barrels & sometimes actions, the dovetail accepts a corresponding part on which a sight is mounted. Dovetail slot blanks are used to cover the dovetail when the original sight has been removed; this gives the barrel a more pleasing appearance & configuration.

DRAM   a unit of apothecaries' weight, equals 1/16 oz. av.

DRAM EQUIVALENT   an obsolete comparison meant to indicate that a certain charge of smokeless powder has the same ballistic efficiency as a given volumetric measure, or dram weight, of black powder. When shotshells were loaded with black powder, 3 drams of powder was the standard charge. When smokeless powders replaced black powder, the dram equivalent was listed on shotshell boxes to give shooters a guideline as to the ballistic efficiency of the smokeless powder charge in the shells. With today's powders, a 3 dram equivalent smokeless powder load may weigh half or less than the stated dram equivalent.

DREYSE   *see* Ignition History.

DRIFT   the left or right deviation from the line of bore of a bullet in flight. Drift is caused by the gyrational spin of the bullet. Right hand twist *(q.v.)* produces a drift to the right, left hand twist produces a left deviation.

DRIFT PIN   a pin or stud that is held in action parts due to its tight fit & slight taper. Removal of a drift pin, called drifting out, is accomplished by pushing on the pin from the point of its smallest diameter.

DRIFT, WIND   *see* Wind Deflection.

DRILLED & TAPPED   *see* Scope Bases.

DRILLING   the three barrel combination gun *(q.v.)* is the classic hunting gun of the German & Austrian hunter. The two shotgun barrels are arranged side-by-side, with the rifle barrel placed directly below them. Two conventionally arranged triggers serve the shotgun, with one of them also serving the rifle barrel when the barrel selector is pushed forward. In most drillings, this barrel selector also erects the folded leaf sight. Scope mounting on a drilling is accomplished by means of the classic German claw mounts (*see* Scope Bases).

DRIVING BAND   originally a brass band around a steel artillery projectile. The driving band took on the engraving (*see* Bullet Engraving), also acted as bearing surface (*see* Bullet Bearing Surface). In two dimensional bullets, the rearmost part or tail of the bullet was slightly over-bore size, and this part of such a bullet was often referred to as the driving band. In cast gas-check bullets where the diameter of the gas-check was slightly larger than bore diameter, the edge of the gas-check cup was often referred to as the driving band, although it also aided in sealing off gases. Wider & stronger bands were needed to prevent the bullet from slipping over the lands, & stronger bearing or driving bands were advocated.

DROP   on a gunstock, is that distance downward from the line of

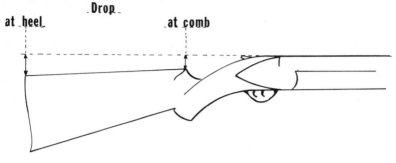

Gunstock drop.

sight or an imaginary line extended to the rear along the top of the barrel to the upper edge of the buttstock. Drop is measured at two points on the buttstock: at the comb and at the heel.

DROP AT COMB   the vertical distance between the line of sight & the forward end of the comb. *Also see:* Stock.

DROP AT HEEL   the vertical distance between the line of sight & the top edge of the butt or heel. *Also see:* Stock.

DROP, BULLET   *see* Bullet Drop.

DROPPED SHOT   *see* Shot Tower.

DROSS   oxidized waste that collects on the top of molten metal, especially when impure lead is being melted for bullet casting. Dross is skimmed off & discarded.

DRUM MAGAZINE   *see* Magazine, Drum.

DRY FIRING   the "firing" of an unloaded gun. Dry firing is often recommended as a means of practicing gun handling & trigger control. Rimfire guns should not be dry fired since this tends to damage the firing pin. Shotguns, especially doubles, should be equipped with snap caps *(q.v.)*. Before dry firing, ascertain that both chamber & magazine are empty, contain no live rounds.

DUMDUM   *see* Bullet, Dumdum.

DUMMY   *see* Cartridge, Dummy.

DUMMY SIDE PLATE   a small plate on the left side of the action that is held in place by small screws, supplied on some rifles so that a side mount *(see* Scope Bases) for a scope can be installed easily without additional drilling & tapping of the action for the mounting screws. At one time, dummy side plates were also installed on box lock shotguns to give the appearance of a side lock gun.

DUPLEX LOAD   a load, primarily used experimentally in rifles, that

91

contains charges of two different powders, one fine-grained & quick burning, the other coarse & slow burning. The two powders must be kept separate in the case to give the sought-after performance. Increased velocity at lower pressure with less muzzle flash led to considerable experimental work, here & abroad, but the duplex loads developed failed to live up to expectations.

DUST COVER   a sliding, easily removable sheet metal device on some military rifles. Installed to protect the bolt or opened action from rain, dust & other foreign matter.

DUST SHOT   *see* Shot Sizes.

DWM   trademark of & abbreviation for Deutsche Waffen und Munitionsfabriken, Karlsruhe, Germany. DWM was founded in 1872, and DWM ammunition is currently being imported into the U.S.

E

EARS a term often applied to the rear sight guard of the British Enfield rifle. In sporterizing the Enfield, removal of these ears becomes mandatory.

EFFECTIVE RANGE the maximum distance at which a bullet can kill game with some degree of accuracy. Effective range depends on caliber, bullet weight, velocity, wind, & is at best a hypothetical comparative term.

EJECTION the forceful mechanical removal of a cartridge or shell, fired or unfired, from the chamber of a rifle, shotgun or handgun equipped with an ejector. Some rifle & shotgun actions are not equipped with an ejector, but have an extractor *(q.v.)* which elevates the head of the cartridge or shell for manual removal. Some double barrel shotguns & rifles have selective ejectors where the ejector kicks out only the fired case, raises the unfired round for inspection or removal.

EJECTOR spring-activated mechanism for the ejection *(q.v.)* of ammunition or fired cases. On ejector doubles, each barrel has a separate ejector.

EJECTOR ROD in double rifles & shotguns, located below the barrel or barrels, the ejector rod is linked to the ejector, activates the ejector when the gun is broken or opened.

EJECTOR ROD in revolvers, the rod that projects forward from the cylinder. By pushing the ejector rod

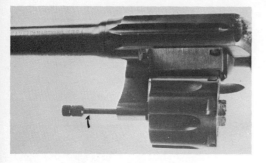

to the rear once the cylinder is swung out, the cartridges or fired cases are removed from the chambers of the cylinder. In some revolvers, pulling the ejector rod forward unlocks the cylinder, allowing it to be swung out. *Also see:* Rod Ejector.

EJECTOR, SELECTIVE, AUTO-MATIC   in some double & single barrel guns, the ejector is linked with the hammer of the barrel. If the shell or cartridge has not been fired & the hammer remains cocked, the ejector rod won't activate the ejector, thus only raising the unfired shell, but ejecting the fired one. *Also see:* Ejection; Ejector.

EJECTOR, SOUTHGATE   a common type of automatic ejector design.

ELEVATION   the up or down movement of any sight that changes the point of impact of the bullet on the target.

ELEVATION ADJUSTMENT on receiver sights & telescopic sights is by means of a micrometer screw. Adjustment screws or knobs are

marked in divisions, sometimes called clicks *(q.v.)* where each such click represents a certain amount of movement of the point of impact at 100 yards in the direction indicated. A click may be a fraction of, or a whole MOA (*see* Minute of Angle).

ENERGY   the capacity for doing mechanical work. In shooting, the energy of motion is of primary concern.

ENERGY, BULLET   the measure of work performed by a projectile in flight, expressed as foot/pounds or ft/lb.

ENERGY FORMULA   to obtain kinetic bullet energy, the following formula is used: V = velocity in fps; W = weight of bullet in gr.; E = energy in ft/lb.

$$E = \frac{WV^2}{450,240}$$

ENERGY, MUZZLE   the energy of a projectile at the muzzle of the gun from which it has been fired.

ENERGY, TERMINAL   the energy of a projectile at the target. The distance from the target to the muzzle of the gun is not the important consideration, but the terminal velocity (*see* Velocity, Striking) of the bullet determines the terminal energy, providing the bullet weight has not changed.

ENGINE TURNED   also called JEWELING or DAMASKEENING. This ornamental polishing is often found

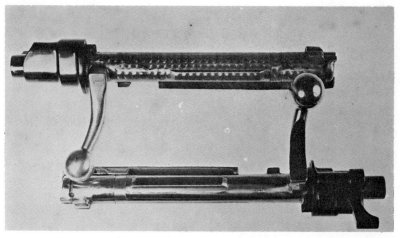

Bolt at top has been decorated by engine turning, bolt below is shown prior to this process.

on bolts, extractors, breechblocks & other gun parts which are not blued.

ENGLISH CHECKERING   *see* Checkering, English.

ENGLISH GUN TERMS   are in some instances identical to those used in the U.S., but a number of the terms can be confusing. The following list is a partial one, covering only the most frequently encountered English gun terms.

BACKSIGHT—Rear Sight
BEND—Drop of Stock
BODY—Receiver
BOLT LEVER—Bolt Handle
BOTTOM PLATE—Floor Plate
CAP—Primer
CAP CHAMBER—Battery Cup
CHARGER CLIP—Stripper Clip
COCKING DOG—Cocking Lever
COMPOUND BULLET—Jacketed Bullet
DRILL ROUND—Dummy Cartridge

ENVELOPE—Bullet Jacket
FIRE-HOLE—Flash Hole
FIRELOCK—Flintlock
FLANGED—Rimmed
FORESIGHT—Front Sight
GUN—Shotgun, usually a side-by-side
GRATICULE—Reticle
HALF-BENT—Half Cock
HALF-HAND—Semi-pistol Grip
HAND—Small of the Stock
KICKER—Part of the ejector system which activates ejector rod
LUMPS—Lugs on barrels of side-by-side
MAGAZINE PLATFORM—Magazine Follower
RETAINING CATCH—Bolt Stop
SELFLOADING PISTOL—Semiautomatic Pistol
SIGNAL PIN—Cartridge Indicator
STALKING MUZZLE—Leather cover for rifle muzzle, removed before firing

STREAMLINE BULLET—
Boattail Bullet
THREADED   HOOD—Receiver
Ring
TUMBLER—Hammer; also same
as Kicker
WATER   TABLE—Action   Bar
Flats

ENGLISHING   a term describing
the British method of aligning the
barrels of a side-by-side shotgun. The
center to center distance of two adjoining shotgun barrels is greater at
the breech than at the muzzle. To
align them so that they shoot to the
same point of impact rather than
crossfire, the barrels are bent or
beveled as they are being assembled.
The process of bending them is Englishing & this is a painstaking, tedious job that requires infinite pa-
tience as well as considerable skill.
Bending the barrels is done by ham-
mering tapered nails inserted under
wires. Only the best English shotgun
barrels are assembled in this fashion.

ENGRAVING   the art of carving
metal in decorative patterns. Scroll
engraving is the most common type
of hand engraving   encountered.
Much of the currently seen factory
engraving is roll-on engraving & this
is done mechanically.

ENGRAVING, BULLET   *see*
Bullet Engraving.

EPROUVETTE   *see* Powder
Tester.

EROSION   *see* Barrel Erosion.

96

EVERLASTING CASE   *see* Reusable Case.

EXPANDER PLUG or BALL
that part of a handloading sizing die
that restores or increases the internal
neck diameter of the cartridge case
being sized.

EXPANDING POINT BULLET
a bullet which has an exposed lead tip
that may be covered with a thin alloy
to delay expansion somewhat. This
tip may have any of several shapes &
expansion of the point is governed by
hardness of the lead core as well as of
the jacket metal, by jacket length as
well as thickness of the jacket walls
from the forward end to the base of
the bullet. In order to increase expansion, jacket edges may be grooved,
scalloped or otherwise shaped or cut.
Also see: Bullet Expansion, Controlled.

EXPANSION   as used in the firearms field, has two meanings: (1)
cartridge cases & shotshell hulls

Bullet at left weighs 250 gr., was loaded for a
wildcat rifle, the 338-06. Bullet at right was
recovered from record moose, shows excellent
expansion and better than 90 per cent weight
retention.

expand when fired. If excessive pressures were created during the firing, the cases do not return to their near-original dimensions. *Also see:* Case Head Expansion. Similarly, primer pockets can become enlarged due to excessive pressures. If a new primer is seated in an expanded primer pocket, the primer will fall out of the primer pocket. *Also see:* Primer Pocket Expansion. (2) bullet expansion is highly desirable in hunting bullets. A bullet that expands properly is said to open up well, or mushroom. *Also see:* Bullet Expansion, Controlled; Bullet, Mushroom.

EXPRESS CARTRIDGES & RIFLES   the term EXPRESS is said to have been coined by Purdey, famed British gunmaker. Express Train cartridges were those black powder loads that carried light bullets at high velocities, & Express rifles were the guns, usually doubles but sometimes single shot rifles, chambered for these rounds. NITRO EXPRESS is the term now used to describe the same or similar cartridges loaded with nitro powders. Nitro Express rifles have also been offered by British gunmakers in bolt action or magazine rifles.

EXTENSION RIB   the small extension of the rib *(q.v.)* on double shotguns, rifles, & a few combination guns that fits into a cut in the upper front of the standing breech. Cross-bolting the extension rib was, at one time, quite popular with gunmakers. The extension rib itself aids in the locking & its use is still common in European gunmaking centers.

EXTENSION STOCK   *see* Stock, Extension.

EXTRACTION, PRIMARY   the first step in extraction & ejection. In primary extraction, the fired case is freed from the walls of the chamber & considerable force may be required to accomplish this. A rough chamber, excessive chamber pressure, & dirty or oversized cases tend to stick. Rapid firing & consequent heating of the gun can also produce sticking. *Also see:* Chamber, Fluted.

EXTRACTOR   a device that withdraws or elevates a fired case or a live round from the chamber as the breech mechanism is opened. *Also see:* Ejector.

EXTRACTOR GROOVE   *see* Case Extractor Groove; Extractor Hook.

EXTRACTOR HOOK   the claw-like device that fits into the case extractor groove *(q.v.)*. In bolt action rifles, the extractor hook engages into the groove when the bolt is closed, accomplishes primary extraction (*see* Extraction, Primary) as well as final extraction as the bolt is moved to the rear.

EXTREME RANGE   maximum distance a projectile is able to travel, regardless of accuracy.

EYE RELIEF   is that distance required between the eye & the ocular lens of a telescopic sight that gives the user of the sight the best image of the object viewed.

F

FABRIQUE NATIONALE d'-ARMES de GUERRE Liege, Belgium. The famed European arms company is the producer of the Browning line of firearms. Abbr: FN.

FACE OF BREECH in double guns, the vertical portion of the action, also called standing breech (*see* Breech, Standing).

FALLING BLOCK *see* Action, Falling Block. *Also see:* Single Shot.

FALSE MUZZLE *see* Muzzle, False.

FANNING the rapid firing of a single action revolver by holding back, or entirely removing, the trigger while rapidly & repeatedly hitting the hammer with the palm of the other, gloved hand. Allegedly a firing method used by the old western gunfighters.

FARQUHARSON *see* Action, Farquharson. *Also see:* Single Shot.

FEEDING process of successively moving cartridges or shells, either manually by activating cams & linkages or semiautomatically by means of gas pressure operating the bolt, from the magazine into the chamber of a firearm.

FEEDING GUIDE also known as FEEDING RAMP or BULLET RAMP. The projecting surfaces or the ramp on the upper part of the inside walls of a receiver that guide cartridges or

98

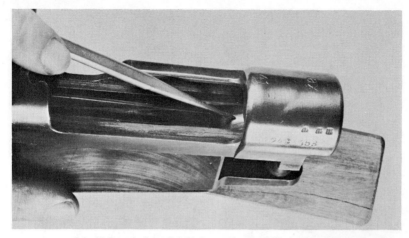

Pointer indicates feeding ramp inside front receiver ring of Mauser M98 action.

shotshells from the magazine to the chamber. Feeding ramp angles in semiautomatic pistols are critical, often are the cause of malfunctions. The lips or edges of a magazine clip *(q.v.)* are thin & easily bent. Bending or other such damages are the primary causes for failure to feed in semiautomatic pistols.

FEED MECHANISM   the group of interconnected parts that feed fresh cartridges or shotshells into the chamber of a semiautomatic or fully automatic gun.

FEET/PER/SECOND   abbr. fps, is the unit of measure of the speed of a physical body. In shooting, the velocity *(q.v.)* of a projectile is measured in fps.

FERRULE   small metal loop, usually going around the entire barrel & stock, that secures & helps to store a cleaning rod or ramrod.

FIELD GUN, FIELD LOAD

Feeding or bullet ramp on barrel of 45 ACP semiautomatic pistol.

shotgun or shotshell load designed exclusively for hunting. This is in contrast to trap or skeet guns or loads.

FIELD OF VIEW   the area seen, at a given distance, through a telescopic sight or binoculars. The field of view is sometimes listed not in feet or inches, but in degrees of angle.

FIELD STRIPPING   *see* Disassembly.

FILLER BLOCK   *see* Grip Adapter.

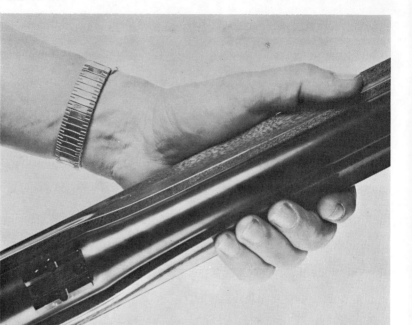

Wide fingerrail incorporated in the custom stock of author's 458 Winchester Magnum.

FINGER RAIL a groove in the forend of some shotguns & occasionally in custom rifle stocks, that permits the grasping hand a better, more secure hold.

FINISH a loosely used term describing the over-all appearance of a firearm. This description often includes the care taken in inletting *(q.v.)*, the quality of the checkering *(q.v.)*, the smoothness of the bluing *(q.v.)*. More specifically, finish also describes the method & materials used to seal the pores of the wood to make it weather resistant & to give it eye appeal.

Some of the most common gun stock finishes are: (1) French polish, a mixture of shellac & boiled linseed oil. A difficult finish, it takes great skill to apply & get smooth, even results. Some finishers add alcohol instead of linseed oil, others use straight shellac. (2) various lacquers, some specifically made for gunstocks, others adapted for stock work. As in all finishing methods, water resistance & easy repair or patching are important & most lacquers fill the bill. (3) oil, especially the various linseed oils & their commercial counterparts. Oil finishing is an art, that is if a professional looking job is desired. Specially made stock oils are relatively easy to use, but the major trouble with oil finishes is the long drying time that can't be hastened successfully. Tedious hand rubbing is the secret to a good oil finish. (4)

plastic coatings are the newest wrinkle in stock finishes, but most of them are factory applied. Some of the newer ones are excellent, but small areas of the finish damaged in field use can't be repaired readily. (5) varnishes are excellent, have all the desired attributes for stock finishing, can be patched easily, & removal of old finish for do-it-yourself stock refinishing is easy.

FIREARM   any device that fires a projectile or a mass of projectiles by means of a propellant charge & a triggering system.

FIREFORMING   *see* Case Fireforming.

FIRELOCK   sometimes used instead of matchlock *(q.v.). Also see:* English Gun Terms.

FIRING CYCLE   the five operations involved in discharging a firearm. Exception should be made here for double rifles & shotguns & for the cylinder revolver, since in the revolver a cartridge is not fed into the chamber with each round fired, nor is each fired case extracted or ejected after firing. Starting with a closed, but empty gun, such as a rifle, the five steps are: (1) opening of action, (2) feeding *(q.v.)* a cartridge from magazine into chamber, (3) closing & locking the action, (4) firing the gun by pulling the trigger, and (5) extraction & ejection of the fired case.

FIRING LINE   in shooting parlance, it is a line of shooters at a rifle or pistol range. The National Rifle Association defines the term as "The firing line is that part of the range immediately in rear of an imaginary line drawn through the several firing points." *Also see:* Firing Point.

FIRING MECHANISM   the pieces of the firearm's mechanism that, through linkages & cams, function in unison to fire the cartridge or shell in the chamber of the gun. Often such parts are spoken of as an assembly *(q.v.)* or group, such as the firing group, trigger group, etc. The firing mechanism consists of firing pin & mainspring, trigger, sear & hammer, plus various other small parts.

FIRING PIN   under tension of the mainspring, is released when the trigger is pulled. The tip or most forward part of the pin hits the primer of the round in the chamber, thus detonating the primer, and this in turn igniting the powder charge. A part of the firing mechanism *(q.v.),* the shape, length & method of linkage to the mainspring vary greatly from gun design to gun design.

FIRING PIN DRAG   occurs when a projecting firing pin indents into the primer cup so much that opening of a break action gun *(see* Action, Topbreak) becomes difficult.

FIRING PIN, FLOATING   sometimes also called a FREE FIRING PIN. A firing pin which is somewhat shorter than its travel in the breechblock *(q.v.),* the pin is held in the breechblock by a spiral spring. As the pin is driven forward by the falling hammer, the spring is compressed, & the compression then forces the pin backwards into the housing. Inasmuch as the firing pin is not in contact with the primer except when being hit by the hammer, a floating firing pin is an additional safety measure. The best known guns with such a firing pin are the Colt Government 45 & the Russian Tokarev 7.62 mm.

FIRING PIN HOLE   the hole in the face of the breechblock or bolt that guides the tip of the firing pin. In old guns, enlargement of the hole leads to extrusion of the primer cup into the hole. Once in a while, a tight firing pin hole prevents free travel of the pin, binding it so that travel is limited or impossible.

FIRING PIN, INERTIA   a type of firing pin that is flush with the breechblock face when the hammer is in the forward position. A spring prevents its forward movement unless that movement is initiated by the falling hammer.

FIRING PIN PROTRUSION that distance the tip of the firing pin projects out from the face of the breechblock or bolt. A certain amount of protrusion is required, & the amount of protrusion depends on the type of action, the size of primer in the cartridge. If protrusion is less than required, due to wear for instance, misfires will occur. If protrusion is excessive, primer cups will be punctured.

FIRING PIN, SPRING-ACTI-VATED   a type of firing pin that

is not activated by a falling hammer, but rather depends on a spring. Cocking compresses the spring, trigger pull releases it. Typical of the spring-activated firing pin system is the Savage M99 lever action rifle. *Also see:* Hammerless.

FIRING POINT   on the firing line *(q.v.),* a place suitably prepared for competitive shooting. This can consist of grading for prone shooting, a small bench for pistol shooting, a solid bench for benchrest shooting, or an unobstructed area which may or may not have a concrete floor. The firing point & its target usually carry matching numbers for easy target identification by the competitor.

FISHTAIL WIND   a wind that changes direction frequently, is virtually unpredictable.

FIVE IN ONE BLANK   sometimes also "5 in 1" blank. A blank round that can be chambered in five different caliber guns: the 38-40 & 44-40 rifles, as well as in 38-40, 44-40 & 45 Colt revolvers. Also known as MOVIE BLANK.

FIXED AMMUNITION   can be either a cartridge or shotshell. Fixed, or SELF-CONTAINED, ammunition is that held within a case, hull, or other container, and consists of a primer, propellant charge, & projectile. Fixed ammunition can be manipulated round by round, & the entire shell or cartridge is placed into the chamber or breech of the gun for firing.

FLANGED   *see* English Gun Terms.

FLASH HIDER   a device that re-duces but does not hide muzzle flash. Fastened to the muzzle of military small arms, the flash hider does not reduce muzzle blast. Also known as FLASH SUPPRESSOR.

FLASH HOLE   small hole in the center of the primer pocket of a car-tridge case or shotshell hull. Through it, the primer flash ignites the powder charge. *Also see:* Primer Pocket.

FLASH INHIBITOR   a coating of potassium sulphate is applied to many of the currently used smokeless propellant powders to reduce, by chemical means, the amount of muz-zle flash *(q.v.)*.

FLASH SUPPRESSOR   *see* Flash Hider.

FLASK   *see* Powder Flask.

FLAT-NOSED BULLET   *see* Bullet, Flat-nosed.

FLATS   on side-by-side shotguns, the lower barrel surfaces near the chambers that make contact with the ACTION BAR FLATS. The action bar flats are the flat sections which extend forward from the breech face, hous-ing at their forward end the knuckle. Located in the knuckle is the hinge pin which engages the hook on the forward (toward the muzzle) lump. *Also see:* Action, Hinged Frame; Knuckle; Lump, Hook of; English Gun Terms (Water Table).

FLAT SHOOTING   a term that describes, not very accurately, the

Arrow (1) indicates barrel flats, arrow (2) the knuckle, and arrow (3) the action bar flats.

trajectory of a specific caliber. Also often used in conjunction with a specific rifle, a description which is erroneous, since it is not the rifle but the caliber that is flat shooting. The term means a trajectory with minimal curvature between muzzle & target.

FLAT SPRING   *see* Spring, Flat.

FLECHETTE   the projectile or projectiles contained in the U.S. Army's experimental SPIW (Special Purpose Individual Weapon) ammunition. Flechettes are essentially small arrows or darts.

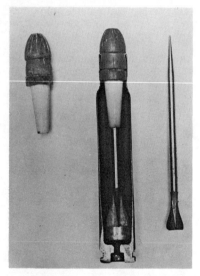

Sectioned XM 144 shows sabot and flechette in case.

FLINCHING   involuntary movement due to anticipation of feeling recoil or gun firing noises at the moment of completing trigger pull.

FLINTLOCK   a term that describes not only a type of action, but also the guns utilizing this type of firing mechanism. The flintlock gun is a muzzle-loading arm that is fired by the action of a piece of flint held in the hammer jaws. As the trigger is released, the flint strikes the steel frizzen, creating sparks. These sparking steel particles from the frizzen fall into the pan that contains finely ground priming powder (black), igniting the priming charge. A touch hole connects the pan with the black powder charge located in the rear or bottom of the barrel. The burning priming compound ignites the main powder charge through the touch hole, thus firing the gun. A DOG LOCK is a variety of the flintlock which carries a hook at the rear of the cock that acts as safety. This hook is known as DOG LATCH.

FLOATING BARREL   *see* Free-floating Barrel.

FLOATING CHAMBER   *see* Chamber, Floating.

FLOBERT ROLLING BLOCK *see* Action, Flobert Rolling Block. *Also see:* Single Shot.

FLOOR PLATE   the often spring-activated metal cover that is underneath the box magazine of a rifle. It forms the bottom of the magazine well, & in most bolt actions serves as fastening point for one end of the flat, zigzag magazine follower spring. Primary purpose of a floor plate is to make removal of unfired cartridges from the magazine easier. Rifles without a floor plate can be emptied

Hinged floorplate on bolt action rifles allows easy access to magazine.

only by moving the bolt fully back, feeding a round in the chamber, & without touching the trigger, pulling the bolt back again, thereby extracting the live round from the chamber. This is continued until all cartridges have been removed from the magazine. Only the Danish Schultz & Larsen rifles are designed so that the loaded cartridges can be placed into the magazine through the floor plate.

FLUX   material used to flux molten lead before casting bullets. Melting lead for casting makes the impurities rise to the top. Lead oxide is one of the major impurities, & fluxing with beeswax reduces the oxides, leaving pure lead. Fluxing should be done before beginning to cast, should be repeated as the surface of the molten metal becomes dull & shows impurities. Fluxing fumes can be ignited with a match, proper ventilation is essential, & fluxing material must be stirred into molten metal. *Also see:* Dross.

FLY   a small part that swings freely through a short arc with one end fastened to the tumbler. In flintlock & percussion guns with double set triggers, the fly blocks the half cock notch as the hammer falls, thus forcing it to travel past that notch.

FLYER or FLIER   bullet that for known or unknown reasons prints or hits outside of the rest of the group fired with the same gun, ammunition, & hold.

FMJ *see* Bullet, Solid.

FOLDED CRIMP *see* Crimp, Star.

FOLDED HEAD *see* Case Head Forms.

FOLDING GUN usually a shotgun that allows folding the gun near the breech. Easily packed & carried, these guns attained only limited popularity in the game fields. Folding shotguns come in all gauges, in single & double barrel models. Because of restrictive gun laws, no folding rifles are offered currently.

FOLDING SIGHT *see* Sight, Folding.

FOLDING TRIGGER *see* Trigger, Folding.

FOLLOWER *see* Magazine Follower.

FOLLOW THROUGH the hard-learned skill of maintaining the sight picture after the trigger has been pulled.

FOOT/POUND abbr. ft/lb, the unit of kinetic energy or the energy of a bullet in motion.

FORCING CONE forward part of the chamber in a shotgun where the chamber diameter is reduced to bore diameter. The forcing cone aids the passage of shot into the barrel.

FOREND, also FORE-END, FORE-ARM that part of the stock forward of the action & located below the barrel or barrels. *Also see:* Beavertail Forend; Stock.

FOREND TENSION also called BEDDING TENSION, is the tension between the wood of the forend & the barrel, expressed in pounds. Some barrels are free-floated *(q.v.)*, that is, there is no contact between wood & barrel steel. Other forends are bedded tightly, that is, contact between wood & barrel steel is very tight, does not allow insertion of a thin paper or metal shim. Tight wood-metal fit is desirable in a hunting rifle, especially if a light barrel is used. Forend fit governs barrel vibration & hence accuracy. Poor accuracy or sudden loss of accuracy is most often due to

This imported folding 410 shotgun has hammers and folds for easy packing.

improper forend tension or stock warpage *(q.v.)*.

FOREND TIP   most forward part of the forend. The tip can be shaped from the stock wood & given various configurations, or a separate forend tip can be fastened. This can be plastic, horn, or a contrasting & exotic wood, often offset from the stock wood by white or black spacers, or yet another wood contrasting in color & grain.

FORENSIC BALLISTICS   police science of identifying fired & recovered bullets, linking them scientifically to having been fired from a particular firearm. A forensic ballistics expert is not the same as a firearms expert witness in court.

FOULING   the residue from burning powder, jacket metal, or lead deposited in a barrel. Fouling, in excess amounts, must be removed every so often to retain accuracy. *Also see:* Bore Leading; Barrel Corrosion.

FOULING SHOT   a shot fired from a clean bore in order to produce slight fouling of barrel. A cleaned barrel will not shoot at the same point of impact as a fouled one, hence the fouling shot. The fouling shot is especially important in competitive target shooting where group size & point of impact can make the difference between winning & losing.

FOWLING PIECE   a shotgun used for bird hunting. A term once used in conjunction with flintlock & percussion guns with locks & stocks especially designed for the newly discovered sport of bird shooting. Fowling piece is now used by some writers who want to sound quaint when describing a shotgun.

FRAME   in usage, has come to mean almost exclusively the forging or casting of a swing-out cylinder revolver. The frame consists of the housing for the cylinder, the lockwork, the grip straps, & at its forward end a threaded housing for the barrel. SOLID FRAME REVOLVERS are similar in construction, have however no swing-out cylinder, depend for ejection on a rod ejector that removes one case or round at a time. HINGED FRAME shotguns (*see* Action, Hinged Frame; Action, Top-Break) are quite common, while the hinged frame revolver design has been phased out. In this type of revolver the frame is hinged at the lower forward end of

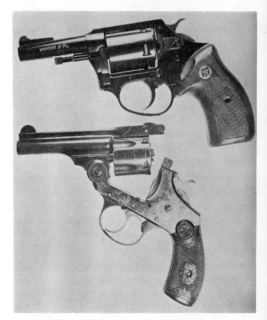

A solid frame **38** Spl. revolver with a hinged frame revolver below.

the frame, with the cylinder pivoting upward as the gun is opened or broken. By moving the muzzle end of such a revolver upward, the action is closed & latched while the cylinder is once again locked against the breech. Some pump action shotguns cannot be taken down, that is the barrel cannot be removed from the action & these guns are sometimes referred to as SOLID FRAME guns. The same term was also used to some extent in connection with centerfire rifles when take-down models were popular. The word frame is also used to describe the solid housing of a semiautomatic pistol which is usually described as the receiver *(q.v.)*.

FREE-BORE the removal of most, if not all, of the rifling from a section of the rifle barrel just forward of the throat. Free-boring is done to reduce the rapid increase of chamber pressure. The bullet travels the length of the free-bore, accepts the rifling when pressure is no longer at peak. The amount of free-bore should never be so long as to make the bullet lose guidance, striking the rifling at an angle. If this happens, accuracy is lost. Measuring of free-bore is simple. Needed are: a cleaning rod, 2 pencils, one loose bullet as is used in the cartridge, one dummy cartridge (a live cartridge should not be used for safety reasons). Insert the cartridge

Paper shim inserted between barrel and forend of rifle indicates that the barrel is freefloated, that is, makes no contact with the wood of the forend.

into the chamber & close the breech. Carefully insert the cleaning rod into the barrel from the muzzle until the tip of the rod makes contact with the tip of the bullet. Mark the cleaning rod where it rests against the muzzle. Remove the cartridge, insert a bullet into the throat, pushing it into place with the pencil. When the bullet makes firm contact with the lands, carefully insert the cleaning rod from the muzzle again. Lower the rod until the tip once again makes contact with the tip of the bullet, holding the bullet in place by pushing on its base with the eraser of the pencil. Again mark where the rod rests against the muzzle. The distance between the first & the second mark on the cleaning rod is the length of the free-boring, or the amount of free-boring, as it is called.

FREE-FLOATING BARREL   to avoid forend tension *(q.v.)* in target rifles, the barreled action is often bedded in such a manner that there is no contact between the wood & the barrel. Fully free-floated barrels usually have an outside diameter bigger than that found on sporting rifles, making the barrel stiffer, hence more accurate & less prone to barrel whip. While target rifles are usually free-floated by the maker, sporting rifles are not. If relieving forend tension only partially cures sudden inaccuracy, a slight free-floating of the barrel often restores accuracy.

FREE PISTOL   a semiautomatic pistol especially designed for target use, & for shooting certain ISU & NRA courses of fire.

FREE RIFLE   bolt action rifle, often a single shot, with a great many refinements for target shooting. The free rifle is fired exclusively with metallic sights & restrictions of the rifle are minimal as is the case with the free pistol *(q.v.)*.

FREE TRAVEL   another term for bullet jump *(q.v.)*.

FRESHENING-OUT   a barrel restoration process by which the lands are somewhat flattened & the grooves are deepened.

FRETTAGE   the process of reinforcing the breech of a cast iron gun by shrinking on hoops of wrought iron or steel to strengthen it.

FRIZZEN   that part of a snaphaunce or flintlock firing mechanism that is struck by the flint. The contact between flint & metallic frizzen creates glowing sparks which ignite the priming charge of fine-grained black powder in the pan.

FROG   *see* Sling Hook.

FRONTAL IGNITION   *see* Ignition, Frontal.

FRONT LOADER   a non-specific term that is sometimes used to describe any type of muzzle-loading gun or a percussion revolver that is loaded from the front of the cylinder.

FRONT SIGHT   *see* Sight, Front.

FRONT STRAP   that part of the revolver or pistol grip frame that faces forward & often joins with the

109

trigger guard. In target guns, notably the 45 ACP, the front strap is often stippled to give the shooter's hand a slip-proof surface.

FULL COCK   *see* Cock, Full.

FURNITURE   on muzzle-loading guns, the metal parts, excluding action parts & barrel, are called furniture. These parts are most frequently made of brass, but silver & other metals are encountered. Furniture is sometimes highly engraved & otherwise decorated.

FUSED SHOT   *see* Shot, Fused.

FUSEE, FUSIL   an early type of flintlock musket.

G

GAGE   a precision instrument for making measurements. Gage & gauge *(q.v.)* are sometimes confused.

GAIN TWIST   *see* Twist, Gain.

GALLERY LOAD   *see* Bullet, Gallery.

GARDEN GUN   low powered 9 mm smoothbored guns, widely used in Europe & England. Designed to protect gardens from varmints, pests, & small game, these garden guns were rimfire guns with a low report. Most of the guns were made in Germany & Belgium. Winchester once manufactured one, the Model 39, but it proved to be a commercial failure. Shells contained shot or a spherical ball, loads were powered by the priming compound only.

GAS   the by-product of the burning of propellant powders. Sometimes the term is used in the plural. Ballisticians & shooters are concerned with these gases since they are hot & under pressure, thus ultimately affect the gun.

GAS-CHECK   a small copper cup affixed to the base of some cast, lead or lead alloy bullets to protect the base of the bullets from the effects of the hot powder gases. *Also see:* Bullet, Gas-check.

GAS CUTTING   the hot powder gases follow the bullet up the barrel at high velocities. Their effect on barrel steel, as well as on lands *(q.v.)* & grooves *(q.v.)* is an erosive one. Gas cutting becomes noticeable visually in the barrels of some high power rifles after several hundred rounds. Gas cutting is also encountered when bullets of less than bore diameter are used to any extent.

GAS CYLINDER in gas operated, semiautomatic guns, the gas cylinder contains the piston which operates the action. The gases enter the cylinder through a small hole in the barrel, forcing back the GAS PIS-TON which acts against the operating rod that activates the moving parts of the action.

GAS LEAK a black smudge or mark around the primer indicating where gas has escaped from the cartridge case.

GAS OPERATED any firearm that depends on the powder gases for its functioning. Gas operated sporting firearms are of the semiautomatic type (*see* Action, Semiautomatic).

GAS PISTON *see* Gas Cylinder.

GAS PORT sometimes called ORIFICE, in semiautomatic guns, is the small hole in the barrel that siphons off powder gases into the gas cylinder.

GAS VENT *see* Vent.

GAUGE abbr. ga., the unit of bore measurement of a shotgun. Originally, the gauge number indicated the number of solid lead balls of bore diameter that could be cast from one pound of lead. The currently used gauges are 10, 12, 16, 20, 28, 410. Only the smallest gauge is ever given in actual bore diameter, .410".

GAUGE ADAPTER a tube inserted in a large barrel that allows the shooter to use shells smaller than those for which the shotgun was

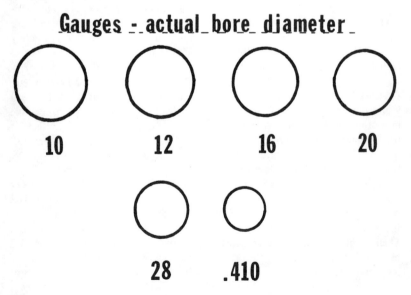

Gauges - actual bore diameter

10   12   16   20

28   .410

designed. Adapters that convert a shotgun from 12 ga. to 410 are popular.

GAUGE EQUIVALENTS, METRIC European shotguns are marked not in gauges, but in bore diameter expressed in millimeters.

10 ga.	19.3 mm	20 ga.	15.7 mm
12 ga.	18.2 mm	28 ga.	13.8 mm
16 ga.	16.8 mm	410 ga.	12.6 mm

GERMAN SILVER widely used alloy consisting of copper 60 parts, zinc 20 parts, nickel 20 parts. Often used in the ornamentation of guns.

GESICHERT the marking found on the German Pistole Parabellum often called the "Luger." When the word gesichert is visible, the gun is on safe; when covered by the safety, the pistol is ready to be fired.

GEWEHR German for rifle.

GILDING METAL an alloy used in making bullet jackets. Gilding metal contains between 90-95 per cent copper, 5-10 per cent zinc.

GLASSBEDDING process of glassbedding is widely used by professional gunsmiths & amateur gun tinkerers. It is done to improve the bedding of the barrel, action, or both in stocks; to reinforce certain areas in the wood, such as the recoil shoulder abutment; to repair minor breaks & splits in stocks. The fiberglass is mixed with a bonding agent & once dried, the resultant surface is smooth, stronger than before & the fiberglass-

covered wood of the stock is virtually impervious to moisture. Various epoxies are used for the same purpose.

GLOBE FRONT SIGHT *see* Sight, Globe Front.

GO GAGE *see* Headspace Gage.

GRAIN abbr. gr., a unit of weight (437.5 gr. = 1 oz. av.), used to designate the weight of a bullet or powder charge.

GRAPE SHOT a cannon projectile consisting of a cluster of small iron balls fired as a unit.

GRAPHITE a chemical form of carbon that is widely used as a lubricant, either in powdered form or mixed with grease or oil.

GRAVITY as it affects a projectile, begins to exert its force the instant the projectile leaves the muzzle of a firearm. *Also see:* Bullet Drop; Air Resistance; Trajectory.

Gesichert.

GREASE GROOVE shallow groove or grooves around the circumference of cast or swaged lead or lead alloy bullets, which are filled with a special bullet lubricant to avoid bore leading *(q.v.)* and to reduce barrel friction. *Also see:* Bullet Casting; Bullet, Inside Lubricated; Bullet, Outside Lubricated; Bullet Lubrication; Bullet, Wadcutter; Cannelure.

GREENER CROSS-BOLT *see* Cross-bolt, Greener.

GREENER SAFETY *see* Safety, Greener.

GREENHILL FORMULA mathematical formula, developed by Sir Alfred George Greenhill, to determine the rate of rifling twist needed to stabilize a specific bullet. Convert bullet length into calibers by dividing its length in inches by its caliber in inches. The Greenhill table is then used to determine twist in calibers, which must be converted to twist per inches by multiplying twist in calibers by bullet diameter in inches. A computerized version of the Greenhill formula can be found in several reloading manuals.

GRIP on pistols & revolvers, the handle or butt *(q.v.)*. Although butt is actually the bottom of the grip, through usage the term is sometimes used to indicate the entire grip. On rifles & shotguns, the grip is the portion of the stock *(q.v.)* that is behind & below the action or breech. If curved to fit the hand, it is a pistol

grip *(see* Grip, Pistol). If the small of the stock is straight, as on British shotguns, the straight grip is sometimes called ENGLISH GRIP.

GRIP ADAPTER a curved attachment, made from plastic, rubber or aluminum, that fits on the front

strap *(q.v.)* of a revolver. In this position it fills the space between the grip & the rear of the trigger guard, gives the shooter's hand a better, firmer hold on the gun. Also called a FILLER BLOCK.

GRIP CAP decorative device added to the base of the pistol grip *(see* Grip, Pistol) on rifles & shotguns. The grip cap can be made of silver, plastic, wood, horn or other materials, is fastened to the stock by means of a visible screw, invisible plugs, or epoxy glue.

GRIP, PISTOL the curved part of the stock behind & below the action on a rifle or shotgun. The pistol grip gives the trigger hand a grasping surface & enables the shooter to pull the gun tighter into his shoulder, thus not only adding support to the gun, but also lessening the effect of recoil *(q.v.)*. The pistol grip is often checkered (*see* Checkering), at the lower edge is often equipped with a grip cap *(q.v.)*.

GRIP SAFETY   *see* Safety, Grip.

GRIP, SEMI-PISTOL   a modified pistol grip that is rounded at the bottom rather than flat. Also called a HALF-PISTOL GRIP.

GRIPS, TARGET   *see* Stock, Target.

GRIP, STRAIGHT   stocks with a straight grip are seen on some lever-action rifles as well as on the stocks of British side-by-side shotguns. It is claimed that the straight stocks on these guns allow shooters to execute a quicker shift from one trigger to the other while the gun is recoiling.

GRIP STRAP   front & rear portion of a handgun frame (*see* Backstrap; Front Strap). In most revolvers, the grip straps are part of the frame *(q.v.)*, while in others, the front strap is a part of the trigger guard while the backstrap is a separate piece.

GROOVE DIAMETER   distance from the bottom of one groove in a rifled barrel to the bottom of the groove opposite it. In the U.S. & Great Britain, the measure is given in decimals of an inch, in Europe the

measure is expressed in millimeters. *Also see:* Bore Diameter.

GROOVES   the spiral cuts in the bore of a rifle or handgun that give the bullet its spin as it moves down the barrel. *Also see:* Twist; Gyroscopic Stability.

GROUP   a number of shots fired at a given range at one target & with one sight setting, with either rifle or handgun, to determine the accuracy of either the gun or the ammunition.

GROUP MEASUREMENT   is for comparison purposes, usually made by measuring the center-to-center distance between the two bullet holes farthest apart. Usage of the term maximum or extreme spread has come to mean the same thing. The actual measurement is called group size. External factors such as barrel heating, warped stock, changing forend tension, can open up

Group measurement.

groups, or it is said that groups spread. Firing of repeated strings (*see* String) will invariably give groups of varying sizes. Measuring the groups then gives maximum as well as minimum spread. *Also see:* Dispersion, Horizontal; Dispersion, Vertical; Flyer.

GUARD SCREWS   the two large screws that hold the trigger guard in the inletting on the underneath side of the stock, & at the same time also pull the receiver of the gun into the stock. Most rifles utilize two of these screws, some use a third one in front of the trigger guard & behind the magazine.

GUEDES-CASTRO DROPPING BLOCK   *see* Action, Guedes-Castro. *Also see:* Single Shot.

GUN   any mechanical device that expels one or more projectiles through a tube or barrel toward a target. This includes shotguns, revolvers & semi-automatic pistols, & rifles. Rifles & handguns can be either centerfire *(q.v.)* or rimfire *(q.v.)*. Included in

the definition of gun should also be those devices which are fired by means of a spring under tension, CO_2 cartridges, & various air guns.

GUN CASE   variety of leather, plastic & aluminum cases, lined or unlined, that accomodate one or two rifles, shotguns or handguns. The use of gun cases for firearms while travelling is not only recommended to protect the guns, but is mandatory in some states. Guns must be unloaded at all times.

GUN FRAME   *see* Frame.

GUN POWDER   *see* Powder.

GYROJET   a patented & trademarked device that fires small rockets. Designed for sporting use, the Gyrojet has not proved popular.

GYROSCOPIC STABILITY   the ability of a bullet to maintain its flight path thanks to the spin imparted to it by the correct twist *(q.v.)* in the gun barrel. *Also see:* Bullet Wabble; Tumbling.

H

HAENEL-AYDT ARC BLOCK
see Action, Haenel-Aydt. *Also see:*
Single Shot.

HAIR TRIGGER *see* Trigger,
Hair.

HALF COCK *see* Cock, Half.

HALF-HAND *see* English Gun
Terms.

HALF-MOON CLIP *see* Clip,
Half-moon.

HAMMER a part of the mechanism that fires a gun. Pivoting around
an axis, the hammer at the end of
its fall (*see* Hammer Fall) transfers
its energy to the firing pin. This is
in contrast to the STRIKER type mechanism that moves in a straight line,

being activated by a spring. The hammer may or may not have a firing pin.
Most centerfire revolvers have a
separate firing pin which is struck at
its rear by the hammer, while rimfire
revolvers have a firing pin that is
integral with the hammer. Some guns
have no visible hammer, are sometimes called hammerless *(q.v.)*, although truly hammerless guns, such
as the Savage M99 lever action rifle,
are made.

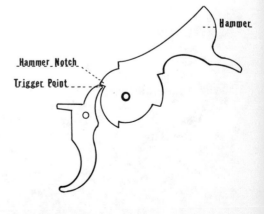

HAMMER BLOCK a small metal block that blocks the rear of the firing pin. Only when the trigger is pulled is the hammer block lowered, allowing the hammer to contact the firing pin. A hammer block is a safety device found on many revolvers.

HAMMER BURR on some exposed hammers, a serrated knob at its upper & rear extremity serves as an aid in cocking.

HAMMER EXTENSION a small & usually off-set device that is screwed onto the hammer spur *(q.v.)*. Used on lever action rifles equipped with telescopic sights to facilitate putting gun on half cock *(q.v.)* or full cock *(q.v.)*, since low mounted scope does not permit easy access to gun's hammer spur.

HAMMER FALL the distance the hammer moves when the trigger is pulled.

HAMMER HOOK in some rifles with a concealed hammer, the bolt or breechblock in its rearward travel over-rides the hammer by moving it back & down. On the top of the hammer is a hook, the hammer hook, that holds the hammer in the cocked position when the trigger, sear, or both engage that hook.

HAMMERLESS while some firearms have hammers which are not visible being located in the action housing, other guns, such as the Savage M99, are truly hammerless. The firing mechanism of the gun is based on a spring-activated firing pin *(see* Firing Pin, Spring-activated).

HAMMER NOTCH a cut or notch in the lower part of the hammer. This notch engages the sear or firing pin, thus putting the gun on half or full cock.

HAMMER SHROUD a small device that is often added to a small frame revolver with exposed hammer. The shroud covers the sides of the hammer, is used to prevent the hammer from catching on clothing while the gun is being drawn. Use of a hammer shroud does not preclude manual cocking for single action shooting.

HAMMER SPUR on exposed hammer guns, the hammer spur extends to the rear & upward, offers a serrated gripping surface as well as leverage for cocking the hammer manually.

HAMMER, STRAIGHTLINE utilized mostly in military arms such as the Reising submachine gun. The cylindrical spring-activated hammer moves forward in a straight line, hitting the floating firing pin *(see* Firing Pin, Floating) located within the bolt.

HAMMER STRUT in double action revolvers *(see* Revolver, Double Action), when shooting the gun double action, the hammer strut serves as cocking mechanism. As the trigger is pulled back, the strut, which is fastened at its upper end to the lower front edge of the hammer & is activated by the trigger at the lower edge, moves the hammer to the full cock position. As full cock is

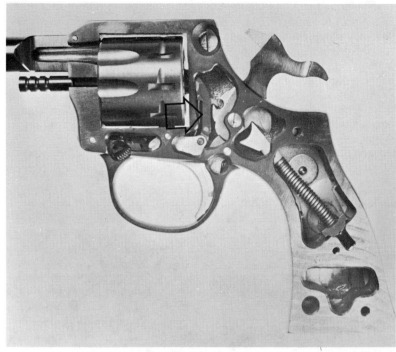

Model shows relationship of hand (arrow) with hammer, ratchet of cylinder, and trigger group.

reached, the trigger moves away from the lower edge of the strut, thus allows the hammer to fall.

HAMMER, TARGET   is a hammer with an extra wide hammer spur that is well serrated for easy cocking. Often installed on target revolvers.

HAND   that part of the revolver lockwork that is connected, by a short lever, with the base of the hammer at one end and the ratchet on the rear of the cylinder at the other. As the hammer is pulled back, the hand moves upward, the upper edge engaging the ratchet on the cylinder, thus moving the cylinder to the next stop as the hammer comes to full cock.

HAND EJECTOR   a Smith & Wesson model designation. Hand ejection, that is removal of the fired cases or live rounds from the cylinder, is accomplished by pushing back on the ejector rod *(q.v.).* This system is now used on all double action revolvers.

HANDGUARD   on military rifles & carbines the piece of wood located atop the barrel & forward of the action. Rapid fire heats the barrel to such an extent that handling of the arm can produce painful burns without this protection. In recent years, wood has been replaced by perforated metal shields.

119

HANDGUN   any firearm designed to be fired with one hand. Classification of handguns can be based on the type of ammunition used, that is centerfire or rimfire. The most common classification is by action types. Revolver *(q.v.)*, which can be either single or double action; semiautomatic pistol (*see* Pistol), which also can be single or double action; & single-shot *(q.v.)* handgun. Revolvers & semiautomatic pistols are sometimes classified by their intended use, hunting, target shooting & defense. The single shot handguns are generally not considered as defense guns, & only three of them are currently imported for target shooting, all of them meeting International Shooting Union requirements. Also included in the handgun classification are the black powder replica guns. Performance of these guns is, on the whole, quite outstanding, both in competi-

Top to bottom: Current production single shot handgun, double action semiautomatic pistol with concealed hammer, a single action revolver, and a double action revolver.

tive matches & in the game fields. *Also see:* Automatic Revolver.

HANDGUN SLING *see* Sling, Handgun.

HANDLOADING also called RELOADING. Centerfire metallic ammunition consists of four components, shotshells of five. There is the case *(q.v.)* or hull *(q.v.)*, the primer, the propellant powder charge, & the projectile—either a bullet or shot. In the case of the shotshell, there is also a wad & a plastic shot collar to prevent shot or pellet deformation while the shot moves up the barrel. There are two basic reasons for reloading the case or hull: economy & better performance from handloads than can be obtained from factory ammunition. The most costly component in ammunition is the case or hull, thus saving & reloading it is definitely worthwhile. Handloads can be tailored for a specific gun as far as performance & accuracy are concerned. Handloading also allows making ammunition that is either obsolete or not made by the ammunition companies (*see* Cartridge, Wildcat).

HANDLOADING METALLICS refers to the reloading of brass cartridge cases for rifles & handguns. RELOADING FOR RIFLE: the fired case is re-sized, that is restored to its original dimensions, in a die *(q.v.)*. During that process, the spent primer is knocked out & a live primer is seated in the primer pocket. With the help of handloading tables *(q.v.)*, a suit-

able powder & powder charge is determined. The correct amount of powder is loaded into the case & a suitable bullet is seated into the case mouth. RELOADING FOR PISTOL: essentially the same process is used as in loading rifle cases, except that the case mouth is belled or turned out somewhat. When the bullet is seated into the case, the case mouth is crimped onto the bullet (*see* Crimp). Belling the case mouth is done to facilitate crimping & to avoid shaving the base of soft lead bullets.

Other steps in reloading metallics may include: gaging diameter of flash hole *(q.v.)*; cleaning primer pocket *(q.v.)* and swaging it if case originally had a crimped primer *(q.v.)*; checking case length *(q.v.)* & trimming to desired length if needed; case mouth chamfering *(q.v.)*; inside or outside case neck reaming to reduce thickness of brass; miking & weighing of bullets; determining case capacity *(q.v.)*; verifying concentricity of bullets with the help of a bullet spinner *(q.v.)*.

HANDLOADING SHOTSHELLS enables shooters to make their own ammunition at a fraction of the cost of factory loads. Reloading the fired hulls also makes it possible to make up special loads, although that practice is not as widespread in shotshell reloading as in handloading metallics. RELOADING SHOTSHELLS: Separate plastic & paper hulls, not only by gauges but also by makes, including high & low base cases (*see* Shotshell). Depending on the loading tools used (*see* Handloading Tools), the handloader collects all the needed components ready to use individually by hand or assembles them to feed into an automatic or nearly automatic loader. The case is first resized to its original dimensions, the spent primer is knocked out & a fresh one is seated. A suitable powder & powder charge for the gauge & intended use, & the size & amount of shot are selected from the handloading tables *(q.v.)*. Over the powder charge is placed either an over-powder wad to prevent the mixing of powder & shot, or a shot cup with collar. The cup & collar keep the shot together so that the entire shot charge travels down the barrel as a single projectile. In determining the powder charge, the total weight of the projectile, that is shot & wad or shot cup, must be taken into consideration. Once the shot charge has been delivered into the hull, the case mouth is crimped *(see* Crimp).

In loading shotshells, it is possible to make up loads identical to factory loads, slug loads, duck, goose & other hunting loads, loads for trap & skeet. It is quite economical to load shells with a simple loading tool that permits making up a box or two of shells in an evening, but there are also loading tools where the handloader merely inserts the empty fired hull, removing, at the other end of the rotating table, the fully loaded shell ready for use. *Also see:* Primer, Battery Cup; Shot; Shot Collar; Wad; Wad Pressure.

HANDLOADING STEPS orderly evolution from the fired case or shell to a fully loaded round. METAL-LICS: Decapping or knocking out the

fired primer is accomplished while the case is being sized in the die. If the case is to be used in the same rifle it was fired in, then it is possible to neck-size *(q.v.)* the case only. This prevents excessive cold working *(q.v.)* of the brass. Pistol & revolver cases are often sized in special dies that make it unnecessary to lubricate the cases. Rifle cases must be lubed. Rifle brass is more prone to stretching, thus case length must be checked. If too long, case is trimmed to specifications with a case trimmer *(see* Handloading Tools). Case mouth chamfering is next; priming is done immediately after the case has been decapped, providing the primer pocket *(q.v.)* is not to be cleaned. Powder selection is based on caliber & bullet weight, the suitable powder & charge being determined from the handloading tables. The powder charge can either be measured volumetrically with a powder measure or weighted on a powder scale. A powder funnel aids in transferring the charge into the case. After all cases are charged, a visual inspection is made to ascertain that all cases contain a powder charge. Then the correct bullet is seated by means of the seater die.

Most rifle die sets contain two dies, the sizing die which contains the decapping pin in the expander plug *(q.v.)*, & the bullet seating die. The dies can be adjusted to some extent. Thus, the full length sizing die normally supplied can be adjusted so that the case is only neck-sized, but special neck-sizing dies are also offered. A few rifle calibers come with three dies, the third one being a special crimping die. Pistol & revolver dies come in sets of three, a fourth one, again a special crimping die, being offered in four-die sets. The first die sizes the case, the next decaps as well as bells the case mouth. The third seats the bullet & crimps, unless there is a fourth die designed for crimping only. The amount of belling, bullet seating depth, & the amount of crimp can be adjusted easily.

Brass for wildcats (*see* Cartridge, Wildcat) is made from standard cases. Special forming dies are offered, often are custom made. Cases are fireformed (*see* Case Fireforming), belts on cases may be cut off in a lathe, case head diameters may be reduced, & case neck or case length may be altered drastically.

SHOTSHELLS: the reloading of shotshells is somewhat simpler than reloading metallics. Powder & shot charges have been worked out carefully by the manufacturers of components & loading tools. Used shells can be run through a shell conditioner (*q.v.*) & those cases with frayed mouths can be trimmed but an adjustment must then be made in the overall length of the charge by reducing wad height so that a case closure can be effected. Many of the shotshell loading tools are supplied with charge bars which deliver pre-determined amounts of a specific powder & shot. Wad developments & improvements have been numerous in recent years. Loaders come in all gauges & some tools come completely set up & ready for use. Some tools will handle plastic as well as paper hulls, others will load only one or the other.

HANDLOADING TABLES are invaluable for handloaders. Carefully worked up tables for all standard & many wildcat cartridges are offered by bullet & powder makers, also by manufacturers of loading tools. Such tables often indicate a wide range of suitable powders & an even wider range of loads or charges. Under no circumstances are the maximum loads to be used as starting loads, and loading manual instructions should be read & followed carefully. Some of the loading tables specify which gun & what primers were used to develop the loads. Often velocities as well as chamber pressures are listed & much pertinent information can be gleaned from the tables & the accompanying textual matter. Many of the tables for metallics also indicate case length, bullet seating depth, primer size, maximum cartridge length, etc. In studying various loading tables, it is often discovered that certain discrepancies exist. Where one table or manual will list a load with a specific bullet as medium or perhaps as maximum (or max) load, another will indicate that the same load is over max. Beginning reloaders should understand that variations in case capacity (*q.v.*), chamber dimensions (*see* Tolerance), barrel length, twist, bullet seating depth, as well as existing range conditions & the type of equipment used in the tests affect load data & performance.

HANDLOADING TOOLS are basically divided into those used for reloading metallics & those designed for loading shotshells. In addition to the tools needed to load the ammuni-

Part of author's reloading bench. Left to right, major components are: Powder scale with powder cannister, loading block with cases and powder funnel, a deburring tool, boxes of bullets, rack for loading dies, loading press with die and case, lube pad, tong tool, another rack with dies, bullet puller of collet type.

tion, there are numerous accessories, some very useful, others falling into the realm of gadgets.

RIFLE & HANDGUN TOOLS: Basic tool set-up is simple, consists of loading press, loading dies, powder scale & funnel, chamfering tool for rifle cases, loading block, & lube pad. Added to this may be a case trimmer (*see* Case Trimming) & case length gage *(q.v.)*, a micrometer & a vernier caliper. For production-line handgun ammunition cleaning, there's even an electric case tumbler on the market. The simplest loading presses are hand-held, can be used to load rifle as well as handgun brass. Bench presses offer a better mechanical advantage, must be bolted onto a solid bench or hefty old table. Offered are simple C, O, & H frame presses, as well as turret presses. In the first three, a ram which moves up & down holds the shellholder which fits the extractor groove of the case. In the turret press, a heavy rotating disc allows mounting several dies instead of the single die mounted atop the C or O frame press. A powder measure is a good investment, but does not replace a powder scale.

SHOTSHELL LOADING TOOLS: Simple loaders are available in nearly all gauges & if only relatively small quantities of shells are to be loaded, this type of loader is suggested. As production rate increases, so does cost & complexity of the loader. Some work in a straight line where the operator moves the case from loading station to loading station, while the bigger machines automatically rotate a number of cases from station to station with each move-

ment of the tool handle. Special primer, powder, shot & wad dispensers are offered on the complex tools. Some tools can deliver up to 700 loaded shells per hour. Many of the loaders can be readily converted from one gauge to another, similar to metallic reloading where only the dies & shellholder need to be purchased to load a different caliber.

HAND STOP predominantly made of aluminum or plastic, the stop is found on target rifles, just behind the front sling swivel. It serves to prevent the left hand from moving or slipping forward, is usually adjustable by means of a sliding nut that travels in an aluminum rail.

HANGFIRE the delayed ignition of a cartridge. If the firing pin audibly makes contact with the primer, but the gun fails to fire, count up to ten before opening the action. Hangfires usually fire before the count of ten is reached. Open the bolt or action slowly, turning ejection port away from your body & any other shooters, pointing the muzzle downrange at all times.

HARD BALL *see* Ball, Hard.

HARQUEBUS an early form of the matchlock ignition system. The original guns of this type were smoothbored, were so unhandy & long that they were fired from a rest formed by two crossed sticks.

HASTY SLING *see* Sling, Hasty.

HEAD DIAMETER diameter of

the case head *(q.v.)* as measured from edge to edge. In rimmed cartridges, this measure is greater than body diameter.

HEADSPACE   that distance from the breech face to that area of the chamber that prevents a further forward movement of the cartridge case as the gun is fired. For a rimmed cartridge, headspace is measured from the breech face to the rear of the chamber where the forward edge of the rim rests. Belted cases, which can be considered a variant of the rimmed case as far as headspace is concerned, headspace on the forward edge of the belt. For a rimless case, headspace is measured from the breech face to a specific point on the shoulder in the chamber, this distance varying with each caliber. Straight rimless cases headspace from the breech face to the square shoulder in the chamber that corresponds to the case mouth. On semi-rimmed cartridges with a rim that has a greater diameter than the case body, headspace extends from the forward edge of the rim to the front end of the chamber, the stop in the chamber

being located somewhat ahead of the case mouth.

HEADSPACE GAGES   are precision ground to rigid specifications to check headspace in rifles & shotguns. Usually a set of two such gages are used, the GO & the NO-GO GAGE. A Field gage is sometimes used. In practice, the Go gage is inserted into a rifle & the bolt should close easily. The Field gage may permit bolt closure, while the No-Go gage will not permit bolt closure. The practice of using a live cartridge as a headspace gage is a dangerous one. Despite SAAMI specifications, factory cartridges from various manufacturers vary enough so that a round may chamber easily, yet despite the fact that the round may be over-sized, it actually chambers in a rifle with too much headspace. If no headspace gage is available, several factory rounds with the bullets & powder charges removed may be used, but care must be taken not to change case neck length or shoulder in any way while removing the bullets.

HEADSTAMP   the impressed

Markings on case head can tell where ammunition was made, what caliber, and in military rounds, when.

mark on the head of a cartridge case or shotshell. Commercially made ammunition shows maker's name as well as caliber or gauge. Military ammunition often bears the mark of the arsenal or contract ammunition maker, the month & year of manufacture, sometimes the specific type of weapon for which the ammunition is to be used. This is important since some military ammunition is loaded to higher pressure levels for use in semiautomatic & automatic rifles, & if fired in a gun not adapted for the higher pressures, gun failure can occur.

HEEL   back end of the upper edge of the buttstock at the upper edge of the buttplate or recoil pad. *Also see:* Stock.

HELICAL SPRING   *see* Spring, Helical.

HIGH BASE   *see* Shotshell.

HIGH BRASS   *see* Shotshell.

HIGH HOUSE   *see* Skeet.

HIGH INTENSITY   *see* Cartridge, High Intensity.

HIGH POWER   *see* Cartridge, High Power.

HINGE FRAME   a type of action (*see* Action, Hinged Frame; Action, Top-break; Single Shot; Frame). The original hinge frame guns were single shot rifles chambered for relatively low power cartridges. The hinge frame design principle is also

used in double rifles & shotguns where the locking & firing systems are considerably more rugged than in the early single shot hinge frame guns.

HIP REST   in off-hand shooting, a position assumed by target rifle

shooters that allows them to rest the left elbow on the left hip, providing the shooter is right-handed.

H-MANTEL   *see* Bullet, H-Mantel.

HOLDING-OFF   a method of sighting a rifle or handgun to compensate for deflection *(q.v.)* of a bullet in flight. A cross-wind will push a bullet off its path of flight. By estimating wind direction & wind velocity, the experienced shooter attempts to compensate for wind effect on the projectile by holding-off or holding into the wind. Light conditions & mirage due to heat may also call for holding-off.

HOLD-OVER a method of aiming a rifle or handgun at a distant target without making a sight adjustment or correction. If a 30-06 rifle is sighted-in to print dead-on at 100 yards with the 150 gr. bullet & the shooter wants to hit a target 300 yards away, the bullet drop *(q.v.)* will be 12.5″. If he were to hold dead-on at the target at that distance, he would miss it. Therefore he compensates by holding-over 12.5″, thus placing his bullet onto the target. In hunting situations, hold-over is a matter of educated guessing of range & wind, requires that the shooter be familiar with the trajectory of the ammunition he is using. *Also see:* Midrange Trajectory; Trajectory.

HOLLOW POINT *see* Bullet, Hollow Point.

HOLLOW POINTER tool used by some handloaders to convert fully jacketed military bullets into hollow point hunting bullets. Also made for lead bullets.

HOLSTER usually a leather sheath, but also made from other materials, that is used to carry a handgun, either suspended from the belt, the shoulder, or concealed in some other fashion on the body, such as ankle holster, wrist holster, etc. Holster design depends on anticipated use of the handgun, such as police, hunting, concealment, western riding holster, etc.

HOLSTER STOCK holster, usually made of wood, that attaches to special hooks on the backstrap of some military pistols such as the Nambu, Mauser, Pistole 08 Parabellum. A flap at the back of the stock allows insertion of the gun into the holster & with the holster attached to the gun, it can be fired from the shoulder in the fashion of a rifle. NOTE: Ownership of such a pistol with shoulder stock falls under the Gun Control Act of 1968 & these guns must be registered with the Alcohol, Tobacco & Firearms Division of the IRS, Department of the Treasury.

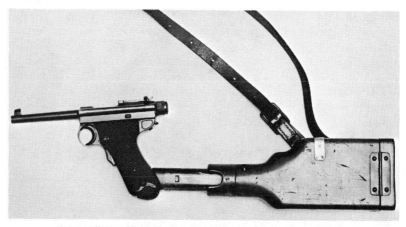

Early type Nambu with shoulder stock attached. Courtesy *Shooting Times* magazine.

HOODED SIGHT   *see* Sight, Hooded.

HOOK OF LUMP   *see* Lump, Hook of.

HOOK PLATE   a buttplate found on some old Schuetzen rifles & also on free rifles *(q.v.)*. The hook fits the upper curve of the shoulder & extends under the arm pit, gives the shooter a better, steadier support for the heavy rifle.

HOXIE BULLET   a lead bullet that carries in its tip a steel ball. The Hoxie Ammunition Co., Chicago, Illinois, around 1907 purchased complete ammunition from Remington & Winchester, removed the factory bullets, replacing them with the Hoxie bullet. The company was in business for only a short time. The steel ball was claimed to give the bullet greater expansion capabilities.

HP   abbr. for hollow point, *see* Bullet, Hollow Point.

HULL   a fired shotshell case, usually paper or plastic. Unless the hull has been damaged or mulitated, it can be reloaded.

HUMIDITY   affects gun performance, stock wood, as well as ammunition. Humidity tends to rust all metal parts of a gun & pitting results.

Corrosion due to high humidity in the chamber of M16.

This in turn hampers, or even prevents, extraction from gun chambers, affects flight of projectiles. Wood, even when properly aged, tends to warp in areas of high humidity, & forend warpage can exert so much pressure on the barrel that the gun becomes virtually useless. Modern ammunition is not as prone to the influence of humidity as the old black powder cartridges, but some malfunctions have been encountered when humidity influences the burning rate of the powder charge or brisance *(q.v.)* of the primer.

I

IGNITION   in firearms, this term refers to the act of setting fire to or igniting the powder charge in a cartridge or shotshell. Ignition depends on a number of factors: the shape of the powder charge within the case & loading density *(q.v.)*. If the case is not full & the powder is concentrated near the flash hole *(q.v.)*, ignition will be different from that obtained with an identical case & powder charge if the charge is spread along the length of the case. Similarly, ignition will differ also when the charge is located near the base of the bullet. Ignition is also governed by the physical shape of the powder granules, the amount or lack of flash inhibitor *(q.v.)*, the brisant quality of the priming compound, the size & concentricity of the flash hole, the burning rate of the powder, as well as powder temperature. *Also see:* Brisance; Powder Burning Rate; Primer.

IGNITION, FRONTAL   a process by which the forward part of the powder charge is ignited first. Frontal ignition originated in Germany; U.S. experiments, both private & military, showed that little was gained by this system. According to the experimenters O'Neil, Keith & Hopkins, the inventors of the O.K.H. cartridges, velocity was increased, pressure was decreased, as were blast & recoil. The O.K.H. group used frontally ignited duplex loads *(q.v.)*. In frontal ignition, a tube inside the cartridge case carried the primer flash to the forward part of the charge. The resultant ignition gave lower but somewhat prolonged pressure peaks,

130

started the bullet into the rifling sooner, reduced recoil. The advantages gained by frontal ignition were minimal, especially when cost & trouble of installing the ignition tube was considered.

IGNITION HISTORY is as old as gunpowder. At first a burning wick or match was applied to the touch hole *(q.v.)*, thus setting fire to the powder charge. The matchlock *(q.v.)* was the next development, this was followed by the serpentine lock, the wheel-lock, the snaphaunce which culminated in the flintlock *(q.v.)*, & still later the percussion system. There seems little doubt that Forsyth was the first to use detonation to ignite a powder charge. The deto-

Belgian pinfire revolver. Arrow points to pinfire mechanism of cartridge in gun's chamber.

nating charge of fulminate was set off by Pauly by having a needle pierce the fulminate package. From this, Dreyse developed the needle gun, the first of the bolt action designs, using a paper cartridge. The primer was attached to the base of the bullet in this cartridge & a needle pierced the bag when the trigger was pulled, hitting the primer which ignited the charge. Pauly's work was continued by Lefaucheux, who is considered the father of the pinfire cartridge *(see* Cartridge, Pinfire).

IGNITION, OVER- occurs when a powerful primer, such as a Large Rifle Magnum primer, is used in a relatively small case. In over-ignition, burning of the powder is too rapid, resulting in excessive & erratic pressures & poor accuracy.

IGNITION, TEMPERATURE OF is that amount of heat required to produce burning. As a powder charge burns, the burning is a progressive process, with each successive layer of powder being ignited as it is heated to its temperature of ignition.

IGNITION TIME the interval of time that elapses from the moment of firing pin impact on the primer to the time when chamber pressure reaches a sufficient peak to begin moving the bullet out of the case neck.

IGNITION, UNDER- occurs when the brisant quality of the primer is insufficient to ignite the charge. In under-ignition only a few grains of the powder burn at the same time. Defective primers, either affected by

131

moisture or oil, are the primary cause of under-ignition, although under-ignition can be produced by using a pistol primer in a rifle case. Under-ignition results in varying velocities, poor accuracy, as well as hangfires.

IMR POWDER   *see* Powder, IMR.

IMPACT   *see* Bullet Impact.

INCENDIARY   *see* Bullet, Incendiary.

INCIPIENT RUPTURE   also called INCIPIENT CASE RUPTURE, is the first indication in metallic cartridge cases of metal fatigue *(see* Case Head Separation; Case Neck;

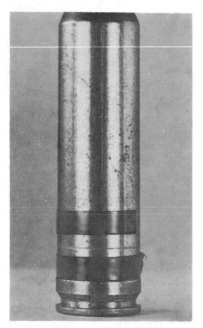

Fine, hairline crack just above belt of 350 Remington Magnum case indicates either excessive pressures or too frequent reloadings with max or near max loads.

Case Rupture). While neck splitting *(q.v.)* & head ruptures are encountered most frequently in rifle brass, incipient ruptures are often encountered on 38 Special cases which have been reloaded too often or when case mouth belling has been excessive. A dark smudge on the case after firing is sometimes the only incipient rupture manifestation that is visible. When this smudge is rubbed away, a fissure or hairline crack becomes apparent.

INDEXING   in mechanics, the system of moving a part a given distance on a lathe, milling machine, etc. In firearms, indexing refers to the rotation of the cylinder of a revolver whereby moving the hammer to full cock moves the cylinder a given distance so that a chamber in the cylinder is aligned with the firing pin on one end & the barrel at the other. In handloading, the turret of a turret loading press must be indexed so that the shellholder & the loading die in the turret are in a straight line.

INDEX MARK   also known as SIGHT LINE, is a mark on the receiver & barrel of some old guns, notably lever action rifles. In replacing a worn-out barrel, the index marks on both parts should align when the barrel has been turned in fully. If the barrel turns in past the index mark, the sights or dovetails for the sights will not line up with the top of the receiver. *Also see:* Witness Mark.

INERTIA FIRING PIN   *see* Firing Pin, Inertia.

INERTIA LOCK   a type of firing system used in two different kinds of automatic or semiautomatic guns, notably pistols. *(see* Action, Blowback; Action, Blow Forward).

INGALLS' TABLES   these tables, developed by Col. J.M. Ingalls, U. S. A., permit the calculation of remaining velocity & trajectory. The tables form the basis for all modern ballistics calculations & many of the data listed in various handloading guides & tables are based on the Ingalls tables. In England, the Hodsock ballistics tables for small arms are used. The Hodsock tables make it possible to calculate striking velocities of bullets at different distances, time of flight over a given distance, & angle of elevation needed to strike the target at that range.

INHIBITOR   *see* Flash Inhibitor.

INITIAL RECOIL   *see* Recoil, Initial.

INLAY   usually decorative, inlays are used on rifle, shotgun, & handgun stocks. Inlays can be made of wood, plastic, silver, gold & other materials, are closely fitted into the wood. Sometimes inlays are used to hide defects in wood. Also encountered on highly decorated guns where metal surfaces have been embellished with inlays, usually gold or silver.

INLETTING   the mortising & shaping of a gunstock so that the barreled action fits into the wood. Modern factory production methods utilize electric shaping machines which inlet up to 24 stocks at the same time by means of a mechanized guide. External stock shaping is accomplished in a similar manner. Hand-inletting is a tedious, painstaking job that requires care & skill. In rifles, custom stockers fit wood to metal tightly, sometimes so tightly that removal of the barreled action becomes tricky. In match rifles, the barrels are free-floated. In rifles with heavy recoil, the bedding of the recoil shoulder *(q.v.)* is particularly critical since poor bedding can split the stock completely. *Also see:* Bedding; Forend Tension; Free-floating Barrel; Glassbedding; Stock.

INLETTING SCREWS   *see* Stockmaker's Hand Screws.

INSERT BARREL   *see* Barrel Insert.

INSERTS, SIGHT   *see* Sight Inserts.

INSTRUMENTAL VELOCITY *see* Velocity, Instrumental.

INTRAFORM PROCESS   a method of producing the rifling in barrels that is claimed to produce superior barrels. Not based on drilling & broaching, the process employs cold swaging of the barrel steel. *Also see:* Broach.

IRIS DISC   a special peep sight containing a diaphragm that permits the shooter to vary the size of the opening. At one time popular on the old target Schuetzen rifles, this type of adjustable disc sight, although still made, no longer has wide appeal. A similar sight with a prescription lens in it is still offered.

IRON SIGHTS   a term originally applied to open sights or those usually furnished on factory rifles. Receiver or peep sights are now often referred to as iron sights to differentiate them from telescopic sights. The rudimentary iron sights have small steps which serve to adjust elevation; better quality rifles often have leaf sights with each leaf being pre-sighted for a certain distance, such as 100 & 200 yards for a 2-leaf sight. The sight notches in the rear sight are frequently square, but have been offered in other shapes, notably the German U-shape which is generally hard to see with the front sight. Many rear sights are adjustable for elevation, a few of them for windage, most of them requiring trial & error adjustments since they are set into dovetail *(q.v.)* cuts. Certain folding leaf

rear sights are seated in a dovetail, but are adjustable for windage & elevation by means of a small sliding bar arrangement that carries the sight notch. Front sights are most often encountered on ramps, may or may not carry a hood which is supposed to protect the sight from damage in the field; however, the majority of these hoods shoot loose & are lost. Front sights vary in shape, rifle sights are often equipped either with a brass, white plastic, or other color inset so that they are more readily visible, are more readily picked up by the eye. *Also see:* Sight.

I. S. U., INTERNATIONAL SHOOTING UNION   the international association that sets up, organizes, governs, & runs the various international shooting events. The I.S.U. rules on technical gun question of competitors, shooting courses, targets, fosters shooting events throughout the world. Even Russia is a member of the I.S.U.

Leaf sights come with many different styles of sight notches. The folding leaf is for 200 yards, the fixed for 100.

J

JACKET   *see* Bullet Jacket.

JAG   tips of various designs that are screwed into the forward end of a cleaning rod to hold patches & other bore cleaning materials. *Also see:* Cleaning.

JAM   the failure of a firearm to function. Most frequently encountered with semiautomatic guns, jams or stoppages are often caused by faulty ammunition. *Also see:* Malfunction.

JANKA TEST   test which determines the relative hardness of wood. When dry, American walnut has a Janka rating of 1000, maple of 1450, pine of 400.

JEWELING   *see* Engine Turned.

JUG CHOKE   *see* Choke, Jug.

JUMP   *see* Muzzle Jump.

K

KEEPER   *see* Sling Keeper.

KENTUCKY RIFLE   a broad term applied to the flintlock rifles of the early U.S. frontier. Around 1770, settlers & pioneers in Kentucky began using these rifles which became known as Kentucky rifles. As a matter of record, most of these guns were made by German & Swiss gunmakers in Lancaster, Pennsylvania. These Pennsylvania gunsmiths reduced gun caliber to about .45″, lengthened barrel & stock, changed the trigger guard, added somewhat improved sights; later added a cheekpiece & altered the butt shape.

KENTUCKY WINDAGE   the early Kentucky rifle *(q.v.)* did not have adjustable sights, hence a certain amount of hold-over *(q.v.)* had to be used to make the ball hit a distant target. Through usage, Kentucky windage has also come to mean "by guess or by gosh" estimation of wind deflection *(q.v.)* of the bullet & compensation for it by holding-off *(q.v.)*.

KERSTEN LOCK   a German locking system, invented by the famed gunmaker, that employs a double Greener bolt. This system is used in some fine double shotguns, combination guns *(q.v.)*, & double rifles.

KEYHOLE or KEYHOLING   occurs when a bullet loses its gyroscopic stability *(q.v.)* & begins to tumble end over end. On the target, the hole in the paper may show the actual outline of the bullet, with cast bullets creating holes that do have the appearance of a keyhole. Keyholing

136

occurs most frequently when cast bullets have not been lubricated.

KICK the physical sensation felt by a shooter when a firearm is being discharged. Kick is a relative term, depends largely on stock shape, mental attitude of the shooter. Shooters often confuse kick & recoil. Kick is only a part of recoil *(q.v.) Also see:* Muzzle Blast; Muzzle Jump.

KICK PAD *see* Recoil Pad.

KICKER *see* English Gun Terms.

KILLING POWER a non-specific & somewhat unscientific comparison of the ability of two bullets to drop game cleanly. Killing power depends on caliber, bullet weight, velocity, energy, range, bullet construction, sectional density of the bullet, as well as the physical condition of the game, the angle of fire, etc.

KINETIC ENERGY the energy of a body in motion. Kinetic energy is expressed by the formula:

$$KE = \frac{MV^2}{2}$$

where M = mass, V = velocity. For kinetic bullet energy, *see* Energy Formula.

KINDLING TEMPERATURE *see* Ignition, Temperature of.

KIRKSITE BULLET a lightweight bullet made from an alloy containing

Kick of 340 Weatherby Magnum.

zinc, aluminum & copper. With a gas-check, it was possible to obtain fairly high velocities with these bullets, but expansion was not the best. Now obsolete.

KNOCK-DOWN EFFECT a mathematical formula was devised by the late John Taylor, noted Africa hunter, to determine bullet knock-down effect. Taylor contended that the ballistics tables did not consider the frontal area of the bullet. Thus, a large, heavy bullet offers more frontal area than a small diameter bullet. As both of them mushroom, the frontal area of the large bullet becomes still larger, hence more effective in bringing down heavy game. Taylor's formula differs from the computerized terminal energy data obtainable from ballistics tables, has proved to be somewhat more reliable providing large bullets are used & the velocity data used are based on actual chronographing

rather than interpolation from ballistics tables. However, since long range chronographing is not always possible, the 100 yard velocity data from the ballistics tables can be used with some built-in margin of error. Taylor's formula determined pounds of knock-down power:

$$KP = \frac{wvd}{7000}$$

where w is the bullet weight in gr., v is velocity in fps, d is the bullet diameter in decimals of an inch.

KNUCKLE the forward part of the action bar flats where they curve & around which the forearm iron rides. *Also see:* Action, Box Lock; Action, Top-break; Flats.

KNURLING the checkering or serrating of sight knobs, bolt handles, hammer spurs & other metal parts of guns to give the hand a better grip or purchase on the part.

L

LANDS   portions of the bore left between the grooves of the rifling in the bore of a firearm. In rifling, the grooves *(q.v.)* are usually twice the width of the lands. Land diameter is measured across the bore, from land to land. *Also see:* Bore Diameter.

LANYARD, LANYARD RING found mostly on military arms especially revolvers & pistols. The use of the lanyard dates back to the days when troops were mounted, had to load & fire guns while in the saddle.

LAPPING   internal polishing of a smoothbore or rifled barrel. Lapping, by means of a tight-fitting lead slug & a fine abrasive, is done to remove slight rust, pitting, or tool marks.

LARGE BORE   *see* Big Bore.

LEAD   forward allowance needed to hit a moving target with a projectile or a load of shot. In shotgunning, two kinds of lead are recognized: SUSTAINED LEAD & SWING THROUGH. The amount of lead required varies

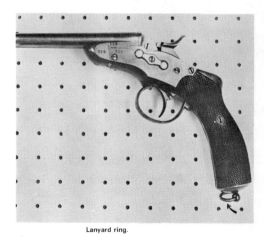

Lanyard ring.

139

from target to target. Lead depends on the speed of the target, its direction, wind, distance from the gun, the type of shell being fired, shooter's reaction time & skill. In SUSTAINED LEAD, the shooter points the barrel of the shotgun at the bird, continues to stay on the bird with the bead of the shotgun, pulls the trigger, & continues moving his gun along the flight course. If he continues his

swing as the target moves through the air, the shot charge will reach the target, providing target course is not altered & shooter does not stop his swing. Skilled shotgunners connect with their targets with considerable regularity by using sustained lead.

In SWING THROUGH, the shooter comes from behind his target with the sight of his shotgun, passes it,

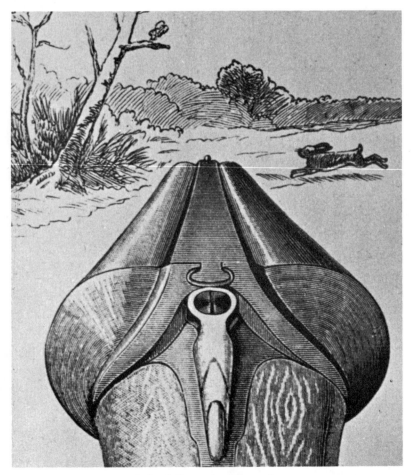

Lead needed for a running rabbit cross shot.

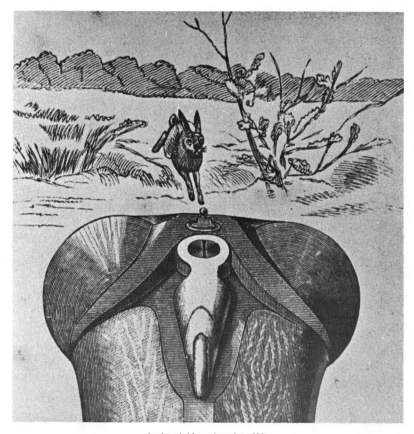

Lead needed for an incoming rabbit.

and pulls the trigger when the distance between sight & target looks right after he has considered target & shot velocity, direction of target, & wind. If the shooter has calculated his lead correctly, the shot charge will intercept the target. Many tables have been computed for leading claybirds in trap & skeet, as well as lead required for most of the game birds. Successful leading depends on the distance of shooter to target & the greater the distance, the more lead is required. The secret in wingshooting or the claybird sports is not to stop the swing of the shotgun. *Also see:* Follow Through.

Similar to the flying target is the running one. Here too a certain amount of lead is required if the bullet is to make contact with the target. As in wingshooting, the speed of the

141

target must be taken into account, but in addition, the shooter must estimate range & take into account the trajectory of his bullet at that estimated range. If a bullet drops 4″ at 250 yards, and the target's speed requires a forward allowance of 1 full body length, the shooter must also hold 4″ high to allow for the estimated distance from the target so that the bullet will strike the de-sired point of impact. The SWING THROUGH lead is probably the most widely used leading technique used by the rifle hunter, although expert hunters often prefer the SUSTAINED LEAD—both systems of course including the necessary hold-over—since the sustained lead allows the hunter to keep the target in sight while the latter travels through brush, up & down hill, & jumps obstacles.

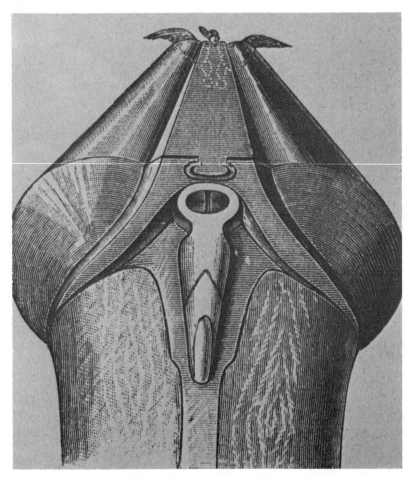

Sight picture shooter should have for rising duck.

LEAD ALLOY, LEAD BULLET
see Bullet Casting.

LEADE   *see* Chamber Leade.

LEADING   *see* Bore Leading.

LEAF SAFETY   *see* Safety, Wing.

LEAF SIGHT   *see* Sight, Leaf.

LENGTH OF PULL   *see* Stock Dimensions.

LEVER ACTION   *see* Action, Lever.

LIGHT GATHERING POWER
see Scope.

LILIPUT PISTOL   once very popular in Germany & Austria, these vestpocket pistols were so small that handling them was difficult & they were generally under-powered. The smallest caliber reported was 4.25 mm (0.167″).

LINE OF BORE   an imaginary line drawn through the exact center of the gun bore. *Also see:* Midrange Trajectory.

LINE OF SIGHT   an imaginary straight line that extends from the shooter's eye through or over the gun's sight to the target. *Also see:* Midrange Trajectory.

LINKAGE   the joining of several parts of a gun where the motion of one part produces a mechanical action of another part, such as the toggle joint in the Pistole '08 Parabellum.

LIP-FIRE   *see* Cartridge, Lip-fire.

LITTLE TOM PISTOL   a 25 caliber pocket pistol, designed prior to WWI, originally made in Pilsen, later in Vienna. This was the first of the double action semiautomatic pistols, is often said to have been the basis for the double action design used in Mauser, Sauer, & Walther pistols.

LIVE AMMUNITION   loaded cartridges or shells capable of being fired, in contrast to dummy cartridges or shells.

LJUNGMAN RIFLE   designed by Erik Eklund, the Swedish Ljungman rifle was adopted by Sweden as the Model AG 42 rifle, was chambered for the 6.5x55 Swedish service round. Egypt adopted the rifle also, but the Egyptian guns were chambered for the 8x57 round. The design of the Ljungman is unique, but despite its many good features, its popularity in military circles was limited & guns are now collectors' items. The owner of one of these rifles should verify the caliber of his gun before firing it.

LOAD   a term with three meaings: (1) to insert ammunition into a gun, as in the range command "Load & Lock" which orders shooters to insert a cartridge into the gun & close the action. (2) to load ammunition, that is to handload or reload. (3) a single round, sometimes also used in conjunction with bullet weight, such as "a 150 gr. load."

LOADING DENSITY the amount of powder contained in a case in relation to its actual powder capacity. The greater the loading density, the better the powder burns. Case capacity varies with cases of different manufacture, also possibly from one lot to another from the same manufacturer. Thus, when cartridge cases are charged with identical amounts of the same powder, loading density will differ with the actual case capacity of each individual case. *Also see:* Case Capacity; Ignition.

LOADING GATE a device for loading found on two different types of guns: (1) a part of the backplate of a single action revolver. Located on the right side of the gun, the loading gate is swung down when the hammer is on the loading notch. This allows free rotation of the cylinder, & as each chamber lines up with the loading port, it can be loaded with a round of ammunition. After firing the entire cylinder or when recharging a partially fired cylinder, the hammer is again brought back to the loading

Left, lever action rifle; right, single action revolver.

notch, the loading gate is lowered, & each fired case in turn is removed by pushing the rod ejector *(q.v.)* backwards until the case is pushed out of the chamber. (2) also used to describe the loading port or loading spring cover of lever action rifles where the gun is loaded, one round at a time, through a machined cut in the receiver that is closed by a spring-activated cover. These guns use tubular magazines (*see* Magazine, Tubular), & depending on manufacturer, eject fired cases either through the side (Marlin) or through the top of the action (Winchester).

LOADING RAMP   *see* Feeding Guide.

LOCK   as originally used, was the firing system on muzzle-loading firearms. On breech-loading, hinge frame guns, the lock or locks are located in the action body, yet the device or system that locks the barrels into place is also sometimes referred to as lock. In bolt action rifles, the bolt carries locking lugs (*see* Bolt Locking Lugs) which fit into machined counterparts, thus effectively locking the action. In shotguns employing the Greener cross-bolt (*see* Cross-bolt, Greener), the bolting system is also often spoken of as the lock.

LOCK ENERGY   is that amount of energy expended on the primer cup by the firing mechanism of the gun that is sufficient to crush & ignite the priming compound. Lock energy depends on the length of travel of the firing pin & its weight, the strength

of the mainspring, as well as on the weight of the other moving parts involved. Insufficient lock energy will not crush the priming compound to ignite it wholly, thus hangfires, loss of velocity & accuracy may result. Too great a lock energy produces pierced primers, with rearward gas leakage & loss of pressure.

LOCK PLATE   metal plate that carries the lock on matchlock, wheellock & flintlock guns. On side lock guns, the lock plate also carries the locks. In better grade guns the lock plate is hand-detachable, although in incorrect usage the locks are referred to as hand-detachable.

LOCK TIME   is the time it takes from completing the trigger pull until the firing pin or striker hits the primer, igniting the priming compound in it. A fast lock time is especially desirable in guns used in competition shooting. Some match guns come with a SPEED ACTION or SPEED LOCK. Shortening lock time can be accomplished by reducing firing pin or hammer fall, installing a stronger mainspring, increasing the weight of the firing pin or hammer, or in revolvers, reducing hammer fall *(q.v.)*.

LOCKING BOLT   sliding blocks that lock the breech bolt in the closed position, such as in the Winchester Model 94.

LOCKING CAM   a rotating cam that, when force is exerted on it, locks the bolt or another part of the firing mechanism. Typical use of locking cams is found in military semiauto-

145

matic & assault rifles, such as the M1949 FN assault rifle.

LOCKING LUG   *see* Bolt Locking Lugs.

LOCKWORK   *see* Action.

LOGWOOD DYE   a dye derived from a tree found in Central America. Blued barrels boiled in a solution of this dye get a deep black finish.

LONG GUN   a term used to differentiate a rifle or shotgun from a handgun or short gun.

LONG RIFLE   abbr. LR, the most popular of the 22 rimfire cartridges. Bullet weights vary between 36-40 gr., the round is manufactured by most ammunition makers; comes with plain lead bullets, copper plated, hollow-pointed; in standard & high velocity loads, as well as in target loads. More 22 LR ammunition is made, sold & used than any other caliber & more guns are chambered for this round than for any other.

LOST   in trap *(q.v.)* & skeet *(q.v.)*, a bird that is either missed completely or had only a chip or two shot out of it. A lost bird is counted as a miss on the shooter's scorecard.

LOW BASE   *see* Shotshell.

LOW BRASS   *see* Shotshell.

LOW HOUSE   *see* Skeet.

LOW POWER   *see* Cartridge, Low Power.

LR   *see* Long Rifle.

LUBALOY   a patented, non-fouling bullet jacket metal.

LUBRICANT   any substance, usually an oil or wax, that makes anything slippery. In firearms, two kinds of lubricant are of importance: (1) those used in the action of firearms, barrels & other parts, either to prevent rust or to make the parts function more smoothly, (2) the lubricant used in bullet lubrication *(q.v.)*. Basically, two types of substances are used for this—waxes such as beeswax or Japan wax, softeners or greases such as tallow, petroleum jelly, or cup grease. Graphite, mixed with either wax or grease, is often incorporated into home-made bullet lubricants. Commercial products are available, are as good if not better than the home-made lubricants, are less messy. Bullet lubrication is done to reduce friction, leading.

LUBRICATION GROOVE   *see* Grease Groove.

LUG   a projection, such as a recoil lug, that aids in holding or supporting one part of a firearm.

LUGER   *see* Pistole Parabellum.

LUMINOSITY   the relative quantity of light passed through an optical system. The degree of luminosity is governed by magnification, diameter of the objective lens, diameter of the exit pupil.

LUMP   in double barrel guns, the

lumps are the projections on the underside of the gun barrels near the breech end that serve to fasten the barrels to the action. *Also see:* Illustration of Flats; Chopper Lump Tubes; Monobloc; Through-lump.

LUMP, HOOK OF the machined cut-out in the forward lump *(q.v.)* that engages the hinge pin between the bars. *Also see:* Bar; Flats.

LUMPS, BIFURCATED in over/under shotguns, thickness of barrels & bar *(q.v.)* gives these guns, especially in 12 ga., greater than desirable depth. To reduce this, the bifurcated or divided lumps are used. Because of the cost in making these, only a few of the best O/U's feature this design. On these guns, the lumps are located one on each side of the lower barrel.

M

MACHINE REST usually a heavy, permanently installed mechanical device that is used to test guns as well as ammunition. Machine rests are used for rifle, pistol, & revolver testing, are of two basic designs: (1) the machine rest locks into its frame the entire gun, or (2) only the stripped gun is used. In semiautomatic pistol & revolver testing, the grips or stocks are removed, in rifle testing, only the barreled action is used. Heavy springs absorb recoil, return gun to battery or original position after each shot. Most machine rests are equipped with electronic triggering devices, thus reducing human errors to absolute minimum. *Also see:* Rest.

MAGAZINE a device for storing ammunition in a rifle, shotgun, or semiautomatic pistol. Magazines are employed in full automatic weapons, semiautomatic rifles & shotguns, bolt action & slide action guns, as well as in lever action rifles. The magazine, with the help of the feeding mechanism, delivers a live cartridge or shell into the chamber of the gun when the firing cycle has been completed & the fired shell or case has been ejected.

The word magazine is also used, primarily in military circles, to designate a storage area for powder or ammunition. Such magazines are re-inforced concrete buildings or bunkers, spaced widely apart to prevent accidental destruction of several magazines.

MAGAZINE, BLIND BOX a magazine that is non-removable. Cartridges are fed into it from the top when the bolt is fully rearward & removal of the cartridges is accomplished by operating the bolt, stripping a cartridge off the top of the magazine, chambering the round, & ejecting the cartridge without pulling the trigger.

MAGAZINE, BOX   similar to the blind box magazine, but has either a floor plate *(q.v.)* which allows removal of unfired ammunition, or a release device, such as the Mannlicher-Schoenauer, that permits the cartridges to be removed from the top without having to run them through

Rifle at far left is a 30-40 Krag with side magazine that somewhat resembles, in design, the Mannlicher-Schoenauer magazine at top center. On Krag, note how scope mount is off-set to left. Below the Mannlicher-Schoenauer is a clip from a Remington Model 870, and far right, a typical tubular magazine as found on 22 RF rifles.

the complete feeding & extraction cycle. Box magazines either store cartridges in a straight line or in a staggered, zig-zag fashion. A box magazine may be located directly below the gun's action, on the side as on the 30-40 Krag, or on the top. The box magazine can either be permanently fastened into the action of a gun, or removable. All box magazines contain a strong spring which pushes against a cartridge platform or follower (*see* Magazine Follower).

MAGAZINE CLIP   *see* Clip.

MAGAZINE CUT-OFF   *see* Cut-off.

MAGAZINE, DRUM   a type of magazine most often seen on the Thompson submachine gun. Drum magazines can hold as many as 100 rounds of ammunition.

MAGAZINE FOLLOWER   the cartridge platform which is supported & moved upward by the magazine spring *(q.v.)* in a box magazine. The follower is shaped on its upper surface so that the next round to be fed into the chamber is in the correct position. The constant push of the magazine spring, which is compressed under the weight of the cartridges, keeps the follower, & consequently the next round, ready for feeding. Tubular magazines also employ a follower, usually plastic, but this type of follower lacks a cartridge platform.

MAGAZINE, MANNLICHER   a

spool or rotary magazine, sometimes considered a type of box magazine. In this magazine, a platform revolves on its axis against the pressure of a spring. The spool type magazine is used in two domestic rifles, as well as in the Mannlicher-Schoenauer rifles.

MAGAZINE, MAUSER   the present box magazine with its floor plate, magazine spring & follower is largely based on the work of Peter Paul Mauser, German arms designer. His first attempts to convert the single shot Model 71 into a repeater rifle were by means of magazine attachments, one fitting around the stock in a curved fashion, the other projecting vertically from the stock.

MAGAZINE PLUG   a wood plug supplied with most semiautomatic & pump action shotguns to reduce magazine capacity to three shots in accordance with the Federal Migratory Bird law.

MAGAZINE RELEASE CATCH on rifles & pistols, a small spring-activated knob or protrusion that, when pushed or moved, permits the magazine to be removed from the magazine housing. The term is also used to describe, erroneously, the latch or catch that releases the floor plate *(q.v.)* of a box magazine in a rifle.

MAGAZINE, ROTARY   *see* Magazine, Mannlicher.

MAGAZINE SAFETY   *see* Safety, Magazine.

MAGAZINE, SPOOL   *see* Magazine, Mannlicher.

MAGAZINE SPRING   the spring in a magazine that exerts its thrust against the follower (*see* Magazine Follower).

MAGAZINE, TUBULAR   usually a metal tube that contains cartridges or shells, end-to-end. Feeding of rounds is accomplished by means of a spring & follower. Tubular magazines are still used in shotguns & rifles, but in the latter, use of this kind of magazine is limited, since only loads with flat-nosed bullets can be used safely. Spitzer bullets, when making contact with the primers in the preceding cartridges in a tubular magazine, could, due to recoil, detonate the primers.

MAGGIE'S DRAWERS   the red flag hoisted by the pit crew in big bore rifle matches. The showing of the flag indicates that a competitor has missed the target completely.

MAGNUM   a cartridge or shotshell that is especially powerful or large. Magnum rifles, shotguns, or handguns are those which fire a magnum cartridge or shell of a specific caliber or gauge. *Also see:* Cartridge, Magnum.

MAINSPRING   the spring that delivers energy to the hammer or striker. The recoil or operating spring in semiautomatic guns is a part of the breech closing system, is not the same as the mainspring.

MALFUNCTION   failure of a firearm to function properly. Three different kinds of malfunctions are recognized: (1) jams or stoppages due to faulty ammunition, that is either failure to feed, seat, or eject a cartridge or fired case; (2) mechanical failure, that is failure or breakage of a part, failure of a linkage pin, bent magazine feed lip, etc.; (3) complete failure due to poor design of parts, inherent lack of accuracy, poor bedding or inletting.

MANNLICHER MAGAZINE   *see* Magazine, Mannlicher.

MANNLICHER STOCK   *see* Stock, Mannlicher.

MANN V REST   *see* Rest, Mann V.

MARK   the call used by the skeet shooter when calling for the low house bird (*see* Skeet). In duck hunting, the usually whispered word means that a hunter has spotted a flight of ducks, is warning others in the blind to stop moving around.

MARK, M, Mk, or MK   a designation widely used by the British military services to designate various models & model changes. To some extent also used by the U.S. military & more recently the term has found its way into model designations in sporting guns, such as the Colt Trooper MKIII.

MARKER   pole-mounted round paddle used by members of the pit crew to indicate the value of a shot fired by a competitor during a match.

151

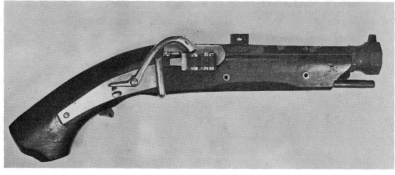

A matchlock pistol of early Japanese origin.

Markers are employed only in big bore, long range matches. A white paddle indicates a hit in the 5 ring, a red one means a 4, a black & white or magpie marker means a 3, a plain black marker a 2. *Also see:* Maggie's Drawers.

MARTINI ACTION   *see* Action, Martini. *Also see:* Single Shot.

MASTER EYE   everyone has one strong or master eye. Ideally, this is also the shooting eye, that is, if the right eye is the master eye, the shooter also naturally is right-handed & shoots from the right shoulder. To determine the master eye: aim your right index finger at some object a few feet away from you, keeping both eyes open while doing so. Now close your left eye. If the finger appears to remain on the object or "target," your right eye is the master eye. If the object appears to jump or move out of alignment when you close your left eye, the left eye is the master eye.

MATCH   a term with two meanings: (1) a slow burning fuse or cord

used in matchlock *(q.v.)* guns. (2) an organized shooting event in which numerous shooters compete. Most matches are held under the auspices of the National Rifle Association, but can be held under the rules of other shooting organizations such as the National Bench Rest Shooters Association. Matches are fired with rifles or handguns, while shotgun events are usually referred to as SHOOTS.

MATCH AMMUNITION   ammunition made with special care & of greater than normal uniformity. Match ammunition is often the only type of ammunition allowed on the firing line during a match.

MATCHLOCK   very early form of muzzle-loading firearm. This ignition system, sometimes also called a FIRELOCK uses a slow burning match *(q.v.)* to ignite the priming charge.

MATTE FINISH   metal finish that is either deep blue or black, but that does not have a sheen. Used widely on sighting surfaces to elimi-

152

nate glare; also used, in several variations, on military arms to prevent light reflections which could indicate troop locations.

MAUSER, PETER PAUL   German arms designer. *see* Action, Mauser; Magazine, Mauser.

MAXIMUM CHARGE, or MAX CHARGE   in handloading, a term denoting that a given amount of a specific powder, with the other components as indicated, delivers the highest allowable chamber pressure (*see* Pressure, Chamber).

MAXIMUM RANGE   the longest range at which a certain cartridge is effective. Most of the published maximum ranges are theoretical, are based on ballistics calculations. In practice, especially in hunting, most of these ranges can be reduced at least 50 per cent for practical game shooting.

ME   abbr. for muzzle energy, *see* Energy, Muzzle.

MEAN RADIUS   a method of measuring group size & ammunition capability. In measuring mean radius, a group is fired, either five or ten shots. The center of the group is located, & distance from that center to the center of each shot is measured. All these measurements are then totalled, & this total is then divided by the number of shots fired. The result is the mean radius. Mean radius specifications are established for military ammunition, & this group measurement is not utilized in civilian marksmanship.

MECHANICAL SAFETY   *see* Safety, Automatic.

MEPLAT   the diameter of the blunt end of the tip of a bullet. The bullet's ballistics efficiency is in an inverse ratio to its meplat, that is the greater the efficiency, the smaller the meplat. *Also see:* Illustration of Bullet nomenclature.

METAL-PATCHED BULLET *see* Bullet, Solid.

METFORD RIFLING   a shallow segmental rifling designed by Metford in 1865. The rifling consisted of 5 very shallow grooves, & was first

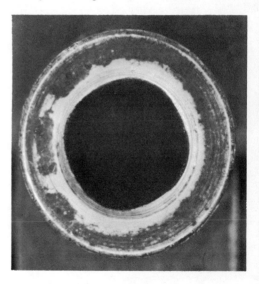

used in a 450 caliber rifle, with a lead bullet hardened with antimony & a paper patch. The shallow grooves were slightly rounded, & this system of rifling proved ideal for black powder cartridges using a lead bullet. In military rifles, the Lee-Metford rifling had 7 shallow grooves .004″ deep, with narrow lands. When cordite was introduced, it was found that the Metford rifling could not withstand the hot gases of the new 303 cartridge & severe erosion of the Metford rifling led to the adoption of the Enfield rifling in 1895. Segmental rifling was also used in the 7.7 Arisaka. Newton used segmental rifling, & one U.S. gun company is now also using segmental rifling, at least in some rifles & calibers. *Also see:* Rifling, Twist.

METRIC CARTRIDGES *see* Cartridge Designations, Metric.

MICROMETER more correctly called MICROMETER CALIPER, but through common usage often shortened to MIKE. A precision measuring device that allows readings to be made to within .0001″ by means of a vernier scale, used to measure bullet diameter, cases, etc.

MIDDLE SIGHT *see* Sight, Middle.

MIDRANGE TRAJECTORY, or MRT midway point of a projectile's trajectory between gun muzzle

& target. MRT is expressed in inches, this representing the highest vertical distance a bullet will attain above the line of sight *(q.v.)* or line of bore *(q.v.)* between muzzle & point of aim. MRT of a bullet, as given in ballistics tables, may be based either on line of bore or line of sight. Based on line of bore, a bullet aimed at a 200 yard target may have an MRT of 2″. If MRT of the same bullet at the same distance is based on line of sight, the line of bore MRT is decreased by half the height of the sight as mounted above the line of bore. Iron sights are usually 0.8″ above the line of bore, so the line of sight MRT in this case would be 2″ minus 0.4″ or 1.6″. Most scopes using standard mounts are about 1.5″ above the line of bore, so in this instance the line of sight MRT would be 2″ minus .75″ or 1.25″.

MINIE BALL designed by Capt. E.C. Minié of France, the cone-shaped bullet had originally an iron cup at the base, was less than bore diameter. Improved by J.H. Burton at Harpers Ferry Armory, the U.S. Minié ball, without iron cup, had a hollowed-out base that greatly helped in expanding the base of the

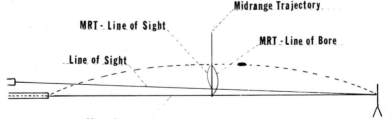

bullet so that a better engagement of the rifling occured.

MINUTE OF ANGLE, or MOA a measure of angle, 1/60th of 1 degree, where one minute of angle at 100 yards means roughly 1″. At 200 yards the same MOA group would measure about 2″, at 400 yards it would be approximately 4″. MOA is used not only to indicate group (q.v.) size, but is also used in sight measurements where one click (q.v.) can mean that moving the sight adjustment knob one division in one direction or the other will move the point of impact at 100 yards one MOA or 1″. Some sights are adjusted so that each point or division on the scale equals 1/2 or 1/4 MOA.

MIQUELET LOCK an early form of flintlock of Spanish origin where the hammer is released through the lock plate (q.v.).

MIRAGE a visual phenomenon created by a layer of heated air that deflects light rays, giving the impression that a distant object, such as a target or a sun-heated piece of road, vibrates. Mirage must be taken into account in long range shooting, especially target shooting.

MISFIRE the failure of a cartridge to fire after the primer has been hit by the striker or firing pin. A misfire is due to faulty ammunition, not gun malfunction.

MOA *see* Minute of Angle.

MOLD or MOULD *see* Bullet Mould.

MONOBLOC the use of a solid forging in the manufacture of side-by-side shotguns. The breech of the barrels & the lumps are machined from the monobloc, with barrels being brazed later to the monobloc. This system of manufacture allows making good doubles at considerable savings in labor. *Also see:* Lump.

MONTE CARLO COMB originally used on live pigeon shotguns & on some trap guns, the Monte Carlo stock is now found more frequently on rifle than on shotgun stocks. The comb of the stock is raised near the butt, while the rearmost part of the comb drops sharply to the heel. The Monte Carlo stock has been claimed to improve the use of a telescopic sight, but a straight stock of the correct height would accomplish the same purpose: to line up the eye quickly with the line of sight. *Also see:* Stock.

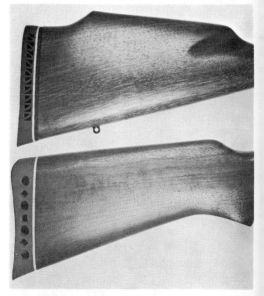

Stock at top has a Monte Carlo comb, the one below is of the straight kind.

MONTE CARLO LACE ON PAD a commercial device that allows the shooter to add a Monte Carlo comblike device to the stock of his gun.

MORRIS TUBE a rifled tube, popular in England & Europe, that fits into the barrel of a rifle or shotgun. The Morris Tube is designed so that the original sights of the firearm can be used, & firing as well as extraction system is that of the gun. The Morris Tube uses cartridges smaller than those used normally in the firearm equipped with such a firing system. *Also see:* Barrel Insert.

MOUNT or SCOPE MOUNT *see* Scope Bases.

MOVIE BLANK *see* Five in One Blank.

MRT abbr. for Midrange Trajectory *(q.v.)*

MULTI-BARREL ARRANGE-MENTS *see* Barrel Arrangements.

MULTIPLE LEAF SIGHT *see* Sight, Leaf.

MUSHROOM *see* Bullet, Mushroom.

MUSKET the term originally described a smoothbore gun, was later applied primarily to military smoothbores. These guns had long forends, were sometimes equipped with a bayonet. When rifling became accepted, some muskets were made with rifled barrels & became known as rifled

muskets. Use of the term musket, as applied to modern hunting rifles, is inappropriate.

MUZZLE the forward end of the barrel where the projectile exits.

MUZZLE BLAST a violent & sometimes noisy disturbance caused by the exit of the hot powder gases from the confinement of the muzzle of a gun after a projectile has left the barrel.

MUZZLE BRAKE a device fastened to the muzzle of a rifle, sometimes to the muzzle of a shotgun, that reduces recoil *(q.v.)* & to some extent also cuts down on muzzle

jump *(q.v.)*. Muzzle brakes are found primarily on heavy recoil rifles, & although they do reduce recoil & jump, the slots in the brake tend to increase muzzle blast somewhat by directing it backward toward the shooter. Muzzle brakes are also known as compensators. *Also see:* Compensator, Cutts.

MUZZLE CAP   small rubber cap, sometimes a toy balloon, pulled over the muzzle of a hunting rifle to prevent entry of rain or snow into the barrel. Muzzle caps need not be removed prior to shooting.

MUZZLE CROWNING   the rounding-off after a muzzle has been cut square & flush. Crowning is done with a special crowning reamer. Crowning protects the critical part of the rifling from accidental damage, & if the muzzle is not squared, powder gases will escape prematurely, thus tipping the bullet base as it leaves the muzzle.

MUZZLE ENERGY   *see* Energy, Muzzle.

MUZZLE JUMP   actually occurs between the moment of ignition of the powder in a cartridge or shell & the moment the projectile leaves the barrel. The vertical jump or rise of the barrel is too fast to affect the trajectory. Jump is sometimes measured as the angle between the bore axis before & after firing. *Also see:* Kick; Recoil.

MUZZLE LOADER   any firearm where powder & projectile are inserted into the barrel through the muzzle. While early muzzle loaders used loose powder & a bullet or shot with or without wadding, some later muzzle loaders used paper cartridges which contained powder & projectile & where the paper acted as wadding.

MUZZLE, FALSE   a short piece of barrel, rifled on the inside & often tapered. The false muzzle carries pins which match corresponding holes in the muzzle of the rifle. The pins serve to align the rifling of the barrel with that of the false muzzle. The false muzzle temporarily seated on the top of the barrel serves only to introduce the bullet into the bore with minimal damage to the soft lead projectile. False muzzles are used on some muzzle-loading rifles as well as on many of the Schuetzen rifles or target rifles made by H.M. Pope & other barrel makers of that period.

MUZZLE FLASH   as the bullet leaves the muzzle, it is followed by hot powder gases & also burning powder particles. As these make contact with the oxygen of the air, the incandescent flash becomes apparent. *Also see:* Flash Hider; Flash Inhibitor.

MUZZLE PROTECTOR   some rifles must be cleaned from the muzzle. In order to prevent accidental damage to the lands by the cleaning rod, a special muzzle protector should be used. Similar in design to the false muzzle *(see* Muzzle, False), the device is presently not commercially offered, but can be made up easily by any gunsmith. *Also see:* Throat Protector.

MUZZLE VELOCITY   abbr. MV, *see* Velocity, Muzzle.

157

N

NATIONAL MATCH BULLET *see* Bullet, National Match.

NATIONAL MATCHES conducted under the auspices of the N.R.A. at Camp Perry, Ohio. The matches are held annually, include centerfire rifle, smallbore rifle & pistol competitions.

NATO CARTRIDGE also known as the 7.62 mm Nato round, identical to the 308 Winchester round which, as a hunting load, is furnished only in soft point ammunition.

NC abbr. for non-corrosive *(q.v.)*.

NECK *see* Case Neck.

NECK ANNEALING reloaders sometimes anneal *(q.v.)* case necks to prevent premature neck splitting, or when drastically changing neck diameter while forming cases for a wildcat cartridge. *Also see:* Cartridge, Wildcat.

NECK-SIZING in handloading, cases that have been fired in one specific rifle & will be fired only in that rifle, need not be reshaped fully, that is full length sized. Neck-sizing only restores case mouth & case neck to proper caliber so that the bullet is held securely in the case mouth. Neck-sizing only prevents excessive cold working of brass, prolongs case life. *Also see:* Case Life; Handloading.

NECK SPLITTING can be due to the age of brass (*see* Brass, Season Cracking of). Neck splitting also occurs when case neck or case mouth has been sized too much & too often. *Also see:* Case Rupture; Incipient Rupture.

NECK TENSION　　amount of tension exerted by the case neck & case mouth that holds the seated bullet in place, especially in uncrimped cases. *Also see:* Bullet Pull.

NECK THICKNESS　　as a cartridge case undergoes repeated firings, the brass has a tendency to flow forward. Eventually case neck thickness increases to a point where no clearance exists between the chamber wall & the outside of the neck. Similarly, brass flowage also reduces inside neck diameter so that brass must be removed or reamed from the inside of the neck before a bullet can be seated.

NECK TRIMMING　　*see* Case Trimming.

NECKING-DOWN　　reducing the inside & outside diameter of the neck of a cartridge case, by means of case forming dies. *Also see:* Cartridge, Wildcat; Handloading Steps; Illustration of Dies.

NEEDLE GUN　　a major development in ignition history *(q.v.).* Invented by Johann Nikolaus v. Dreyse in 1829, the rifle version of the needle gun was adopted by several European armies. The Dreyse system with the paper cartridge became obsolete with the invention of the metallic cartridge in the 1870's.

NIPPER　　a bullet hole that just touches a higher value scoring ring than the ring which contains the greater part of the bullet hole *(see* Target).

NIPPLE　　on percussion guns, the nipple is a small, threaded tube on which the percussion cap is placed.

Reaming the inside of a case neck.

CONE is an early term for nipple. The nipple connects with the chamber, so that when the cap is exploded by the hammer, the flash of the cap travels through the nipple into the chamber, igniting the powder charge there. Nipples are removable by means of a NIPPLE WRENCH, and NIPPLE PICKS are used to clear obstructions from the inside of the nipple.

NITRO EXPRESS   *see* Express Cartridges & Rifles.

NO BIRD   *see* No Target.

NO-GO GAGE   *see* Headspace Gage.

NON-CORROSIVE   abbr. NC, used to describe primers or cartridges not containing any of the compounds that tend to cause rust or corrosion. Military ammunition made after 1952 is usually non-corrosive, but if such ammunition has been used and there is any doubt about it containing corrosive components, the gun should be cleaned promptly & thoroughly. Currently produced factory primers & ammunition are non-corrosive.

NOSE   the bullet tip or forward portion, which may be any of numerous configurations. *Also see:* Bullet.

NOSLER   *see* Bullet, Nosler.

NO TARGET   in certain circumstances, the referree at a registered trap shoot, that is one held under the auspices of the Amateur Trapshooting Association (ATA), may declare "no target" especially while doubles are being shot. A "no target" call allows the shooter to repeat shooting at that station. *Also see:* Skeet; Trap.

NRA   abbr. for National Rifle Association. A non-profit organization that formulates rules, regulations & targets as well as guns for rifle & pistol competitions. The official organ of the NRA is *The American Rifleman,* published monthly.

NUTCRACKER TOOL   *see* Tong Tool.

NYDAR SIGHT   *see* Sight, Nydar.

O

OBJECTIVE LENS the lens at the front of the telescopic sight. This is the lens that forms the first image as an object is viewed through the scope.

OBTURATE to seal the breech of a gun by the expansion of the brass cartridge case to prevent the escape of gas.

O'CLOCK *see* Clock System.

OCULAR LENS a single, but more frequently a compound, magnifying lens in the eyepiece of a telescopic sight.

OFF-SET MOUNT *see* Scope Bases, Off-set.

OGIVE *see* Bullet Ogive.

OIL DENT occurs in handloading during the sizing process when too much lubricant has been used. Although cases with severe oil dents can be used since firing them will restore

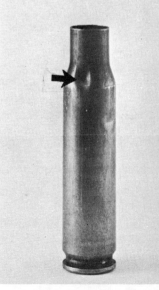

Arrow points to the oil dent in cartridge case.

case shape, it is generally recognized that the oil dent areas have been weakened due to cold working of the brass, hence these areas are prone to case rupture *(q.v.)*.

OIL FINISH   *see* Finish, Oil.

OPE   *see* Bullet, Open Point Expanding.

OPEN BOLT FIRE   a system of breech closure used most frequently in semiautomatic military small arms, but also used at one time in the M55 22 RF Winchester rifle, now used by Gevelot, France, in several 22 RF rifles. In this system, the breech remains open until the trigger is pulled. This releases the spring-loaded bolt from its rearward position, strips a round off the top of the magazine & when the cartridge is chambered, the gun fires. The Gevelot guns do not have a firing pin, but the bolt face has two ridges which contact the rim of the base of the cartridge in the chamber. This gives ignition at two opposite points on the rim. Gas pressure throws the bolt rearward where it is locked in place by the mainspring & ejection is accomplished due to the gas pressure rather than through mechanical means.

OPERATING HANDLE   has the same function as the bolt handle on bolt action rifles. The operating handle is located either on the operating rod or on the bolt of a semiautomatic gun, either gas or recoil operated, & when moved back manually, permits opening the action.

OPERATING LEVER   *see* Action, Lever.

OPERATING ROD   *see* Action Bars.

OPERATING SPRING   in fully automatic weapons & semiautomatic firearms, the powerful spring that closes the action. Also known as RECOIL SPRING or RETRACTING SPRING.

ORDNANCE   a branch of the military services concerned with arms & ammunition design, development & testing. Also, military materiel including artillery, ammunition & small arms.

OUTSIDE LUBRICATED BULLET   *see* Bullet, Outside Lubricated.

OVER AND UNDER   abbr.O/U, a type of barrel arrangement where two barrels are aligned one on top of the other. Though technically a "double" since two barrels are described, the latter term is reserved for side-by-side guns. "Superposed" is a tradename to describe an O/U shotgun. Most O/U's are shotguns or smoothbores, but rifle-shotgun combinations are sometimes arranged in the over-under fashion. Many O/U's are of German origin, where Bock-Doppelbüchse is an O/U rifle, a Bock-Doppelflinte is an O/U shotgun, & the Bock-Büchsflinte is an O/U arrangement of one rifle & one shotgun barrel. *Also see:* Combination Guns; Barrel Arrangements.

OVER-BORE CAPACITY is of concern to handloaders & cartridge designers, especially those working with wildcat cartridges (*see* Cartridge, Wildcat). Over-bore capacity is that combination of caliber, barrel length, bullet weight, & case volume which does not allow the complete burning of the charge of ballistically correct powder within the volume of case & barrel.

OVER-POWDER WAD *see* Wad, Over-powder.

OVER-SHOT WAD *see* Wad, Over-shot.

OVERTRAVEL *see* Trigger Overtravel.

163

P

PAD   *see* Recoil Pad.

PALM REST   shaped support for the hand extending downward from the forend of a match rifle. The palm rest is usually fully adjustable, sliding in the same aluminum rail as the hand stop *(q.v.)*.

PAN   part of a firing mechanism found in early locks including matchlocks, wheel-locks, flintlocks. The pan contained the priming charge that was ignited by various means: by a slow burning cord in the matchlock, by sparks created by the flint striking the frizzen in flintlocks, etc.

PAPER-PATCHED   *see* Bullet, Paper-patched.

PARABELLUM   a bastardized Latin phrase that has many meanings to the shooter & gun collector. Based on the Latin "Si vis pacem, para bellum" ("If you want peace, prepare

Only match rifles come with a palm rest (arrow).

for war.") & attributed to Vegetius 400 B.C., the word Parabellum is the protected tradename of Mauser & D.W.M. In the U.S., the term is often used to designate exclusively the 9 mm cartridge for which the Pistole Parabellum *(q.v.)* is chambered. However, the 7.65 mm cartridge for which this pistol has been chambered is seldom linked with the Parabellum name, which is equally as incorrect since there are numerous similar, and therefore confusing, 7.65 mm pistol cartridges (the Bergman No.8, Borchardt, Browning, Francotte, Frommer, Glisenti, French Long, Mannlicher, Roth-Sauer, & the Pickert revolver cartridge). Besides referring to the 9 mm pistol ammunition, Parabellum is used to describe the semiautomatic pistol refined by Georg Luger. During WWI & to a limited extent in WWII, the German Army used a Parabellum machine gun, basically a refined version of the Maxim machine gun made by D.W.M. *Also see:* Pistole Parabellum.

PARABELLUM PISTOL   *see* Pistole Parabellum.

PARADOX   guns & ammunition patented by G.B. Fosberry in England. The guns were essentially side-by-side shotguns, but the choke-bored barrels were rifled for a few inches near the muzzle. The type of rifling used was sometimes called ratched rifling & consisted of sharp spirals. The solid ball projectile was a severely cannelured & crimped conical lead slug that often was covered by a light brass jacket. Offered by several

At left, a Paradox load; at right, the Westley Richards Explora load.

British gunmakers, the guns were sold under such names as Paradox, Explora, Jungle Gun, etc. Usually 8 to 10 bore in their original designs, the bullet weight varied between 735-750 gr. with an approximate MV of 1300 fps. The original Paradox round carried a soft lead slug & the jacket was added later since it was found that this gave better penetration. The rifling did not preclude the use of buckshot, and the guns were widely used in India against tiger as well as in Africa against heavy game. The 8 to 10 bore guns were considered as large bores, but later, sometime around 1890, these guns were also offered in the smaller gauges, such as 12 ga.

PARALLAX   occurs in telescopic sights when the primary image of the objective lens does not coincide with the reticle. In practice, parallax is detected in a scope when, as the viewing eye is moved laterally, the image & the reticle appear to move in relation to each other.

PARALLAX ADJUSTMENT a feature found on most of the telescopic sights with a power greater than 8X & on all target & varmint scopes. Since parallax in the higher power optical sights can be critical, the objective lens of these scopes is adjustable so that the target image can be brought onto the same plane as the reticle. This is accomplished by rotating the objective lens. The quality scopes have the parallax adjustments pre-set so that the shooter need only turn the objective lens until the correct distance mark corresponding to the target distance is set on the indicator or zero mark of the scope's objective housing or bell.

PARALLAX CORRECTION in quality telescopic sights used for hunting, is seldom needed since most of these scopes are corrected for all possible parallax errors at the factory. However, some low-priced scopes do have parallax. To correct parallax, at least partially, ascertain that the crosshairs are in sharp focus by adjusting the eyepiece until maximum sharpness is obtained. If the objective lens can be turned, do so until no more parallax is apparent. However, adjusting the turret & therefore the location of the reticle is not recommended. In some cases of parallax, especially at close ranges, some correction of parallax can be obtained by adjusting the eyepiece, although sharpness & definition of the reticle will suffer accordingly.

PARKERIZED FINISH a process of finishing the steel parts of a gun so that it does not have the high degree of polish & light reflection found on sporting arms. Military arms are often parkerized to give the finish longer wear & life expectancy, since the finish is rust-resistant.

PARTITION BULLET *see* Bullet, H-Mantel; Bullet, Nosler.

PASTER a small piece of paper, usually black or white, that is pasted over a bullet hole in a target. Self-adhesive pasters have nearly obsoleted the lick & stick variety.

PATCH a term with two meanings: (1) in muzzle-loading guns, the often greased cloth, paper or leather patch that nearly covers the bullet or ball as it is seated in the barrel atop the powder charge. (2) a piece of cloth, usually flannel, used to clean the bore of a gun. *Also see*: Cleaning.

PATCH BOX inletted into the buttstock of a muzzle-loading long gun, the often ornately decorated patch box with either a hinged or sliding lid was used to store balls, patching materials & grease. *Also see:* Patch; Furniture.

PATRIDGE SIGHT *see* Sight, Patridge.

PATTERN distribution of a load of shot fired at a sheet of paper placed vertically 40 yards from the gun. To

The Pedersen Device. Courtesy Col. B. R. Lewis, photo by K. F. Schreier, Jr.

pattern a shotgun, a mark or aiming point is made on the sheet of paper & after firing one shell, a 30″ diameter circle is drawn around the aiming point. Counting the pellet holes within the circle & knowing the number of pellets contained in the load fired, allows the shooter to calculate the percentage pattern. Divide the total number of pellets in the circle by the number of pellets in the shell. To obtain a valid pattern percentage, no less than five such patterns should be fired & an average should be calculated from those data.

PATTERN, BLOWN   pattern that shows an irregular distribution of the pellets on the patterning paper or board. Blown patterns are usually caused by faulty ammunition, permit targets to fly right through the pattern despite the fact that the shooter had the correct lead & sight picture at the moment he fired.

PEABODY FALLING BLOCK SINGLE SHOT   a particularly strong

falling block action (*see* Action, Falling Block). *Also see:* Single Shot.

PEDERSEN DEVICE   top secret of WWI, the Pedersen device was manufactured too late to see service. Designed for trench warfare, the device was used in a modified Springfield rifle where it replaced the bolt. The rifle became, in effect, a 40-shot, blowback semiautomatic rifle firing an 80 gr. & also a 90 gr. .30 caliber bullet at approximately 1300-1500 fps. Maximum effective range of the lighter bullets was only 350 yards. Remarkably, the Pedersen device ejected the cases to the left.

PEEP SIGHT   *see* Sight, Peep.

PELLET   two types of pellets are recognized: (1) shotgun pellets, better known as SHOT and (2) air or spring gun pellets or projectiles. Air gun pellets come in two calibers, 177 & 22, are produced mainly in Germany. The Diabolo pellet is a skirted or waisted pellet that, because of preci-

167

sion manufacture, is widely used in competitive air gun matches.

PENDULUM, BALLISTICS an early device to determine bullet velocity. Invented by Benjamin Robins (1707-1751), the pendulum essentially consisted of a block of wood of known weight suspended by means of a chain of known weight. At the bottom of the block a length of tape was fastened. When a bullet of known weight was fired into the block, the block moved backward. This distance was measured by means of the tape on the block. With the weight of the block & bullet known, as well as the weight of the chain & distance of rearward travel of the block, velocity of the bullet was readily calculated. Although the ballistics pendulum has long ago been replaced by modern electronic chronographs, it is still being used today to some degree to measure recoil.

PENETRATION   *see* Bullet Penetration.

PENNSYLVANIA RIFLE   *see* Kentucky Rifle.

PEPPERBOX PISTOL   a percussion pistol with multiple barrels which rotated with each pull of the trigger, aligning a chamber of the non-removable barrel arrangement with the firing mechanism of the gun. The Sharps 4 barrel pepperbox pistol is perhaps the most widely known example of this type of handgun.

PERCUSSION ARM   any type of

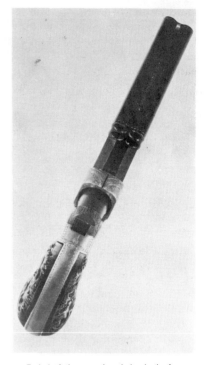

Typical of the pepperbox design is the four barrel Sharps.

gun fired by the percussion system. In this ignition system (*see* Ignition History), the powder charge was ignited by a percussion cap, the forerunner of the modern primer. The cap was placed on the nipple *(q.v.)*, & when the hammer hit the cap, the flash of the detonating charge in the cap travelled through the hollow nipple, thus igniting the charge in the barrel. Black powder shooters of today often use replica percussion arms in competitive shooting events.

PERCUSSION CAP   the small cap that contains a detonating charge of fulminate. *Also see:* Percussion Arm.

PERCUSSION LOCK the external lock system which succeeded the flintlock ignition system. Various locking systems evolved from the basic form, including several devices which fed caps onto the nipple or nipples.

PIECE in military jargon, the soldier's rifle, also used in conjunction with any military small arm.

PIEZO-ELECTRIC CRYSTAL a specific type of quartz or related mineral that is capable of creating its own, minute electric charge when acted upon by some outside source. This system is widely used in ballistics research in conjunction with determining pressure (*see* Pressure Determination). In practice, a small steel stud is placed into contact with the piezo-crystal. As pressure builds in the chamber or barrel, equal pressure is exerted on the stud which transfers the pressure to the crystal. The crystal creates minute amounts of electric waves which, when passed through an amplifier, can then be recorded on a cathode-ray oscilloscope.

PILL LOCK a transitional percussion system that pre-dates the copper percussion cap. In the pill lock, a pellet of fulminate, placed into a special tube which connected with a floating firing pin, was used to ignite the powder charge. The fulminate, in pill shape, was coated with wax or varnish. Design of the pill lock is generally credited to Joseph Manton, famed British gunmaker & he was issued a patent for this system in 1816.

PINFIRE *see* Cartridge, Pinfire.

PINWHEEL a bullet that has printed in the exact center of the target.

PIPES identical to ferrules *(q.v.)*.

PISTOL a gun held & fired by one hand, with a chamber that is permanently aligned with the rifled bore. Magazine as well as single shot pistols are being made. In recent years, the word pistol has been used more & more to describe SEMIAUTOMATIC PISTOLS in contrast to revolvers or sixguns. Although the term semiautomatic is technically correct—that is, one round is fired for each pull of the trigger until the magazine is empty—the use of "automatic pistol," "auto pistol," or simply "automatic" has become widespread.

PISTOL, DOUBLE ACTION some semiautomatic pistols can be fired, if a cartridge is chambered & the hammer is not cocked, by merely pulling the trigger. This will first cock the hammer, then permit the hammer to fall, thus firing the first shot. When that first round has been fired, the gun ejects the empty case, rechambers a fresh round & pulling the trigger will then fire the newly chambered cartridge. A DA (double action) semiautomatic pistol can safely be carried with one round chambered & the safety on. The Walther P38 is a typical DA pistol. *Also see:* Revolver, Double Action.

169

PISTOL, FOREIGN semiautomatic or selfloading pistol saw its major development in Europe. The first autoloading pistol was introduced in 1892 in Austria, although German authorities claim that the first truly selfloading pistol was designed & made in the U.S. European arms companies & designers devoted considerable time & effort to the development of semiautomatic pistols & a great many of the action designs & numerous cartridges were the result of some 50 years research. Currently, only 4 U.S. companies manufacture semiautomatic pistols, while there are three or four times as many European concerns making autoloading pistols.

PISTOL GRIP *see* Grip; Grip, Pistol.

PISTOL GRIP ADAPTER *see* Grip Adapter.

PISTOL GRIP CAP *see* Grip Cap.

PISTOL RUG a zippered & lined bag used to move handguns. Although some of the pistol rugs are treated with a rust-inhibiting agent, guns should never be stored for prolonged periods in such a rug unless periodic checks for rust are made on the inside & the outside of the gun. Pistol rugs are used for revolvers as well as pistols.

The pistol rug.

PISTOL, SINGLE ACTION design typified by the Colt 45 ACP. If a single action pistol is carried with one round in the chamber, the hammer can be left in the cocked position providing the slide safety is applied. However, this is not considered to be wholly safe & lowering the hammer is recommended. If the hammer is lowered while a round is in the chamber, it is then necessary to cock the hammer manually before the chambered round can be fired. *Also see:* Revolver, Single Action; Revolver, Double Action.

PISTOLE PARABELLUM semiautomatic toggle-linkage pistol originally designed by Borchardt & later somewhat modified by Georg (not George, as some writers would have it) Luger. The first of these guns were introduced by DWM in 1898, were chambered for the 7.65 mm Parabellum cartridge. The 9 mm Parabellum cartridge was adopted for that pistol by the German army in 1908, hence the gun is officially known as Pistole '08 Parabellum. However, the name of Georg Luger has been linked to the gun to such an extent that the gun is often simply called the "Luger." That name is trademarked in the U.S., & its use is restricted to those guns produced by the holder of the trademark, Stoeger Arms Corp. A great many manufacturers made these guns over the years for numerous armies & collecting these pistols has become somewhat of a science. This pistol has seen much military use despite the fact that it is relatively costly to produce & somewhat of a nightmare to maintain

under combat conditions.

PITCH a term with three meanings: (1) pitch of rifling, *see* Twist. (2) the relationship of grip angle to bore axis of a handgun. This is of particular importance to match shooters who fire the three gun course (22 RF, 38 Spl., & 45 ACP) with semiautomatic pistols, where gun heft, feel, & grip pitch should be as similar as possible for maximum shooter performance. (3) the angle formed by the intersection of the line of bore & a line connecting the heel & toe of the butt on long guns. Pitch

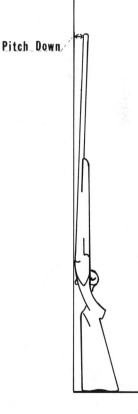

Pitch Down

is particularly important in shotguns. The point of impact may be raised or lowered by altering the slant of the butt, thereby changing the angle of pitch. If a shotgun shoots high, it is said to have a LONG TOE or a small amount of pitch down. If a gun shoots low, it has a SHORT TOE or a large amount of pitch down. To measure PITCH DOWN, place the butt of the gun flat on a horizontal surface & move the gun against a vertical surface until contact is made in the receiver area. The distance between the gun muzzle & the vertical surface, in inches, is pitch down.

PITTING of barrel & chamber, is the result of rusting or improper gun care, especially with black powder guns. These must be cleaned immediately after shooting & any fouling must be removed. If this is not done, rust, & eventually pitting, will result. Even guns fired with non-corrosive primers & smokeless powder loads should be cleaned occasionally to remove fouling & prevent rust formation. Although some shallow pitting can be removed by a gunsmith, deep pitting may call for either a new barrel or a barrel relining *(q.v.)* job.

PLINKING the shooting at various targets which are not of the formal or match variety. Targets most often selected are tin cans, claybirds, boxes, etc. The word was coined by Elizabeth "Plinky" Toepperwein, often called the greatest woman trapshooter of her time. She used to call for her targets by calling "plink."

PLUGGED SHOTGUN *see* Magazine Plug.

PLUNGER a term sometimes used to describe the firing pin in double rifles & shotguns.

PMVF MAGNUMS a series of wildcat cartridges, also known as the Powell-Miller-Venturi-Freebored, which were said to have exceptional power of penetration. Velocities were extremely high, trajectories exceptionally flat. Published reports ranked these cartridges as "big game" cartridges, yet recommended that they not be used for game larger than deer. The PMVF Magnums never became very popular, with most of them being badly over-bore.

POCKET RIFLE *see* Bicycle Rifle.

POINT BLANK when shooting at a target so close that no sighting or sight correction is needed, the target is said to be at point blank range. Such a range is usually figured in feet, or at most a few yards.

POINT OF AIM is that point at which the shooter aims the sights of his gun. If the bullet strikes at that point, it is often said to "print (at the) point of aim."

POINT OF IMPACT if point of aim *(q.v.)* is dead-on at 100 yards, & bullets strike the target high & to the right, for instance, the point of impact differs from the point of aim. A sight correction is indicated. Each time the sight setting is changed, point of impact & point of aim must be compared until the desired location of point of impact in relation to point of aim is reached.

POISON BULLET *see* Bullet, Williams.

POPE RIB a rib integral with the barrel. Designed by Harry M. Pope, famed barrel maker & shooter, the rib made it possible to mount a target scope low over the barrel.

POPE RIFLING was designed especially for lead alloy bullets. This type of rifling is distinguished by: (1) slightly rounded corners of the grooves, (2) a left-hand twist, (3) gain twist (*see* Twist, Gain) rifling from breech to muzzle, (4) a bore diameter that tapers toward the muzzle, (5) narrow lands. Pope rifles, due to the meticulous finish of the barrels, are super-accurate guns, holding their own even against today's rifles. Bullets were seated either from the muzzle (*see* Muzzle, False) or from the breech.

PORT a machined cut or opening, such as the gas port or ejection port.

POST *see* Reticle.

POWDER must be considered as two separate entities—black powder & the modern smokeless propellant powders. The Chinese are generally credited with the invention of a chemical mixture which was used in fireworks. Roger Bacon, in 1263, appears to have used a refined version of a similar compound which, with but minor changes, is still being used today—the black powder used in muzzle-loading guns. As the use of the old black powder became more general, it underwent changes. Gun cotton, & later Nobel's work, ultimately let to the smokeless powders of today. Black powder still consists of the same ingredients as it did in the days of the first firearms: sulphur, saltpetre & finely ground charcoal. The only major difference between the gunpowder of the old days & today's product is the greater uniformity of the powder which is offered in a number of granulations (*see* Powder, Black).

A few of the powders used by handloaders.

POWDER, BALL   also known as spherical powder. The ball powders burn at lower temperatures than the rod or stick powders, hence produce less barrel wear. Widely used by reloaders, ball powders meter easily, that is, they pass through the powder measure *(q.v.)* readily & without trouble since the powder particles need not be sheared off by the rotating drum of the powder measure.

POWDER, BALLISTITE   also known as Nobel powder, was the first of the modern smokeless powders. First made in 1887, Ballistite consists of 40 per cent nitroglycerine & 60 per cent nitrocellulose. In its general behavior, it strongly resembles the British Cordite *(q.v.)*.

POWDER, BLACK   still manufactured today for muzzle-loading guns, black powder comes in four granulations: Fg, FFg, FFFg, & FFFFg, with the Fg powder being the coarsest granulated, the FFFFg being the finest. In flintlock guns, the priming is done with a fine grain powder, the actual charge in the barrel consisting in most cases of FFFg. Black powder, also called gunpowder, ignites readily, burns violently, & must be handled with extreme care.

POWDER, BULK   a now obsolete smokeless nitrocellulose base propellant powder. When it was introduced, reloaders were able to switch from black to smokeless powder loads by simply measuring the amount of powder bulk for bulk.

POWDER, BULK, SMOKELESS same as Powder, Bulk *(q.v.)*.

POWDER BURNING RATE   depends on the exact chemical composition of a powder & its physical configuration. Burning rate is controlled by the distance fire must travel through each powder granule before it is entirely consumed. Powders are usually classified from the fastest burning one to the slowest burning one. Many of the smokeless powders now on the market have somewhat over-lapping burning rates, are therefore suitable for a wide variety of cartridges. When a handloader talks about fast or slow powders, reference is made to the burning rate, not to the velocities obtained. If equal amounts of a fast & a slow powder are ignited, the fast one will develop higher peak pressures than the slow one.

POWDER CHARGE   that amount of a propellant powder that is suitable for specific cartridge-bullet combination, or in the case of shotshells, for a specific weight of shot & wad column. In handloading, charges are either weighed on accurate scales, or are thrown by a powder measure *(q.v.)* which works on the volumetric system. If factory loads of different manufacture are broken down or taken apart, it will be found that powder charges often vary quite considerably. The powder used by ammunition makers is not identical to that sold to handloaders, & each new lot of powder is first tested for burning rate & other properties. Factory ammunition is loaded to specific pressure/velocity levels, & therefore load variations in factory cartridges only indicate that different powders & powder lots were used in loading those rounds.

POWDER, DENSE a modern smokeless powder, frequently combined with nitroglycerine, that gives ballistics results identical to those obtained with black powder. However, loads with dense powder are always considerably smaller & they are loaded by weight in contrast to bulk powder (*see* Powder, Bulk).

POWDER, DOUBLE-BASE a powder which has as basis nitrocellulose, as do all modern smokeless powders, to which has been added between 10-40 per cent nitroglycerine. *Also see:* Powder, Single-base.

POWDER, FLAKE a general descriptive term that describes the physical configuration of the powder.

POWDER FLASK a container fashioned from wood, leather, metal or other material & furnished with a closure, usually spring-operated. Antique powder flasks are of great value, are often ornately decorated, were used to carry black powder afield. Replicas are now widely used by black powder shooters.

POWDER HORN usually fashioned from a steer horn with the larger end permanently closed, powder horns were used to carry powder. Sometimes two such horns were used, the larger one for the powder used as main charge, the smaller one, sometimes known as the primer horn, containing the finer-grained priming powder.

POWDER, IMR or Improved Military Rifle, a DuPont designation of a series of powders with a deterrent coating to control the burning rate. IMR powders produce higher velocities at lower pressures than the powders used prior to the introduction of the IMR powders. The IMR designation precedes the numerical powder designation, e.g. IMR 3031.

POWDER MEASURE mechanical device that allows a handloader to throw charges of a propellant powder. The charges are determined by setting a rotating & adjustable drum or slide, the powder being supplied, by gravity feed, from a powder storage tube. With the setting adjusted, a charge thrown is then weighed on an accurate powder scale. Further adjustments are made until the powder measure delivers the desired amount of powder volumetrically. Coarse-grained powders are sheared or cut by the sharp edge of the rotating drum of the powder measure, ball powders

At left, a powder flask, at right, an antique priming horn used to carry a fine grain powder.

because of their physical configuration are said to meter easily. *Also see:* Powder Charge.

POWDER, PROGRESSIVE a powder with a burning rate that increases in proportion to the pressure created within the case or shell. Older powders burned at a uniform rate & rate of burning was not related to pressure levels.

POWDER, SEMI-SMOKELESS a mixture of black & smokeless powder which is now obsolete. Powder charges were not critical, velocities low, & this powder was ideally suited for loading the old black powder cartridges.

POWDER, SINGLE-BASE a type of powder in which the main constituent is nitrocellulose. The powders offered by DuPont are single-base powders.

POWDER, SMOKELESS all of the currently used powders, excepting the black powders, are of the smokeless type. The basis for these powders is nitrocellulose. *Also see:* Powder, Single-base; Powder, Double-base; Flash Inhibitor.

POWDER, SR or Sporting Rifle Powder, now obsolete.

POWDER TESTER or EPROU-VETTE. A pistol-like device, fired by a flintlock mechanism & used to test the strength of black powder. When uniformity of black powder was improved, the use of the powder tester declined.

POWER as far as the shooter is concerned, is most frequently the optical power, that is the power of magnification of a telescopic lens or the eyepiece of a pair of binoculars. A four power scope has a magnification of 4 X, an eight power has 8 X, etc.

PRESS *see* Handloading.

PRESSURE as the propellant powder charge burns, it creates gases which are under pressure. The thrust of these gases against the inside walls of the case or shell, against the base of the projectile, the chamber walls, & the bore, is the pressure that is of concern to the shooter. Pressure, in the U.S., is expressed as pounds-per-square-inch, or psi.

PRESSURE, AVERAGE as given here, is the average obtained with a pressure barrel *(q.v.)* under ideal laboratory conditions. Pressure depends not only on the powder charge & the burning rate of the powder *(see* Powder Burning Rate), but also on case wall thickness, age or brittleness of the case, bullet pull *(q.v.)* tightness of chamber, free-bore *(q.v.)* if present, condition of bore, brisance of primer, as well as other conditions. The following pressure figures are averages, determined in pressure barrels.

RIFLE PRESSURES, MEAN

22 Long Rifle, High Velocity	24,000
222 Remington	40,000
22-250 Remington	55,000
243 Winchester	50,000
270 Winchester	54,000

30-30	38,000
30-06	50,000
308 Winchester	50,000
338 Winchester Magnum	53,000
375 H&H Magnum	53,000
458 Winchester Magnum	50,000

PISTOL & REVOLVER
PRESSURES, MEAN

38 Special	15,000
357 Magnum	43,000
44 Magnum	40,000
45 Long Colt	15,000
9 mm Parabellum, U.S. loads	33,000
9 mm Parabellum, German loads	44,000

The above pressure figures are in psi, were determined by means of the crusher system (*see* Pressure Determination).

PRESSURE BARREL   a specially made, extra heavy & long barrel used to measure pressures & velocities. The pressure barrel may be drilled for crusher gage *(q.v.)* pressure determinations, it may be set up for piezoelectric crystal *(q.v.)* measurements, or it may be calibrated for strain gage *(q.v.)* measurement. The chamber of the pressure barrel is cut with extra care so that its dimensions conform exactly to those set forth by SAAMI *(q.v.)*. Although ballisticians often talk about a pressure gun, most laboratories use some sort of universal receiver, such as the Modern-Bond unit, & screw the suitable pressure barrel into the receiver. Most laboratories determine pressure & velocity simultaneously. Hence, the velocity data published may be some-

what misleading since they were arrived at with the long pressure barrel which, of course, gives higher velocities than the barrel of a sporting rifle would with identical loads.

PRESSURE, CHAMBER   the gas pressure created within the chamber. Chamber pressure, sometimes called breech pressure, & back thrust *(q.v.)* are often confused. The back thrust on the bolt face is not identical to chamber pressure. For instance, the back thrust on the breechblock or bolt face in a rifle chambered for the 22 Hornet is 1850 lb., while the chamber pressure is in the area of 40,000 psi.

PRESSURE CURVE   as the powder burns progressively, chamber pressure is increased until the inertia of the bullet in the case neck has been overcome & the bullet begins its travel the length of the barrel. Although elapsed time from the beginning of powder ignition to the bullet leaving the barrel is extremely short, it is possible to record, photographically, the entire pressure curve by means of a cathode-ray oscilloscope.

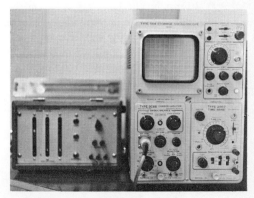

Equipment used to obtain velocity and pressure readings at the same time.

PRESSURE DETERMINATION can only be undertaken in a well-equipped ballistics laboratory. At one time the Petavel mechanical gage was widely used, but was replaced by the crusher gage *(q.v.)* method which is also known as the RADIAL PRESSURE GAGE. The piezo-electric crystal *(q.v.)* has been widely used, & most recently, the strain gage *(q.v.)* system for determining pressures has been shown to be more reliable than the crusher system. The oiled case system, in use in Great Britain, is essentially very much like our crusher system, except that the crusher is contained in the bolt face & the case is oiled to permit its free movement to the rear against the bolt face. Currently, ammunition companies are working on development of a system that will establish an industry-wide standard, with pressures to be indicated in LUP (lead units of pressure) & CUP (copper units of pressure).

PRESSURE ESTIMATION is of importance to the handloader. Pressure manifestations are: (1) difficult or hard bolt lift, indicating that back thrust on the bolt was sufficient to make contact between locking lugs & corresponding cuts tighter than usual; (2) difficult extraction, including possible case head separation, where pressure was high enough to expand the case to such a point that the brass did not spring back; (3) cratering or severe flattening of the primer in the primer pocket; (4) shiny marks on the case head where the case was set back against the bolt face; (5) case body splits, especially

in cases which have been reloaded numerous times with maximum loads; (6) case head expansion beyond .002″. These signs are indicative of higher-than-normal pressures, but it is not possible to estimate the exact amount of pressure by these signs.

PRESSURE, PEAK or pressure peak, is the maximum chamber pressure which occurs when the projectile, either bullet or shot, has travelled less than 1/4 its distance through the barrel.

PRESSURE, RESIDUAL is that amount of pressure left in the chamber after the bullet has left the gun. Residual pressure must drop to zero or a safe limit before the mechanism of a fully automatic rifle allows safe opening of the bolt.

PRIMER a small metal cup, held friction-tight within the primer pocket of a centerfire cartridge case or a shotshell hull. The primer contains a priming compound which is explosive, & the ANVIL. The anvil is posi-

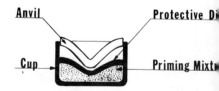

tioned in such a manner that a small amount of priming compound is between the inside wall of the primer cup & the anvil. When the firing pin hits the outside of the primer cup, the blow crushes the priming compound between the anvil & the inside wall of the primer cup, detonating the

178

compound. This in turn ignites the powder charge in the case, the primer flash passing through the flash hole in the case (*see* Cartridge, Centerfire). Today's primers are non-corrosive, & U.S. factory ammunition is primed with Boxer primers exclusively (*see* Primer, Boxer; Primer, Berdan). The thickness of the primer cup wall varies with the ultimate use of the primer. Thus, pistol primers have thinner cup walls than rifle primers, since the firing pin fall of rifles is heavier than that of pistols. There is also a considerable difference in the brisance *(q.v.)* of the priming compound in rifle, pistol & shotshell primers.

PRIMER, BATTERY CUP   two piece primer used in shotshells. Shotshells do not have a primer pocket with a flash hole as do metallic cases. The battery cup primer consists of a separate metal cup, the battery cup, which contains the primer or cap. This primer design is needed since the shotshell base does not offer adequate support to the type of primer used in metallic rifle or handgun cases. The cap used in the battery cup primer is very similar to the primer used in metallic cartridges.

PRIMER, BENET   invented by Col. S.V. Benet, Chief of Ordnance, the Benet primer was adopted by the U.S. Army in 1866. It was a cup primer, but lacked the anvil. The priming compound was extremely sensitive & the primer had to be handled with great care.

PRIMER, BERDAN   invented by

Case at left is for Boxer or American primer; case at right is suitable for the Berdan primer.

A.C. Hobbs of the Union Metallic Co., the primer was named after Col. H.W. Berdan who cooperated with Hobbs on many ammunition developments. The Berdan primer consists of a primer cup, priming compound, & a foil cover. The anvil is not part of the primer, but is a part of the cartridge case. Berdan primed cases have two flash holes in the primer pocket. Use of Berdan primed ammunition has declined in the U.S., but much European ammunition is still Berdan primed. Berdan primed ammunition can be reloaded, however, since Berdan primers & special decapping tools are available.

PRIMER, BLOWN   a primer that has been blown out of the primer pocket. Excessive pressure is the primary cause for a blown primer & when this occurs hot gasses are allowed to escape toward the rear.

PRIMER, BOXER   also called "American primer," it was invented by British Col. E.M. Boxer in 1867. Today, the Boxer primer is the most widely used one (*see* Primer).

PRIMER, CENTERFIRE   any

179

primer that fires a centerfire cartridge (*q.v.*), but the term is most frequently used when the Boxer primer is considered. (*see* Primer, Boxer).

PRIMER, CORROSIVE is one that contains potassium chlorate, a mercuric compound, or both. The use of corrosive primers required careful cleaning of the bore as soon as possible after firing & more guns corroded internally due to lack of care than due to any other cause. U.S. military ammunition made after 1952 is all non-corrosive & no corrosive priming is currently used in U.S. commercial sporting ammunition.

PRIMER, CRATERED an almost certain indication of higher-than-normal pressures, but can also be caused by mechanical faults of a gun. On a cratered primer, a small ridge of primer cup metal is formed around the firing pin indentation, a feature that can be seen as well as felt. If cratered primers occur with factory ammunition, the gun should be checked for mechanical defects. If it occurs with handloads, the loads may be too hot for the gun, for the bullet used, or may be simply over maximum. *Also see:* Handloading Tables, Maximum Charge.

PRIMER, EXTRUDED a condition where the primer has been partially pushed out of, or protrudes from, the primer pocket of a cartridge case due to excessive pressure. This occurs most frequently with revolver handloads that exceed the maximum powder charge. An ex-

truded primer often locks or freezes the cylinder of a revolver. *Also see:* Recoil Shield.

PRIMER FLASH when the firing pin fall crushes the priming compound between the inside wall of the primer cup & the anvil, the priming compound explodes. This explosion creates heat & pressure in the primer & the resultant flash passes through the flash hole of the case to ignite the powder charge. Priming compound mixes vary greatly chemically & in their explosive properties, the exact mix depending on the ultimate use the primer will be put to. Small pistol primers vary considerably in brisance (*q.v.*) from large rifle primers & these in turn vary a great deal from large rifle magnum primers. The amount of primer flash is carefully controlled by various tests during primer manufacture & large grained, slow burning powders in large cases require a hotter & longer primer flash than a small powder charge of a fast burning propellant powder in a small case such as the 222 Remington case.

PRIMER, FLATTENED a condition where the normally somewhat rounded edges of the primer in the primer cup are completely flattened & have become level with the surrounding case head. A certain sign of excessive pressure, flattened primers can occur with factory loads in guns with extremely tight chambers or bores.

PRIMER LEAK a gas leak

around the edge of the primer, usually detected by a dark smudge around the edge of the primer & case head. A leaky primer is due either to excessive pressure or a loose primer pocket. If primer leakage occurs, brass should not be reloaded unless the primer pocket gage indicates that the pocket is not over-sized. Over-sized primer pockets occur only when brass has been subjected to excessive pressures.

PRIMER, MERCURIC any primer containing fulminate of mercury in the priming compound. Upon firing, the resultant chemical change will leave a mercuric salt residue that leads to rapid corrosion of bore, chamber & brass cases. Mercuric compounds are no longer used in the manufacture of priming compounds. *Also see:* Primer, Corrosive.

PRIMER, NON-CORROSIVE abbr. NC, any primer not containing potassium chlorate or fulminate of mercury. U.S. made primers are now all non-corrosive. *Also see:* Primer, Corrosive; Primer, Mercuric.

PRIMER POCKET a round depression in the base of a cartridge case that provides access, through the flash hole, into the body of the case. The primer fits into the primer pocket friction-tight. U.S. military 30-06 ammunition used to have crimped primers & when that brass was to be reloaded, the primer pocket had to be swaged up to accept the new primer. The explosion of the priming compound leaves a RESIDUE in the bottom of the primer pocket. If precision

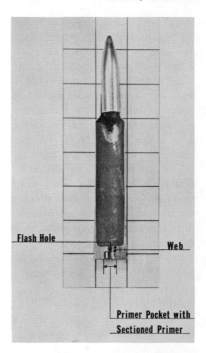

Flash Hole

Web

Primer Pocket with Sectioned Primer

ammunition is to be handloaded, this residue must be removed, either mechanically or chemically. Mechanical cleaning can be accomplished by means of special, manually operated scrapers or reamers, or by small wire brushes in either a manually turned chuck or a hand-held small electric tool, such as manufactured by Dremel Mfg. Co. Special primer pocket gages are often used by handloaders to determine if PRIMER POCKET EXPANSION has occurred due to pressure. The flash hole, located centrally in the base of the primer pocket, must be of a specific size to permit entry of the primer flash *(q.v.)*.

PRIMER, PUNCTURED or PIERCED can have two causes: either a firing pin that is too long, or, more likely, excessive pressure within the primer. As the firing pin falls & depresses the base of the primer cup, it also weakens that area of the cup. If either primer pressure or pressure from the burning powder within the case exceeds the strength of the firing pin depression, the primer is set back against the firing pin. If the gun mechanism is such that the firing pin can be moved back even slightly by that force, it may not puncture or pierce the primer. However, if either the pressure is too great or there is no firing pin rearward movement, then the primer is pierced, permitting the hot gases to escape to the rear.

PRIMER RESIDUE   *see* Primer Pocket; Primer Seating.

PRIMER, RIMFIRE   in contrast to centerfire ammunition that contains a separate primer, the priming compound in the rimfire cartridges is contained within the rim of the cartridge case. The nearly liquid priming mix is placed in the base of the rimfire case & cases are then rotated on large turning tables, thus distributing the priming mixture into the rim. A gradual drying of the liquid leaves the priming compound distributed within the rim of the case. The firing pin crushes the priming compound between the walls of the rim, thus exploding the priming compound.

PRIMER SEATING   is the insertion of a new primer into the primer pocket of a cartridge case or shotshell hull (*see* Handloading). While seating primers in shotshells hulls is

not too critical, primer seating in rifle & handgun cartridges is critical. If the primer pocket *(q.v.)* contains a large amount of PRIMER RESIDUE, the thin walls of the primer cup can be crumpled while forcing the primer into the primer pocket. A damaged primer may not fire or may produce a hangfire *(q.v.)*. Properly seated, the primer anvil should be making contact with the bottom of the primer pocket & the primer should be seated below the level of the case head by about .005″. If a primer is not seated deeply enough, erratic ignition can occur & in revolvers, a protruding primer can lock up or freeze the cylinder so it won't rotate.

PRIMER, TAPE   perhaps better known as the MAYNARD PRIMER for its inventor Dr. E. Maynard of Washington, D.C. The Maynard primer strongly resembles the paper-covered strips of caps made for today's toy cap pistols. The tape primer was an important improvement in ignition *(see* Ignition History), since it did away with the hard-to-handle percussion cap.

PRIMER TUBE   on some handloading presses for metallic ammunition as well as on fast-operating shotshell loaders, priming of cases or hulls is done by means of an automatic primer feed. Primers are stored in the primer tube, open end up, are gravity-fed into the primer seating mechanism. Like primers for metallic cases, primer tubes come in two sizes. Small primers, stored inadvertently in a large primer tube can become cocked & jammed. Extreme

182

caution is required to clear the tube since careless insertion of a wire into the tube can set off the primers in the tube.

PROJECTILE a bullet or a load of shot in flight. Shot is properly considered a projectile & to the weight of the shot must be added the weight of the shot collar or wad with collar since either contributes weight, although small, to the total weight of the shot load. This consideration must be kept in mind when developing special shotshell loads where projectile weight governs the powder charge.

PROOF the firing of a deliberate over-load to test the strength of a barrel, action, or firearm. Proofing is done under strictly controlled conditions. When a barrel, action, or gun passes proof, a proof mark *(q.v.)* is stamped into that gun or gun part that has been tested.

PROOF HOUSE a place where guns or gun parts are being tested or proofed. In Europe & Great Britain, the government closely supervises the operation of the proof house & each gun manufactured must undergo proof. Once a gun is proofed, it receives a proof mark *(q.v.)*. Many official, state-operated proof houses also issue a certificate of proof with each gun or gun part tested.

PROOF LAW governmental rules controlling the proofing of guns or gun parts. While most European countries proof only new guns, British law requires that every second-hand gun be re-proofed. Failure to supply a proof certificate with such a

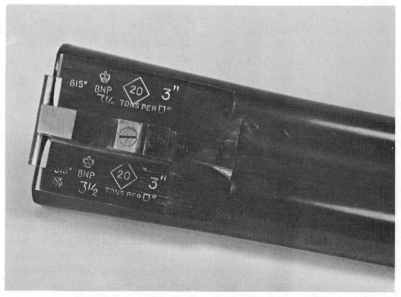

British proofmarks on modern British side-by-side Webley & Scott shotgun.

gun is "an absolute offence . . ." The penalty for selling a non-re-proofed shotgun is £40 or about $122.

PROOFLOAD also commonly called "Blue Pill," despite the fact that U.S. proofloads are marked with brilliant red lacquer or paint. Proofloads used by U.S. gun companies are about 25 per cent overloads, are fired under strictly controlled safety conditions. Since the U.S. does not have a proof law, some gunmakers do fire proofloads, while others do not.

PROOF MARK on European guns is quite specific, indicating all of the proofs the gun or gun parts underwent.

PROOF MASTER the head of a government owned or operated proof house.

PROPELLANT powder charge within a cartridge or shotshell. The term is now used almost exclusively in conjunction with smokeless powders, but since a propellant serves to move a projectile out of a gun barrel, black powder is also included.

PSI abbr. for pounds-per-square-inch, the measure used to indicate the amount of force or pressure exerted upon the chamber *(q.v.)* during the combustion of powder & given in psi. *Also see:* Pressure.

PULL a call used by the trap shooter to indicate that he is ready for the claybird's release. In skeet, "Pull" is used to call for the bird

from the high house. *Also see:* Skeet; Trap.

PULL THROUGH a string-like device, sometimes found in old military rifles, that permits a cleaning patch to be pulled through the bore of a gun. A pull-through can come in handy on a hunting trip if a takedown or collapsible cleaning rod is not available.

PUMP ACTION *see* Action, Pump.

PUNKIN BALL round lead ball, cast to bore diameter, used in smooth-bored & rifled muzzle-loading guns.

PUNT GUN usually a large-gauge smoothbored gun mounted on a small boat resembling a Barnegat sneak box. Punt guns were widely

used for market hunting ducks, geese & swans, but their use is now illegal in the U.S. In England, punt guns are still used, can be either breech-loaded or muzzle-loaded, come with one, two or more barrels. Usually loaded with black powder, some punt guns can handle up to 2 lb. of shot. Punting brings down lárge numbers of birds which are then retrieved by means of the boat. Dogs are seldom used to bring in cripples.

PURDEY SIDE LOCK   perhaps the most famed & best of all side lock actions (*see* Action, Side Lock). The Purdey design differs in several important points from the standard side lock design. Invented by F. Beesley who was employed by Purdey's, famed English gunmakers, the design has not been altered since it was patented in 1880 & even a well-used Purdey is considered a "good buy."

PUSHBUTTON SAFETY   *see* Safety, Pushbutton.

Q

QD SWIVELS *see* Swivels, Quick-detachable.

QUICKLOADER popular with many of the single shot military rifles, the quickloader was usually made of a block of wood, held up to 10 cartridges at the side of the stock for ready use. Home-made quickloaders are occasionally encountered on single shot match rifles, especially 22 RF guns where the course of fire calls for five rounds. Such a five round quickloader allows the shooter to eject & then load his rifle with a minimum of movement & subsequent change of position.

R

RADIAL PRESSURE GAGE   *see* Pressure Determination; Crusher Gage.

RADIUS SHOULDER   the type of case shoulder found in all Weatherby centerfire cartridge cases.

RAMP   word with two meanings: (1) mechanically, a ramp is a slanting

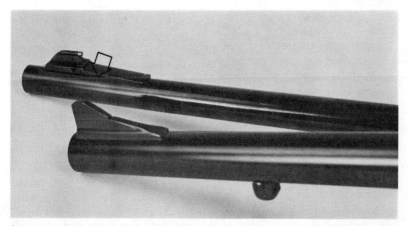

Arrow on upper barrel shows machined cut that will hold hood that can be slipped on this ramped, bead-equipped rifle sight. Below, a type of ramp sight found on handguns.

187

or sloping surface that connects two uneven levels; in mechanically operated guns the sloping surface in the rear of the chamber is called the FEEDING or BULLET RAMP (*see* Feeding Guide); (2) a SIGHT RAMP is used on some front sights for revolvers & on nearly all such sights for rifles, such a ramp serving to elevate the actual sighting device.

RAMROD   rod, usually wooden but sometimes metal, that is used in muzzle-loading guns to ram wads & bullets down the barrel. The ramrod, housed in ferrules below the forend, is also sometimes used as cleaning rod. The ramrod should not be confused with the cleaning rods found on some military rifles, especially European ones of WWI & later vintage.

RANGE   a term with several meanings, some of them being only comparative at best: (1) a target or shooting range, a place with a safe backstop & some sort of target butts or stands, usually equipped with benches for shooting as on rifle ranges; ranges designed for pistol shooting sometimes have benches for shooting equipment at the specific distances from the targets; (2) effective range *(q.v.)*; (3) extreme range *(q.v.)*; (4) the estimated distance a hunter or shooter is from the intended target; (5) point blank range *(q.v.)*; (6) accuracy range or the extreme distance at which a gun can be expected to show the greatest, most consistent accuracy.

RANGEFINDER   an optical de-

vice that, by manipulation of two optical images, gives, or is supposed to give, the user an accurate range measurement.

RANGEFINDER RETICLE   *see* Reticle.

RAPID FIRE   one phase of the National Match Pistol course of fire.

RATCHET   a toothed or notched wheel at the rear of a revolver cylinder. Each tooth in turn engages the pawl of the hand *(q.v.)* to rotate the cylinder. The number of teeth in

Arrow points to ratchet on rear of a revolver cylinder.

the ratchet depends on the number of chambers in the cylinder. If the cylinder contains five chambers, the ratchet will have five teeth; if the cylinder has nine chambers, such as some 22 RF revolvers, there will be nine teeth in the ratchet.

RATE OF TWIST   *see* Twist.

REAMER   one of several metal-cutting tools used either (1) to rough out—a roughing reamer, (2) to chamber—a chambering reamer, or (3) to finish—a finishing reamer, used in the chamber of a barrel or the chambers in a revolver cylinder.

REAR SIGHT   *see* Sight, Rear.

REBARREL   the replacement of an old, shot-out barrel with a new barrel which may or may not be chambered for the same cartridge. Shotguns & handguns are sometimes rebarreled if the barrel has been damaged in some way without damage to the action or functioning mechanism of the gun.

REBATED HEAD   cartridge case where the rim is smaller in diameter than the body of the case *(q.v.)*.

REBOUNDING LOCK   a type of lock that is designed so that, when the trigger is pulled, the hammer after falling is acted upon by the mainspring & is forced back into its safety position.

REBOUND SLIDE   a sliding device under spring tension that, in some revolvers, prevents, by means of a stud fastened to the slide, the rearward movement of the trigger except when sufficient force is exerted on the trigger.

RECEIVER   that part of a rifle or shotgun (excepting hinged frame guns) that houses the bolt, firing pin, mainspring, the trigger group, & the magazine or ammunition feed system. The barrel is threaded into the some-what enlarged forward part of the receiver, called the receiver ring. At the rear of the receiver, the butt or stock is fastened. In semiautomatic pistols, the frame or housing is sometimes referred to as the receiver.

RECEIVER BRIDGE   the rear part of the receiver that arches over the bolt raceway *(q.v.)*. The bridge is often drilled & tapped to allow placing the rear scope mount. Some receiver bridges have a cut through the bridge to permit passage of the bolt handle when the bolt is pulled rearward. This type of bridge is encountered on the Mannlicher-Schoenauer rifles, & such a SPLIT BRIDGE requires special scope mounting methods as well as special mounts. *Also see:* Scope Bases.

RECEIVER RING   the forward portion of the receiver into which the barrel is screwed. Some military receivers have large rings, others, chambered for smaller cartridges, have small rings. Large & small receiver rings are also encountered in sporting rifles.

RECHAMBER   process of enlarging the chamber of a rifle or handgun so that a larger cartridge can be fired in the gun, with this larger cartridge having the same diameter bullet as the cartridge for which the gun was originally chambered.

RECOIL   rearward push of a gun upon being fired, often called kick *(q.v.)* although kick is only a part of recoil. The gases of the burning powder force the bullet out of the case

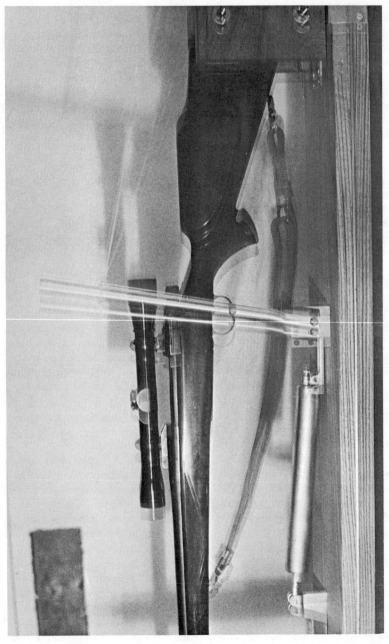

High speed photograph of recoil of big game rifle in wildcat caliber.

mouth & at the same time push the gun to the rear. The process of recoil is identical with all firearms. Recoil force is measured or computed in ft/lb & occurs in line with the bore axis. Because this thrust or force occurs above the hand holding or supporting the firearm, there is also an upward movement of the gun muzzle, the muzzle jump *(q.v.)*.

Recoil depends on several factors: (1) the size of the cartridge, including bullet weight. A 458 Winchester Magnum has more recoil than a 300 Weatherby Magnum which has more recoil than the 30-06, which kicks more than the 22 LR cartridge. (2) gun weight is an important consideration. Even a relatively light recoiling rifle, such as the 30-06, can, if the gun is built so that its weight is insufficient, kick so hard that the inexperienced shooter will soon begin flinching. The British double rifles, chambered for the big Express cartridges, often weigh over 10 lb., thus reducing the recoil since the inertia/weight ratio is such that the weight of the gun absorbs a part of the recoil. Guns with heavy recoil usually are equipped with a recoil pad *(q.v.)*. (3) stock shape can help considerably in absorbing recoil, the straighter the stock, the less recoil is felt by the shooter. (4) recoil is accompanied by muzzle blast *(q.v.)* & muzzle jump *(q.v.)*. The effect of recoil, especially on the heavily recoiling rifles, can be reduced somewhat by the installation of a muzzle brake *(q.v.)*.

RECOIL, CALCULATED　a simple formula, with a few given data, allows ready calculation of free recoil, also sometimes referred to as kinetic energy. Recoil is expressed in ft/lb. In calculating recoil, consideration must be given the muzzle velocity of the powder gases as they leave the muzzle. This figure has been determined with cannon & it has been found that the same gas velocity at the muzzle holds true for the great majority of cartridges. This gas MV or the constant "C" has a value of 4700 fps. To calculate recoil energy, use this formula:

$$RE = \frac{1}{2\,GW} \left[\frac{bwbv + cwC}{7000} \right]^2$$

where:

RE = recoil energy
G = gravitational constant of 32.2 ft/sec/sec.
W = weight of the gun in lb.
bw = bullet weight in gr.
bv = bullet velocity in fps.
cw = weight of the powder charge in gr.
C = the constant of 4700 fps, also known sometimes as the "velocity of the charge."

RECOIL CROSS-BOLT　as found on some military rifles as well as on a few conversions, is a cross-bolt that holds a small steel plate in the stock to act as a recoil abutment in the stock.

RECOIL, INITIAL　occurs before the bullet leaves the barrel. Initial recoil energy is identical to the energy exerted on the base of the bullet to move it through the barrel. However, the velocity of the initial recoil or rearward movement of the gun is in a direct mathematical relationship between gun weight & projectile weight, disregarding barrel friction & the weight of the air column in the barrel ahead of the bullet.

RECOIL LUG   a metallic block or projection, integral with the bottom part of an action, that, when properly inletted (*see* Inletting) into the stock, abuts against the recoil shoulder in the stock, thus transfers much of the recoil force onto the stock. In guns with severe recoil & in military rifles, a recoil cross-bolt *(q.v.)* is sometimes used.

RECOIL, MEASURED   there are two highly accurate methods of determining recoil. The most frequently used system employs a device known as a dynamometer, the other method is an adaptation of the ballistics pendulum (*see* Pendulum, Ballistics).

RECOIL MOVEMENT   in the strictest sense, is only a rearward movement of the gun. However, as pointed out under recoil *(q.v.)*, there is also muzzle jump *(q.v.)*. In heavily recoiling handguns, such as the 44 Magnum, there is not only the rearward push as well as muzzle jump, but depending on the grip shape & the shooter's hand, there may also be considerable torque *(q.v.)*, that is a lateral movement of the gun & hand.

RECOIL OPERATED   *see* Action, Semiautomatic.

RECOIL PAD, or KICK PAD

usually made of rubber & fastened to the butt of the stock to help absorb recoil & to prevent the gun from slipping off the shooter's shoulder. Buttplates, made from wood, steel, hard rubber, horn, plastic & other materials are sometimes erroneously called pads.

RECOIL REDUCTION DEVICES *see* Muzzle Brake.

RECOIL SHIELD   a metal flange, integral with the standing breech of the action of a revolver. Located directly behind the rear face of the cylinder, the recoil shield prevents cartridges from backing out of the chambers due to recoil. However, if too hot a handloaded cartridge is fired, the case can, nevertheless, back out of the chamber, thus stopping cylinder rotation, a condition sometimes referred to as a frozen or locked cylinder. Similarly, if a primer is pushed out of the primer pocket, even partially, cylinder rotation can be prevented, the gun is then frozen or inactivated.

RECOIL SHOULDER   that mortised part of the stock that accepts the recoil lug *(q.v.)*. The shoulder, if the lug is inletted properly, transfers recoil to the stock. *Also see:* Inletting; Recoil Cross-bolt.

RECOIL SPRING   *see* Operating Spring.

REDUCED CHARGE or LOAD   a term usually applied to handloads for rifles with jacketed bullets. Reducing the charge of powder below

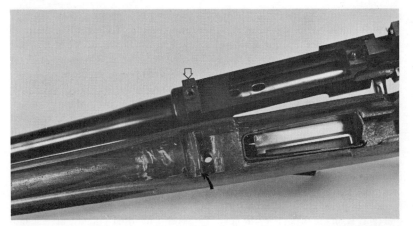

Arrow on barreled action indicates the recoil lug that fits into the abutment in stock. Arrow on stock indicates recoil shoulder in stock which, on this stock, has been glassbedded.

a minimum load listed in any of the available loading tables affects the ballistics of the cartridge. By reducing loading density *(q.v.)*, the burning rate of the powder is altered drastically, position of the powder in the cartridge case becomes critical & pressure becomes erratic & sometimes excessive. *Also see:* Squib Load.

REGULATING BARRELS   a tedious job needed to make both barrels of a side-by-side or O/U gun shoot to the same point. Good quality double rifles & shotguns, contrary to popular belief, do not have the axes of the respective bores parallel. Double rifles usually have the center of the bores closer together at the muzzle than at the breech. In firing the right rifle barrel, the muzzle is thrown to the right, while the left barrel moves the muzzle to the left on firing. With proper regulating, both barrels can be set so that the average two shot group measures about 3″ at 100 yards. In hot climates where such

double rifles are most frequently used, CROSS-SHOOTING becomes a problem. The faster a bullet travels, the faster it leaves the barrel, hence the less chance there is of muzzle movement. As external temperatures rise, the burning rate of the powder is altered & the right barrel will shoot to the left, while the left barrel will place the projectile to the right. Hence, many of the British double rifles regulated in England have their barrels set so that they actually shoot farther apart in England, but will shoot closer together, due to the effects of the external heat, in the tropics.

REINFORCE   the rear part of the barrel of a rifle, shotgun, or handgun, just ahead of where it is threaded into the action. On most guns, the reinforce gently slopes down to actual barrel diameter, but in other guns, such as the Japanese Arisaka, there are barrel steps *(q.v.)* to help in barrel diameter reduction. The reinforce

193

provides extra strength in the chamber area where barrel walls are thinned due to chamber reaming & where pressure reaches maximum peaks. Although reinforce is usually round, octagonal ones are encountered sometimes, especially in German custom rifles.

RELAY   a group of competitive shooters slated to fire a rifle or pistol match at the same time. The number of shooters in a relay depends on the number of available firing points. As one relay is on the firing line, the next relay assembles on the ready line. In the clay target sports, skeet *(q.v.)* & trap *(q.v.)*, the team is called a squad.

RELOADING   *see* Handloading.

REMINGTON-RIDER   *see* Action, Rolling Block.

REPEATER   any firearm capable of firing more than one shot without having to be reloaded.

RESIZING   *see* Sizing.

RESOLVING POWER   the ability of a lens or a system of lenses, to render details more readily visible. Resolving power depends on aberration corrections & objective lens diameter.

REST   any means of supporting a gun, most frequently a rifle, while firing it. A shooting stick was issued to musketeers who rested their heavy guns in the forked end of the stick while the other end of the stick, usually sharply pointed, was rammed into the soil. Today, in Germany as well as in Scotland, the use of the ALPENSTOCK or climbing stick is extended to serve as rifle rest.

Harry Pope, the barrel maker, & Dr. Franklin W. Mann devised, separately, rifle rests that removed all human aiming & trigger pull error from shooting. Guns or barrels were locked into these rests, & DR. MANN'S "V" REST has served as the basis for the modern machine rest *(q.v.)*. MACHINE RESTS often weigh several hundred pounds, are set into concrete stands, permit the use of either the entire rifle or only the barreled action. Trigger release is accomplished either manually or electronically.

A modified Bench Rest is shown in the illustration of Recoil *(q.v.)*. Not as heavy as the conventional machine rest, this rifle cradle can be moved easily, yet performs nearly as well as a heavy machine rest. For sighting-in, the shooter should use a rest of some kind. Leather bags, or tightly woven canvas bags filled to maximum capacity with fine sand will do very well. The forend of the rifle should lie on the rest, with the toe of the butt being rested either on another, slightly smaller sand bag or on the clenched left fist of the shooter if he is right-handed. If sand bags are not available, a wooden or G.I. ammo box covered with a heavy blanket to protect the forend will do.

In benchrest shooting, special PEDESTAL RESTS are used. The rest carries a specially shaped leather sand bag, & another shaped bag supports the rifle at the butt. In shooting

A metal pedestal rest with fitting sand bag for forend and buttstock is best for sighting-in. The same rest equipment is used in benchrest matches.

from a rest, it is not necessary to hold the forend, but the rifle should be nestled tightly into the shooter's shoulder. The left hand can either support the rifle at the toe of the butt or can be used to push the rear leather bag into position.

Varmint hunters shooting at long ranges as well as big game hunters often use a portable rest of one kind or another. Most of the commercially manufactured ones vary only slightly from the forked stick of the musketeer. In field shooting, the big game hunter will assume any possible position, kneeling, prone or sitting, often resting his rifle across a rock or tree trunk, using his jacket or hat as padded rest for the forend of his rifle. In the widest sense of the word, the sitting position with a tight sling *(q.v.)* can also be considered a rest.

For determining the accuracy of handguns and handgun ammunition, special machine rests have been designed, the BROADWAY REST being the best known one. For sighting-in a handgun, the shooter can use either a padded box, a sandbag, or the padded forend rest of the benchrest shooter. Sighting-in a handgun is a two-handed job & care should be taken, especially with revolvers firing magnum cartridges, not to scorch or otherwise damage the rest. The hot gases emerging from the muzzle can damage leather bags or hunting jackets.

RESTOCK the process of equipping a rifle or shotgun with a new stock. Various suppliers carry semi-inletted as well as nearly finished stocks for most rifles & shotguns. If special features are desired, such as a cheek-piece *(q.v.)* or a Monte Carlo comb *(q.v.)*, many gunsmiths can do the job, or the gun can be restocked by one of the custom stockers.

RETICLE also erroneously called reticule, the sighting device in a telescopic sight or scope. The reticle, which may consist of various arrangements of crosshairs, post or dot, is

195

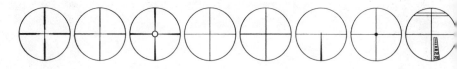

Types of reticles.

adjusted so that it appears to be on the same plane as the target. The use of scopes on shotguns, once quite popular, has declined. Today, nearly all varmint & big game rifles are equipped with scopes, & even brush guns, such as the venerable 30-30 & the 444 Marlin, are being equipped with telescopic sights. While rifle use governs the power or magnification of the scope, the scope buyer usually has a wide choice of reticles. Scopes for handguns presently come only with standard crosshairs. Several types of reticles have been developed into fairly accurate means of estimating the range from the hunter to the target. These include the crosshairs equipped with an MOA *(q.v.)* dot, duplex crosshairs that subtend one minute of angle at 100 yards, and specially designed RANGEFINDER RETICLES which remove all range guessing right out to 500 yards.

Thin reticles or crosshairs are generally best used on long range guns, while heavier reticles, with greater & faster visual pickup, are good for brush hunting. Reticle designs vary widely, not only from country to country, but also among U.S. manufacturers. *Also see:* Scope.

RETRACTING SPRING   *see* Operating Spring.

REUSABLE CASE   also known as EVERLASTING CASE. Although most brass cartridge cases can be reloaded a number of times, the everlasting case, made from especially heavy brass, had a longer life, was widely used in Schuetzen rifles *(q.v.)* where the bullet was loaded by means of a false muzzle *(see* Muzzle, False). Semi-fixed ammunition, that is a cartridge case (often an everlasting one) containing primer & powder but not the bullet, was also referred to as a semi-fixed round *(see* Round).

REVOLVER   a handgun, usually fired by holding it in one hand, in which 5-9 cartridges, depending on caliber & gunmaker, are loaded into a cylinder that rotates in the frame of the gun as the gun is being cocked. Cocking the gun aligns a chamber in the cylinder with the bore, firing expels the bullet from the case & cylinder into the bore where it then exits from the muzzle. This cycle continues as long as the shooter pulls the trigger after every shot & cartridges remain in the cylinder chambers.

In order to permit cylinder rotation, there must be a slight clearance between the forward face of the cylinder & the breech end of the barrel. As the bullet leaves the case mouth, it jumps into the bore, & there is some gas leakage between the cylinder & the rear end of the barrel. Moreover, the bullet, because of the jump from

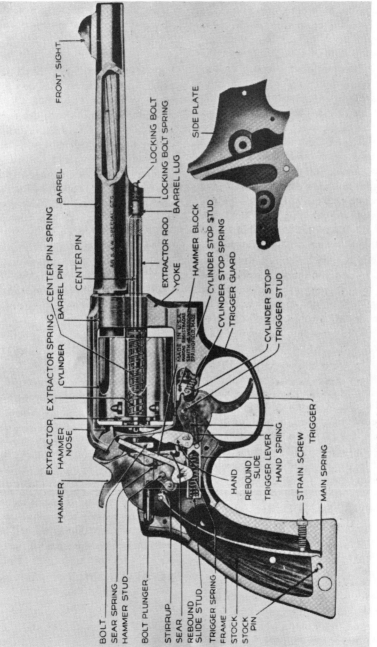

FRONT SIGHT

BARREL

LOCKING BOLT

LOCKING BOLT SPRING

BARREL LUG

SIDE PLATE

CENTER PIN SPRING

BARREL PIN

CENTER PIN

EXTRACTOR ROD

YOKE

HAMMER BLOCK

CYLINDER STOP STUD

CYLINDER STOP SPRING

TRIGGER GUARD

CYLINDER STOP

TRIGGER STUD

EXTRACTOR SPRING

CYLINDER

EXTRACTOR

HAMMER NOSE

HAMMER

38 S & W SPECIAL CTG

MADE IN U.S.A.

HAND

REBOUND SLIDE

TRIGGER LEVER

HAND SPRING

STRAIN SCREW

TRIGGER

MAIN SPRING

BOLT

SEAR SPRING

HAMMER STUD

BOLT PLUNGER

STIRRUP

SEAR

REBOUND SLIDE STUD

TRIGGER SPRING

FRAME

STOCK

STOCK PIN

Cutaway of Smith & Wesson revolver shows the relative simplicity of revolver mechanism.

197

case mouth to bore, does not accept the rifling as quickly as the same bullet fired from a semiautomatic pistol. Both of these points are often used to point out the relative ineffectiveness of the revolver when compared to the semiautomatic pistol. However, the fact remains that, because of the over-all structure of the revolver—either double action or single action—this type of handgun is capable of handling cartridges much more powerful than those fired in any of the semiautomatic pistols.

REVOLVER, AUTOMATIC British invention, the Webley-Fosberry was issued to the British services, but did not prove satisfactory. The gun looks like a revolver, but functions on the firing principle of a semiautomatic pistol. The gun had to be cocked manually for the first shot, was issued at first chambered for the 455 Cordite service round, later for the 38 ACP. If not gripped tightly while firing, the gun would malfunction; dirt & dust put the gun out of action quickly, as did rapid fire shooting. The gun was introduced in 1900 & early Mauser revolvers are based, at least in part, on the design of this unique gun.

REVOLVER, DOUBLE ACTION abbr. DA, a revolver that can be fired, without having to be cocked previously, by merely pulling the trigger. Many of the DA revolvers have an exposed hammer, can therefore be cocked by moving the hammer fully rearward until the gun is completely cocked. Then only slight pressure on the trigger is required to fire the gun.

In double action shooting, a pull of 10 or more pounds must be exerted on the trigger to cock & fire the gun.

REVOLVER, SINGLE ACTION abbr. SA, a revolver that does not have a swing-out cylinder, but a loading gate where each cartridge is inserted separately into the cylinder. The single action gun must be cocked, by means of the hammer that usually carries a large hammer spur, before the trigger can be pulled. In contrast to the DA revolver, the SA revolver has a safety notch on the hammer, as well as a loading notch. When the hammer is placed on this loading notch, it allows free rotation of the cylinder for either removal of the fired cases by means of the rod ejector *(q.v.)*, or filling the cylinder with fresh rounds.

REVOLVER, SOLID FRAME *see* Solid Frame.

REVOLVER TIMING a revolver is said to be out of timing when the cylinder is not locked in place properly aligned with the bore when the gun is fully cocked. Checking for timing should always be done with an empty gun & the hammer should be cocked slowly in single action style. Fast cocking may spin the cylinder into place, thus giving the impression that the timing is all right.

REVOLVER, TIP-UP *see* Action, Top-break.

RF abbr. for Rimfire, *see* Cartridge, Rimfire.

RFM   abbr. for Rimfire Magnum. The 22 Winchester Rimfire Magnum surpasses field performance of the 22 Long Rifle rimfire round. Rifles, handguns, as well as a combination gun, are chambered for this round. The 40 gr. bullet has a muzzle velocity of 2000 fps.

RIB   a raised metal strip on the top of a barrel used for sighting. If the rib is made from solid metal, it is known as a SOLID or BOX RIB. If the rib is merely a thin strip of metal or plastic that is supported by studs, it is known as a VENTILATED RIB. The ventilated rib helps to dissipate the heat from the barrel during shooting, therefore is of special importance on trap & skeet guns where a great number of rounds are fired & where the heat mirage would make accurate shooting difficult. The terms upper & lower rib are sometimes used to describe the rib that is formed when two barrels are joined side-by-side.

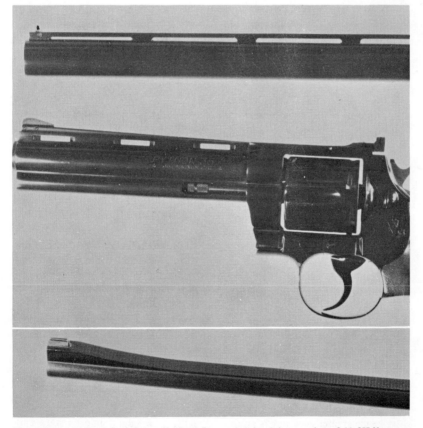

Ribs on three types of guns. Top to bottom: Ventilated ribs on a single barrel shotgun and on a Colt's 357 Magnum Python. Below, a solid rib on a sporting rifle.

However, the upper rib is not a sighting plane or rib in the usual sense. *Also see:* Extension Rib.

RICOCHET   a bullet that has struck a hard surface & glanced off. Ricochets are dangerous. The long-lived theory that high velocity bullets readily break up on contact, even if that contact surface is only a leaf, is not correct. An immediate bullet break-up on such contact only occurs when the bullet has all or nearly all its original muzzle velocity. As velocity decreases, ricochet possibilities increase, even with such fast moving bullets as those from the 240 Weatherby Magnum or the 22-250 Remington.

RIFLE   a shoulder arm with a rifled barrel. The longitudinal & spirally cut grooves (*see* Twist) impart to the bullet a spinning motion which stabilizes the bullet's flight. Rifles can be divided into several classifications: (1) by intended use, military, big game, small game, varmint, target & match rifles; (2) by barrel length, with a rifle having a barrel of less than 22″ being classified as a carbine *(q.v.);* (3) by the type of action *(q.v.)* used, such as single shot, bolt, pump, or semiautomatic action.

RIFLED SLUG   a finned projectile loaded into a shotshell & fired from a shotgun. Rifled slugs are used for big game hunting, have however a relatively limited range in comparison to bullets. The fins on the rifled slug give the projectile greater flight stability, hence greater accuracy is attainable than with slugs not having fins.

Best used in one of the special slug guns which have open bores, the rifled slug usually has a wad attached to the base that acts as gas seal in the barrel.

RIFLE SLING   *see* Sling.

RIFLING   the spirally cut grooves in the bore of a rifle or handgun. The rifling stabilizes the bullet in flight. The rifling may rotate to the right or to the left (*see* Twist), the higher parts of the bore being called lands *(q.v.),* the cuts being referred to as grooves *(q.v.).* Since the invention of rifling in barrels, many different systems have been tried, such as oval, Newton, Newton-Pope, parabolic, Haddan, Enfield, segmental rifling, etc. Most U.S. made barrels have a right hand twist *(q.v.),* while British gunmakers prefer a twist that rotates to the left. In practice, there seems to be little difference. *Also see:* Broach; Bullet Engraving; Button Rifling; Cleaning; Deep-hole Drilling; Intraform Process; Metford Rifling; Pitch; Pope Rifling; Twist, Gain.

RIFLING HEAD   that part of the rifling cutter that contains the cutting or reaming edges. A chatter in the rifling head as it proceeds down the barrel will produce uneven rifling which, in turn, prevents the bullets from attaining any degree of accuracy *(q.v.).*

RIFLING MARKS   *see* Bullet Engraving.

RIM   a ledge found on some cartridge case heads, as well as on shot-

Semi-rimmed 225 Winchester at left, the rim of a shotshell, and the rimmed 30-30 round. Arrow indicates rim.

shells. The rim permits the extractor hook *(q.v.)* to extract the case or hull after firing. *Also see:* Case, Rimmed.

RIMFIRE   *see* Cartridge, Rimfire.

RINGED BARREL   a readily visible bulge in the barrel of a gun, most frequently a shotgun, that is due to the presence of a foreign object in the bore as the gun was being fired. Since shotgun barrels have considerably thinner barrel walls than either rifles

or handguns, they tend to bulge or ring more frequently.

RINGS   *see* Scope Rings.

RIOT GUN   shotgun with a short barrel, often cylinder bored & sometimes equipped with special sights, extra large magazines, etc. Primarily a police arm, some outdated riot guns have found their way into the hands of hunters who do quite well with them on closely rising birds.

RISING BLOCK   *see* Action, Rising Block. *Also see:* Single Shot.

ROCKWELL HARDNESS SCALE a mechanical method that permits determination of the relative hardness of any metal. A pre-determined scale serves as basis & most readings on the Rockwell for gun steel are made on the Rockwell C scale. *Also see:* Brinell Hardness Scale.

ROD EJECTOR   often confused with an ejector rod *(q.v.)*. The rod ejector, as found on single action revolvers, is located on the lower right side of the barrel, is brought into use only to eject, from inside, a fired case from the chamber of the

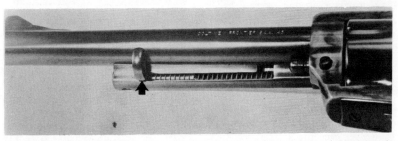

Coil spring on rod ejector of single action revolver is clearly visible. By pushing on finger rest (arrow), the rod ejector is moved to the rear so that fired case can be removed from chamber of cylinder.

cylinder of a SA revolver. The spring-activated rod ejector is operated manually & the cylinder must be rotated one stop each time a fired case is to be removed from one of the chambers. *Also see:* Frame; Revolver, Single Action.

ROLLED CRIMP *see* Crimp, Roll.

ROLLING BLOCK *see* Action, Rolling Block. *Also see:* Single Shot.

ROOK RIFLE rifle firing a low power but highly accurate cartridge used primarily in England for pests, small varmints, & rooks, crow-like birds. Many of the rifles were chambered for centerfire rimmed cases (*see* Case, Rimmed; Rim), originally loaded with black powder.

ROTARY MAGAZINE *see* Magazine, Mannlicher.

ROTATING BAND *see* Driving Band.

ROUND a word with two meanings. (1) a round of skeet or trap indicates the firing of 25 shotshells at thrown claybirds (*see* Skeet; Trap). (2) a single cartridge or shotshell, although the term round is not usually associated with a single shell. Round is also widely used to describe the number of cartridges, such as 5 or 10 rounds, that were carried or fired by a hunter. At one time, when fixed ammo—that is a self-contained cartridge or shell containing powder, primer & projectile in one container —became popular, the word round

was often used to describe one of these cartridges. A SEMI-FIXED ROUND is a cartridge case that contains only primer & powder, with the bullet either being seated into the throat (*see* Chamber Throat) or by means of a false muzzle (*see* Muzzle, False). Extra heavy brass cases for extended use, so-called EVERLASTING CASES, are said to have been made popular by Harry Pope, famed barrel maker & target shooter. *Also see:* Pope Rifling; Reusable Case.

RULE OF THREE a method of sighting-in a scoped hunting rifle. Developed by Warren Page, shooting editor of *Field & Stream,* this method of sighting is suitable for most of the currently used calibers. Sight the rifle in so that the shots print 3″ high at 100 yards. At close range, the bullet will still hit a lethal area, except when head or neck shots are taken where a dead-on hold would overshoot the mark or point of aim. At 200 yards, the bullet will still be about 3″ high, at 300 yards, the bullet will print on point of aim, at 400 yards, the bullet drop will be 8-12″ low, depending on the ballistic coefficient *(q.v.)* of the bullet. In practice, if the target is around 350 yards away, by holding dead-on the bullet drop will be such that the projectile will still land in a lethal area. Cartridges such as the 300 Winchester Magnum & the 7 mm Remington Magnum fall into this class. Using cartridges such as the 30-06 and the 270 with the lighter bullet, the range should be reduced to about 275-300 yards. If the Rule of Three system is used, shooting tests at actual ranges should be performed with the same ammunition as is to be used on the hunt.

RUNNING DEER, BOAR   *see* Target, Running Deer.

RUNOVER   *see* Checkering Runovers.

RUPTURED CASE   *see* Case Rupture.

RUST   the process of oxidation of iron & steel.

RUST PREVENTION   can be divided into two gun care classifications—gun storage & guns in use on hunting trips. For short-term storage, rust proofing can be accomplished easily by wiping all metal parts with a silicone wiping cloth. For prolonged storage, a heavy coating of a special grease is best. There are a number of vaporizing sprays on the market, but a great many of them, when they have dried, leave a hard-to-remove film that is almost as bad as the gummy gunk left by the old oils popular for rust prevention around the turn of the century. For the prevention of rust in the field, a good coat of paste wax that does not contain any abrasive is best. One coat of such a wax will protect a gun for an entire day during heavy rainfalls.

RUST REMOVAL   can sometimes be done easily without damage to the steel or bluing, but if actual pitting has occurred, then the rust removal must be turned over to a gunsmith. For light surface rust removal, take a pad of the finest steel wool available & soak it in oil. Then gently polish all areas, even if there are no rust traces. If the surface remains rough, some pitting has taken place.

S

SA abbr. for single action.

SAAMI abbr. for Sporting Arms & Ammunition Manufacturing Institute. Most major arms & ammunition makers are members of SAAMI & this organization determines many of the basic measurements for chambers, bores, cartridges, etc.

SABOT from the French, literally a wooden shoe or the shoe of a horse. In bullet designing, a sabot was tried on bullets that had both ends pointed to give them the best possible flight characteristics. The sabot was needed to provide an area on which the gases could exert the push the bullet required. The sabot was designed so that it would drop from the bullet as soon as the projectile left the muzzle.

However, the sabot-equipped bullet remains an experimental one, being dug out every once in a while for possible military use.

SADDLE RING a metal ring fastened by means of a small metal stud to the receiver frame of some carbines. Originally designed to allow a mounted man to fasten the carbine to the saddle horn by means of a leather thong. Several manufacturers are now producing carbines with saddle rings, with many of these models being made to commemorate various historical events.

SAFETY a mechanical device incorporated into the firing mechanism of a gun to prevent the accidental firing of the gun. A number of different

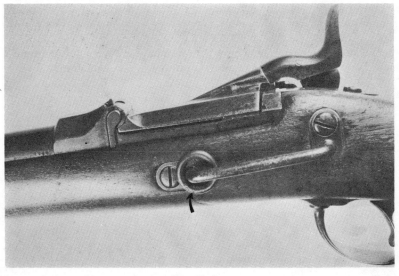

The saddle ring.

safeties are used, but basically a safety blocks the sear, trigger or hammer, or any two of the three functioning parts. On some bolt action rifles, application of the safety also locks the bolt, thus preventing the opening of the action or lifting of the bolt handle. The safety can be located in a number of positions on or near the action, depending on the type of gun & its use. Some bolt action rifles have a three position safety, where the SLIDING SAFETY *(q.v.)* in the rearward position makes the gun safe & also locks the bolt. The center position prevents the firing of the gun but permits the bolt to be operated, while the forward position allows the firing of the gun. In hunting rifles more than in shotguns, the silent safety is highly desirable. The audible clicking off or on of a safety can spook game or can provoke a charge if a dangerous animal is involved.

SAFETY ADJUSTMENT a job generally best left to the gunsmith. Some safeties can be jarred loose, or the safety half cock *(q.v.)* can become worn so that it does not engage. Similarly, if a sear is worked down to a certain point, it is possible that the movement of the safety from safe to fire would discharge the gun.

SAFETY, AUTOMATIC a safety system most frequently encountered in side-by-side & O/U shotguns. When the action is closed, the safety device is activated automatically & must be moved to the fire position before the gun can be fired. This type of safety is sometimes known as MECHANICAL SAFETY. Some trap & skeet guns come with NON-AUTOMATIC or MANUAL SAFETIES, since competitive claybird shooters feel that the automatic safety is a hindrance. Some firearms, although not equipped with a visible safety mechanism, are said to have "automatic" safeties; actually, these guns must be cocked manually before they can be fired, hence are "safe" when the action is locked on a live round in the chamber. Most of these actions have a special blocking mechanism that prevents the hammer from making contact with the firing pin (*see* Safety Block).

SAFETY BLOCK   a small steel block that, in some actions, rises up when the hammer is lowered manually. This prevents the hammer from making contact with the firing pin & even a hard blow on the hammer will not fire the gun as long as the block is in position.

SAFETY, CROSS-BOLT   pushbutton safety found on many pump & autoloading shotguns. The button is located in the trigger guard, and when pushed to the left, readies the gun for shooting. Most of these safeties lock sear & trigger, are not easily jarred into the firing position.

SAFETY DISCONNECTOR   *see* Safety, Magazine.

SAFETY, GREENER   thumb-operated safety located on the left side of the lock plate or the stock. Based on a pivot, the safety was developed by W. W. Greener, famed British gunmaker, in 1875. In addition to side-by-side shotguns, the Greener safety is also seen on continental guns, especially combination guns such as drillings *(q.v.)*.

SAFETY, GRIP   a type of safety usually found on the backstrap *(q.v.)* of semiautomatic pistols. Consisting of a lever or plunger that projects out from the backstrap, the grip safety prevents the gun from being fired unless the safety is depressed

by the shooter's hand. This occurs when the gun is gripped in the normal fashion. Most grip safeties reset automatically the moment the pressure of the shooter's hand is released.

SAFETY, HALF COCK   a type of safety found particularly on lever action rifles & carbines. When the hammer is moved partly back, the safety notch in the hammer is engaged & the gun cannot be fired until the hammer is brought to full cock & the trigger is pulled. If the safety notch is worn, a sharp blow can permit the sear to slip out of the notch, thus firing the gun.

SAFETY, LEAF   *see* Safety, Wing.

SAFETY LOCK   a now obsolete

term describing the safety & its parts. Sometimes used to describe the slide safety of semiautomatic pistols such as the 45 ACP (*see* Safety, Slide).

SAFETY LUG   an extra lug on the bolt of some bolt action rifles. Located about 1/3 of the total bolt length in front of the bolt handle, the lug was designed to hold the bolt in place should the locking lugs fail. Some bolt action rifles do not have a safety lug, but use the bolt handle itself as an additional lug.

SAFETY, MAGAZINE   a mechanical system in some semiautomatic pistols that prevents the firing of the gun if the magazine is not securely locked in the gun. The magazine safety is occasionally called a SAFETY DISCONNECTOR.

SAFETY, MAUSER   *see* Safety, Wing.

SAFETY, MECHANICAL   *see* Safety, Automatic.

SAFETY NOTCH   on single action revolvers, the first notch that is felt when the hammer of such a gun is moved to the rear. In its action it is similar to the half cock safety (*see* Safety, Half Cock) of the lever action rifle & carbine. If the notches in the base of the hammer have not been damaged, placing the hammer into the safety position or notch prevents the gun from being fired. If, however, the notches are worn or have been stoned to unsafe limits, a blow on the hammer or a mis-engagement of hammer & trigger can fire the revolver.

SAFETY, PUSHBUTTON   indefinite term that is sometimes applied to cross-bolt, Greener, sliding or top-tang safeties.

SAFETY, SLIDE   a safety device on the left rear of the frame of the 45 ACP & other pistols. When moved up, the slide safety engages a cut in the slide, prevents the gun from being fired. This safety can only be engaged when the hammer is fully cocked.

SAFETY, SLIDING   usually located on the right side of a bolt action rifle. Also called thumb safety, some of these safeties lock the bolt as well as hammer, sear or trigger, or any two of the three. Some sliding safeties are flat, stamped pieces of metal with two humps to give the thumb leverage, others are solid metal blocks which are serrated. *Also see:* Safety.

SAFETY, THUMB   an indefinite term to describe any safety operated by the shooter's thumb. The sliding safety, the top-tang safety, as well as the safety that blocks the slide on some semiautomatic pistols are considered thumb safeties.

SAFETY, TOP-TANG   a sliding safety located on or near the top tang of the action (*see* Tang). This type of safety is most frequently found on double barreled shotguns & rifles, although some bolt action rifles feature the top-tang safety. The location of this safety is nearly ideal, is readily operated by the thumb, hence is sometimes called a thumb safety (*see* Safety, Thumb).

SAFETY, WING   also known as

207

Sliding top-tang safety of a side-by-side shotgun and the slide safety of a 45 ACP.

MAUSER or LEAF SAFETY. This rotary safety rides on the rear of the bolt, is found primarily on bolt action rifles. Designed by Peter Paul Mauser, this safety is found on many military arms, especially those based on the Mauser action. Some air rifles as well as a few bolt action shotguns have wing safeties.

SAWED-OFF SHOTGUN *see* Shotgun, Sawed-off.

SCABBARD a leather sheath, sometimes called a BOOT or RIFLE BOOT, that is fastened to a saddle & in which a hunter can carry a rifle. Scabbards come in a variety of styles, are furnished for scoped & unscoped guns. In fastening a scabbard to the saddle, attention should be paid not only to the rider's comfort & quick accessibility to the gun, but also to the comfort of the horse. A scabbard that hits the horse in the side of the neck or chafes the haunch can make the most docile mount difficult to handle.

SCATTERGUN a term that is often used to describe a shotgun.

SCHNABEL FOREND erroneously also called shnobel or schnobel. A curved, & sometimes carved, shape at the forend that resembles the beak of a bird (Schnabel in German). This type of forend is common on German & Austrian guns & was popular in the U.S. In recent years, there

208

The Schnabel forend.

has been a revival of this type of forend on factory as well as custom rifles.

SCHONZEITPATRONE German term designating any of the smaller centerfire cartridges, such as the 222 Remington. The phrase also embraces the more powerful rimfire cartridges such as the 22 RFM *(q.v.)*. Many of the German & Austrian Jaeger or game wardens carry a small caliber rifle afield during the closed season (Schonzeit) to shoot varmints as well as undesirable birds. The small caliber cartridges have a low noise level, little recoil, are adequate for the taking of such game. Many combination guns *(q.v.)* are either barreled for one of these cartridges or one of the shotgun barrels is equipped with a barrel insert *(q.v.)* which is chambered for one of these cartridges.

SCHUETZEN RIFLE a special target rifle of single shot persuasion.

Use of these rifles was once very popular in the U.S. for off-hand matches. The long, heavy barrel carries target sights & the gun is equipped with double set trigger (*see* Trigger, Double Set), palm rest *(q.v.)*, a high & often extremely pronounced cheekpiece *(q.v.)*, hook plate *(q.v.)*. Many of these guns carried a false muzzle (*see* Muzzle, False), were chambered for such black powder cartridges as the 32-40 or the 38-55.

SCOPE a special telescopic sight that magnifies the target, chiefly used on rifles & handguns, although equipping shotguns with 1X or one power magnification scope was popular for a brief period. The use of scopes on hunting & target rifles is not new, but the widespread use of scopes is relatively recent & vast improvements in scopes have been made since the end of WWII.

Scopes are sometimes referred to as telescopic sights, optical sights, & as "glassware" by some writers. The power of magnification, expressed by 4X for four power or 6X for six power, governs the ultimate use of the scope, as well as the field of view *(q.v.)* & the LIGHT GATHERING POWER. This latter optical quality of a scope depends on several factors: relative brightness & light transmission, as well as magnification. The higher the magnification, the smaller the field of view. The relative ability of the optical system to control image brightness depends on the amount of light transmitted through the scope—on the diameter of the objective lens *(q.v.)* & therefore on the area of the exit pupil. Under full light conditions, the light gathering power of most scopes will be adequate. As the available light is reduced, the relative brightness of the image is reduced. A properly arranged set of quality lenses has a greater light gathering power than a set with lenses of poorer quality & this becomes apparent as light intensity is decreased. *Also see:* Aberration; Definition; Elevation Adjustment; Eye Relief; Objective Lens; Parallax; Resolving Power; Reticle; Sighting-In; Windage Adjustment.

SCOPE BASES or BLOCKS or MOUNTS are metal blocks mounted, by means of screws, on the receiver, action or top strap *(q.v.)* of a firearm. On some rifles, the bases, because of the overall length of the scope, are mounted either wholly or partially on the barrel. Most factory rifles are DRILLED & TAPPED for scope bases, that is holes have been

drilled & threaded for the screws to hold the scope bases in place.

Mounts for all domestic & most foreign military & sporting rifles are available. Blocks for handguns, primarily revolvers, are also offered, since hunting varmints & big game with scoped handguns has become popular in the last few years. Shotgun bases are also available, although low rifle bases can be used on some shotguns. The scope bases must be equipped with scope rings *(q.v.)* of the same manufacture as the bases, since rings & bases must mate to hold the scope securely on the gun. Bases & rings are manufactured by most scope makers, also by some firms that specialize in blocks & rings only.

The type of scope & gun, the ultimate purpose of the gun, as well as such mechanical features as the amount of bolt lift, dictate the height of the scope bases. Hunting scopes are generally mounted low, as close

Off-set scope on 30-40 Krag, tip-off scope mount that permits instant use of iron sights, and low-mounted scope of low power on brush hunting rifle.

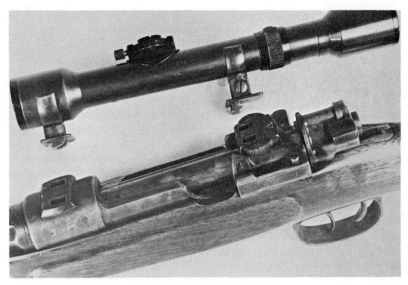

Claw mounts are popular on the Continent.

to the line of bore *(q.v.)* as possible, while target & varmint scopes *(see* Scope, Target & Varmint) often are mounted high over the line of bore by means of special target blocks.

Scope bases or blocks come in various styles. The majority of hunting scopes on standard length actions use a TWO PIECE MOUNT, one base being mounted on the forward receiver bridge, the other on the rear bridge. Some action designs necessitate the use of a one piece or BRIDGE MOUNT, while still other actions, such as the Krag or the Mannlicher-Schoenauer with its split rear bridge, requires a special mounting technique with a SIDE or OFF-SET MOUNT. While most scope rings are easily detached from the bases, sometimes a quick removal of the scope from the rifle is desirable or essential. Here is where the TIP-OFF MOUNTS are of great help.

Some old German mounts & at least one currently produced U.S. mount places the scope fairly high over the line of bore. The bases are of standard design, but the scope rings *(q.v.)* are fashioned in such a manner that they can be used in lieu of a rear or peep sight, with the shooter simply using the front & rear sighting holes in the rings in conjunction with the front sight of the rifle. Some mounts allow rapid scope removal, the rear base being equipped with a flip-up peep sight that takes the place of a rear sight on the rifle barrel, but does require a front sight on the barrel.

A mount that has never become very popular in the U.S. but is encountered fairly frequently abroad is the CLAW MOUNT. The origin of this mount is European, with the rings having claws that fit into machined & spring-locking cuts in the bases. While most of the U.S. mount-ring combinations require the use of a screwdriver or coin to loosen the screw that holds the ring to the base, the claw mounts require only slight finger pressure to release the rear ring from its mount. Re-mounting requires only hooking the front claws into the slots of the front mount, and slight pressure on the rear of the scope to re-engage the claws of the rear mount. Many of the currently produced 22 rimfire guns have the receivers grooved for scope mounting & most of the scopes suitable for these guns come with tip-off mounts that readily engage the grooves in the receiver. While some scope bases have no provision for the adjustment of either elevation *(q.v.)* or windage *(q.v.),* others allow some degree of coarse windage adjustment. The majority of scopes have internal adjustments (*see* Scope, Internal Adjustment) for elevation & windage. However, one U.S. manufacturer offers scopes which have no internal adjustments, all adjustments being made in special mounts which permit accurate changes.

SCOPE BLOCKS *see* Scope Bases.

SCOPE CAPS or COVERS plastic, rubber or leather covers that fit over the ocular & objective lenses of a scope. Connected by means of rubber or leather bands, scope caps are used to protect the lenses from rain, snow, scratches, & from dust while the scoped gun is stored. Special scope covers which can be flicked off the scope for field use are sometimes encountered, although their use

has not become as widespread as might be expected. Some target & varmint scopes are equipped with metallic scope covers which are threaded so that they screw into the ocular & objective lens housing.

SCOPE, EXTERNAL ADJUST-MENT a few hunting & most target & varmint scopes have provision for the external adjustment of windage & elevation. While the hunting scopes require special scope bases *(q.v.),* the target & varmint scope bases, though higher than usual, are of standard design & adjustments for windage & elevation are made by means of special scope rings *(q.v.).*

SCOPE, ILLUMINATED a telescopic sight, usually with a fixed power of magnification, that contains a light source, often a small dry cell. When a button is pushed & the electric circuit is closed, a small beam of light is projected onto the target. A number of military sniper scopes, including infra-red light scopes for night use, have been developed. An illuminated hunting scope was developed some years ago, but failed to gain consumer acceptance.

SCOPE, INTERNAL ADJUST-MENT a telescopic sight containing two sets of mechanical systems which make possible windage & elevation adjustments. These systems are housed in two TURRETS, one containing the windage adjustments, the other the elevation adjustments. The adjustment dials are protected from tampering & accidental movement by means of screw-on turret caps which, through the use of neoprene rings, also seal the turret & prevent dirt & moisture from getting into the turret & the adjustment system. Scopes are usually positioned in the rings so that the elevation adjustment turret is on top; this places the windage adjustment turret to the right side of the gun. The adjustment dials clearly indicate in which direction the dial must be turned to obtain the desired movement, this usually being shown by an arrow. To aid adjustment, a graduated dial surrounds the adjustment screw & a click may be audible when the screw is turned one division on the dial. Some scope makers adjust the elevation & windage systems so that one click or division on the dial moves the point of bullet impact 1/2 MOA, others adjust the divisions for 1/4 MOA, or for one MOA. Moving the 1/4 MOA scope adjustment one click will move the point of bullet impact 1/4" at 100 yards. A scope that has MOA adjustments moves the bullet impact one inch at 100 yards for each click or division on the dial. *Also see:* Elevation Adjustment; Rule of Three; Scope Rings; Windage Adjustment.

SCOPE MOUNTING HEIGHT a measurable factor that is often neglected during sighting-in *(q.v.).* Since a scope is usually mounted about 1.5" above the line of bore, this extra elevation must be taken into consideration during sighting-in & in calculating the midrange trajectory *(q.v.).*

SCOPE MOUNTS   *see* Scope Bases.

SCOPE, RANGEFINDER   a type of telescopic sight that has built into it a means of determining range. To a certain extent, these rangefinder scopes require knowledge of game size as well as the ability to interpolate quickly the range from the known size of the dot or the known distance between two spaced horizontal crosshairs in the reticle *(q.v.).* Over the years, further refinements have been made on this basic principle of comparing game size with reticle size for range estimation. The latest development in scopes eliminates all guess work on range determination by the use of a trajectory-compensating cam which acts as a mechanical hold-over *(see* Holdover). To allow for variations in trajectory, cams have been designed for each bullet weight in any given caliber.

SCOPE RINGS   although one piece rings that simply slip over the objective lens in the front & over the ocular lens at the rear of the scope are still being offered, two piece rings are by far the most popular and most reliable way of fastening the scope to the scope bases *(q.v.).* The scope rings must be mated to the bases; with only a few exceptions can the rings from one manufacturer be used with the bases of another manufacturer. These exceptions occur primarily with target scopes, & with a few varmint scopes that are mounted in target-type rings.

In the two piece rings, the scope is held securely by 2-4 screws per ring, this arrangement permitting the scope to be moved forward or

Internally and externally adjustable target scopes.

Scope rings hold scope securely on two-piece scope base.

backward to obtain the proper eye relief *(q.v.)* before the screws are tightened. The standard rings, sometimes referred to as hunting rings, offer no windage or elevation adjustments. The target scope rings contain windage & elevation adjustments, the scope being suspended in the rings by means of spring-activated plungers which bear against the scope tube. Most of the target rings have 1/4 MOA clicks (*see* Click; Scope, Internal Adjustment) & the adjustment knobs on the rings are not protected from accidental movements as are the adjustment dials of an internally adjusted scope. Occasionally, a shooter selects an internally adjustable varmint scope (*see* Scope, Target & Varmint), yet equips it with externally adjustable target rings for greater convenience in making sight adjustments. While the hunting-type rings can absorb considerable abuse in the field, the very sensitive target rings must be carefully protected from accidental knocks.

SCOPE, SNIPER   military scope, often painted in camouflage colors & equipped with rangefinding reticle (*see* Scope, Rangefinder), usually of fairly high power, 6X-10X. Infrared sniper scopes (*see* Scope, Illuminated) have also been used to some extent.

SCOPE, SPOTTING   telescope used on the range or in the hunting field, often with a variable power or magnification adjustment. It is used by target shooters to see their score on the target & by hunters to evaluate game heads or to spot game at great distances.

SCOPE, TARGET & VARMINT a telescopic sight, usually of high power, that incorporates several special mechanical & optical refinements. Target & varmint scopes may either have internal adjustments or may be adjusted externally by means of special scope rings *(q.v.)*. Target & varmint scopes are usually of fixed power or magnification, with the lower powers, 10X or 12X being used for varmint hunting, while the higher power scopes, 20X, 25X, & 30X, are used for competitive shooting. All of these scopes are equipped with parallax *(q.v.)* adjustment, many come with special sun shades that are screwed onto the objective lens housing, special rubber cups that fit over the ocular lens housing to exclude disturbing light rays while sighting. Some of the older target & varmint scopes carry a spring around the scope tube that helps in absorbing recoil, thus preventing damage to either the optical system or to the elevation & windage adjustments. The majority of these scopes also come with scope caps, either slip-on or the aluminum ones that screw onto the objective & ocular lens housings.

SCOPE, VARIABLE POWER a telescopic sight that allows the shooter to change the degree of magnification, from 3X to 9X for example. Any telescopic sight must be water & fog-proof to give a clear sight picture of the object viewed. The special optical system required to permit magnification changes poses an extra problem in sealing the scope from moisture. Only during the last decade have scope makers succeeded in fully sealing the scope tubes so that variable scopes are now as fog & moisture-proof as fixed power scopes.

SCORING PLUG   device used in competitive rifle & pistol shooting to determine precisely where a bullet entered the target paper. Scoring plugs come in sizes corresponding to bullet diameters, are frequently equipped with magnifiers so that the value of the bullet holes in the target can be determined without question.

SCROLL GUARD   trigger guard *(q.v.)* extension that sweeps downward & to the rear on some Schuetzen *(q.v.)* rifles. Muzzle-loading rifles often have a brass scroll guard.

SEAR   a pivoting bar in the firing or lock mechanism of a gun. The sear engages in one of the hammer notches *(q.v.)*. If the sear engages the full cock notch *(see* Cock), it holds the hammer in the cocked position. The sear is linked with the trigger, either directly or by means of a connecting rod or bar. Pulling the trigger permits the sear to slip out of the notch at the base of the hammer, thus allowing

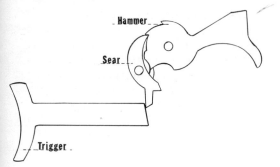

the hammer to fall. In truly hammer-less *(q.v.)* guns, the sear may engage the cocking piece or the firing pin.

SEAR SPRING   in some guns, a small helical spring working with the sear.

SEASON CRACKING   *see* Brass, Season Cracking of.

SEATING DEPTH   the precisely measured depth to which a bullet is seated in the mouth of a metallic cartridge case. Seating depth is critical in handloading, especially when a long bullet is seated so far out of the case mouth that the bullet tip engages the rifling of the throat (*see* Chamber Throat). This increases chamber pressure (*see* Pressure, Chamber) to excessive levels. Cases with short necks therefore often preclude the use of a long bullet in handloading. Similarly, a short magazine may also prevent the use of a long bullet.

SECANT OGIVE   a bullet de-signed so that the cylindrical surface of the bullet is secant to the curve of the bullet head, the latter being the distance from bullet shoulder to

bullet tip or point. *Also see:* Illus-tration of Bullet nomenclature.

SECTIONAL DENSITY   ratio of a bullet expressed in pounds to the square of its diameter expressed in inches.

SEGMENTAL RIFLING   *see* Metford Rifling.

SELECTIVE EJECTOR   *see* Ejector, Selective.

SELECTIVE TRIGGER   *see* Trigger, Single Selective.

SELFLOADING   *see* Action, Semiautomatic. *Also see:* Action, Automatic.

SELF-LUBRICATING BULLET *see* Cartridge, Self-lubricating.

SEMIAUTOMATIC   *see* Action, Semiautomatic.

SEMIAUTOMATIC PISTOL *see* Pistol.

SEMI-FIXED AMMUNITION *see* Round, Semi-fixed.

SEMI-PISTOL GRIP   *see* Grip, Semi-pistol.

SERPENTINE   a part of the firing mechanism of a matchlock gun. In the upper jaws of the serpentine, so named becaused of its serpent-like S shape, is held the slow match, while the lower part of the serpentine that extends below the stock acts as the trigger of the gun.

SET GUN sometimes also known as trap gun, but no connection with a gun used for trapshooting. Now outlawed in most states for killing of small game & varmints, these guns are also under the jurisdiction of the ATFD & must be registered. Set or trap guns are usually single shot small caliber rifles, sometimes shotguns, which fire when an extension of the trigger system, being hooked up with some bait, is tripped. The gun is usually mounted on a spike driven into the ground, with the muzzle directed toward the bait.

A somewhat similar system of firing a gun was used in the now illegal alarm or burglar guns. These were tripped by means of string or catches fastened to windows or doors. Most of these guns were loaded with shot & the earlier models were often home-made.

SETSCREW two types of setscrew are encountered in guns: (1) the screw that controls the amount of trigger pull. In match guns, the trigger is often equipped with a second setscrew that controls the amount of travel before the trigger breaks (*see* Trigger Pull). (2) a setscrew is often used to anchor another screw in place that could be loosened by heavy recoil or hard usage of the gun.

SET TRIGGER incorrectly called Sett Trigger, *see* Trigger, Set.

SHARPS *see* Action, Sharps. *Also see:* Single Shot.

SHARPS-BORCHARDT *see* Action, Sharps. *Also see:* Single Shot.

SHEATH TRIGGER *see* Trigger, Sheath.

SHELL more commonly called shotshell *(q.v.)*, a loaded shotgun shell. Sometimes the term is used colloquially to describe a quantity of metallic ammunition; thus, one might hear that a hunter bought a box of 30-30 "shells" for deer hunting.

SHELL CONDITIONER tool used by those who reload shotshells to restore the hull to its original size & also to shape the brass head of the hull to its former shape & size if needed. Some shell conditioners also knock out the spent battery primer, while others, operated electrically, are used to "iron out" used paper hulls.

SHELLHOLDER device that fits into the ram of a loading press (*see* Handloading Tools) to hold a cartridge case. The circular shellholder

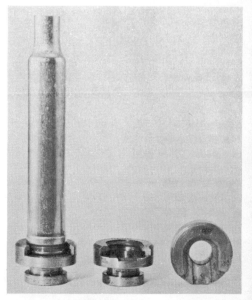

Shell holders.

is bored through from top to bottom to permit expulsion of the spent primer from the primer pocket of the cartridge case by means of the decapping pin in the sizing die. The primer seater of the loading press is moved into the machined slot of the ram with a live primer & the ram is lowered so that the live primer is transferred from the primer seater to the primer pocket in the case. *Also see:* Primer Seating. Shellholders are made for virtually all currently available U.S. & European cartridge cases, but the shellholders from one maker should not be used with a loading press from a different manufacturer. Thickness variations in the shellholder could affect sizing operations, may in effect alter the case sufficiently that a condition similar to excessive headspace *(q.v.)* can be created.

SHOOT   a term widely used to denote a competitive shooting event in skeet *(q.v.)* or trap *(q.v.)*. A registered shoot is one sanctioned by either the National Skeet Shooting Association (NSSA) or the Amateur Trapshooting Association (ATA). The registered birds broken or lost are counted on the competitor's shooting record which determines his over-all standing or classification. *Also see:* Shoot-off.

SHOOTING GLASSES   used by most competitive shooters, are slightly larger than regular glasses, have tempered & hardened lenses. The glasses may or may not be ground to the shooter's regular prescription if he normally wears correc-

tive lenses. Shooting glasses come in several colors which aid considerably in seeing the target more sharply & clearly under differing light conditions. The tempered lenses also serve to protect the eyes in case a cartridge or shell bursts due to excessive pressure & hot powder gasses leak backwards.

SHOOTING POSITIONS   depend on the type of competitive shooting. Not only do the body positions in skeet & trap vary from each other, but they also differ from station to station in both claybird sports. In competitive rifle events, four positions are recognized, although not all matches fired use the four positions: prone, sitting, kneeling, & offhand. In the conventional pistol matches, the handgun is held in one hand, either right or left, depending on the shooter's natural inclination. In firing the PPC (Police Pistol Course) or any of the other combat courses, gun handling, body stance, & even gun hand changes, for the shooter uses his strong or regular hand as well as his "weak" hand. Some combat course forms prescribe the use of a two-hand hold, & this two-handed hold is the approved form of using a handgun when hunting unless some sort of rest is utilized. In hunting with a rifle & especially when taking long range shots, the hunter must improvise to the best of his ability & as quickly as possible before the game is spooked. *Also see:* Rest.

SHOOTING REST   *see* Rest.

SHOOT-OFF   when in a registered trap or skeet shoot *(q.v.)* two or more competitors tie for first place, a shoot-off is held. Depending on the event, a shoot-off may mean one extra round of 25 targets, or as many as 100 targets.

SHORT   abbr. S, for the 22 Rimfire Short cartridge. Although not obsolete, the 22 S is not very popular & relatively few guns are capable of handling the small cartridge. The bullet weighs between 15-29 gr., with an MV of 1045-1710 fps. As a light plinking load, the 22 S is adequate, & certain I.S.U. *(q.v.)* events are fired with this cartridge.

SHOT   a small spherical mass of metal. Most shot is formed from lead alloyed with other metals, to facilitate forming of the shot & to give it hardness. Shot comes in many sizes, from "dust" to 00 buckshot & shot sizes vary greatly from country to country. While most of the popular shot sizes are loaded commercially & shot is available for the handloader, some shot sizes, notably the smaller ones, are not readily available. Many recommendations have been made as to what shot size to use on certain game species, much of the information being, at best, one man's opinion. Not only does every shotgun vary in performance somewhat from shot to shot even when the same factory ammunition is used, but similarly, shot performance varies from shell to shell. The smaller shot sizes, such as #9 & #8, are used for claybird shooting, woodcock & other small birds, while the larger sizes, such as #4 & #2 are often recommended for geese & turkey.

SHOT, BRIDGING OF   occurs in the shot reservoir of a shotshell loading tool when the shot pellets, in passing through the narrow orifice of the shot measure, get jammed or bunched up. The soft lead pellets sometimes undergo the shearing action of the charge bar & bridging must be re-

SHOT NUMBER	12	9	8	7½	6	5	4	2	BB
	•	•	•	●	●	●	●	●	●
APPROXIMATE PELLETS PER OZ.	2385	585	410	350	225	170	135	90	50

BUCKSHOT NUMBER	4	3	1	0	00
	●	●	●	●	●
APPROXIMATE PELLETS PER LB.	340	300	175	145	130

moved promptly if the charge bar of the shotshell loading tool is to deliver the correct amount of lead shot into the next shell to be loaded.

SHOT CARTRIDGE   a metallic cartridge case loaded with shot instead of a bullet. Commercial shot cartridges are only offered in 22 Long Rifle ammunition, but handloaders often load handgun cartridges with shot loads, using them for pest, varmint, or snake shooting. Sometimes these loads are used to take small game such as rabbits, ptarmigan, spruce grouse.

SHOT, CHILLED   sometimes called hardened shot. Pure lead shot is soft, hence deforms easily, affecting shot performance (*see* Shot Deformation). Shot is now hardened with antimony which also aids in the forming of the lead pellets as the lead is dropped from the shot tower *(q.v.)*. Chilled shot is now used as the standard in U.S. made shotshells & experiments with plated shot (*see* Shot, Plated) are continuing. Metals other than lead have been tried, but lack the many good properties of lead.

SHOT COLLAR   a plastic band, sometimes combined with a plastic over-powder wad (*see* Wad, Overpowder) inside a shotshell. The shot collar is wrapped around the shot, dropping away after the shot column leaves the muzzle. The collar prevents the pellets from bouncing off each other & the inside walls of the barrel, thus preventing shot deformation *(q.v.)*. The use of a shot collar also

appears to boost velocity of the shot column, hence also that of the individual shot pellets.

SHOT COLUMN   the mass of shot contained in a shotshell. The shot, without the use of a shot collar *(q.v.)*, as it travels the length of the barrel, does not do so bunched up, but the pellets are strung out. Thus, the pellets that were in the bottom of the load may occupy a central location or may be in the forward part of the shot column.

SHOT DEFORMATION   occurs as the soft lead pellets bounce off each other as well as off the inside walls of the barrel. Shot that is out of round has decreased ballistic efficiency as well as poor flight pattern. Preventing deformation of shot has been tried by plating of pellets (*see* Shot, Plated).

SHOT, FUSED   occurs mostly with handloaded shotshells when hot powder gases leak into the shot, fusing the pellets, making the massed pellets especially lethal at short ranges. At the normal & longer ranges, fused shot becomes virtually useless since its effectiveness, that is pattern *(q.v.)*, has been destroyed.

SHOTGUN   a long gun designed to fire shotshells, the muzzle *(q.v.)* of the smoothbored barrel containing a constriction known as choke *(q.v.)*. *Also see:* Gauge. Basically, there are six types of shotgun actions *(q.v.)*: single shot, side-by-side, over & under, pump, semiautomatic, bolt.

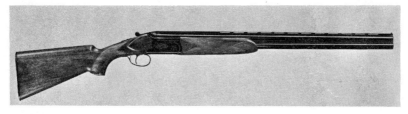

Typical over/under shotgun with ventilated rib and single, selective trigger.

Also see: Double; Combination Guns; Over and Under; Stock, Shotgun.

SHOTGUN, DOUBLE   two barrel shotgun where the barrels are arranged side-by-side, the term side-by-side being frequently used to describe such a shotgun. Although over/under guns are also doubles in that they have two barrels, they are never described as such. The double shotgun had its origin in England. The various action designs have been copied in the U.S. as well as in Europe, but the classic, high-grade double still comes from one of the British gunmakers. The basic action designs are the box lock & the side lock (*see* Action, Box Lock; Action, Side Lock). These are usually based on the hinged frame (*see* Action, Hinged Frame), a relatively simple design where the action body houses the entire action. Doubles come with either ejector *(q.v.)* or extractor *(q.v.),* are offered with double or single triggers (*see* Trigger, Double; Trigger, Single). In contrast to rifles, the locks of the double fire the gun, have nothing to do with the actual locking of the gun which is accomplished by the bolt (*see* Bites). The safety of most doubles is automatic (*see* Safety, Automatic), but the skeet or trap gun may have a manual safety (*see* Safety, Automatic). *Also see:* Cocking Lever; Cocking Rod; Doll's Head; Chopper Lump Tubes; Face of Breech; Flats; Lock; Lump; Lump, Hook of; Top-lever.

SHOTGUN PLUG   *see* Magazine Plug.

SHOTGUN, SAWED-OFF   usually a double barrel shotgun on which the barrels have been cut to an illegal length. Possession of such a gun is in violation of the Gun Control Act of 1968.

SHOT PATTERN   *see* Pattern.

SHOT, PLATED   copper & nickel have been used to plate shot pellets. Plating is claimed to leave shotgun barrels cleaner than does lead shot, is said to increase shot velocity, reduce or eliminate shot deformation, hence give better patterns. Wildfowl authorities have shown that unplated lead shot ingested by ducks is toxic to the birds. However, plated shot has not found wide sportsman's support & its manufacture is expensive. No shotshells with plated shot are loaded commercially & the hunter who wants to use plated shot must handload his shotshells.

SHOTSHELL a self-contained round of ammunition consisting of a case with a brass head, a primer (*see* Primer, Battery Cup), a powder charge, wads (*see* Wad) & a load of shot *(q.v.)*, being closed by means of a crimp *(q.v.)*. Early shotshell cases

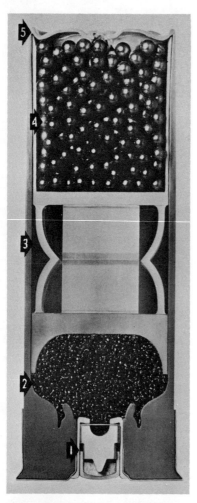

Cross section of shotshell shows (1) primer, (2) powder charge, (3) plastic wad, (4) shot charge, (5) crimp of plastic case. Shell is Winchester's AA trap and skeet load.

were made of brass, were reloaded many times by the shooter. Paper hulls with brass head replaced the brass cases & the paper hulls have now been replaced by plastic hulls with brass heads. Some all plastic shells without brass heads are also manufactured & these will probably be the shells of the future. Commercially loaded shotshells are offered in 10, 12, 16, 20, 28, & 410 ga. (*see* Gauge), are manufactured for every shotgun use & loaded with a wide choice of shot *(q.v.)* sizes. Handloading shotshells *(q.v.)* is a necessity for many shooters, especially those who shoot skeet & trap. Brass & other metals have been used to make hulls for handloaders, but their use has declined in the last few years.

U.S. shells are manufactured in two lengths: 2 3/4'' & 3''. Most European guns currently imported are chambered for U.S. shell lengths, but some with shorter chambers do show up once in a while. When U.S. shells are fired in them, chamber pressure (*see* Pressure, Chamber) becomes dangerously excessive.

Shooters often differentiate between HIGH & LOW BASE, HIGH & LOW BRASS shells, but there is a frequent misunderstanding of the terms base & brass. The height of the outside BRASS head of the shell is not necessarily in a direct ratio to the height of the BASE wad (*see* Wad, Base) inside the shell. A low brass shell may have a high base wad & vice versa. The internal construction of the shell, that is the size of the powder charge, the amount & size of the shot, plus the height of the base wad & other wads used, depends on the ultimate use of the shell. When paper hulls were the only ones manufactured, light skeet & trap loads were found in hulls with low brass heads, while hulls with high brass heads were used when maximum shotshell power & range were needed. These terms are still being used, but with the introduction of plastics, the discussion becomes academic, since ammunition makers can now load virtually any desired ballistic performance into the hulls.

SHOT SIZES   *see* Shot.

SHOT STRINGING   as the shot charge leaves the barrel of the gun, the individual pellets have not only slightly varying ballistic properties, but also have been given varying velocities. The shot column *(q.v.),* after the shot collar *(q.v.)* drops away, begins to stretch & at 30 or 40 yards, not all of the pellets hit the target at the same time. This shot string—or shot stringing—was thought to be a major reason for many misses, but has recently been shown to be of relatively little importance, especially with the modern powders, shot collars & wads.

SHOT TOWER   lead shot has for many years been made in shot towers. Liquid lead is dropped—& the purer the lead the more likely it is to form perfect spherical shot—from the 8th or 9th story of the tower into a 40 ft. deep water tank. The molten lead is poured through a pan that has perforations in the bottom the size of the shot desired. As the lead droplets fall, they become round. Chilled shot

(q.v.) made by the tower method is still the primary source of shot today, although a newer method that obsoletes the 100 year old shot tower is now being used to produce equally as good shot & at a greater rate of speed.

SHOULDER   *see* Case Shoulder.

SHOULDER HOLSTER   a leather holster *(q.v.)* or pouch with straps that makes it possible to carry the holstered handgun under the arm pit or in a similar location. Shoulder holsters are widely used by law enforcement officers & sometimes by hunters who use a handgun. While the standard shoulder holster is designed for maximum concealment of a small gun, hunters use custom-made holsters for their big frame handguns, thus allowing them greater use of their hands for riding, climbing, camera use. *Also see:* Scabbard.

SHOULDER PAD   a leather or rubber pad on a shooting jacket or shirt. Shoulder pads are designed either to reduce recoil or to prevent slippage of the gun butt from the shoulder. Heavy leather or rubber pads are used on coats designed for competitive rifle shooting, anti-slip pads are found on garments designed for skeet & trap shooters.

SIDE ARM   military term designating any arm worn on the belt, including revolvers, semiautomatic pistols, as well as daggers, bayonets, etc.

SIDE-BY-SIDE   abbr. S/S, *see* Shotgun, Double.

223

SIDEHAMMER the locating of the hammer at the side of the lock plate or action was a developmental step, ultimately resulting in the center location of the hammer. The Colt Root pistol & the Springfield 45-70 rifles & carbines are typical side-hammer guns.

SIDE LOCK *see* Action, Side Lock.

SIDE PLATE a shaped metal plate that either covers the working parts of a gun, such as the side plate of the revolver, or, as in the case of side lock guns, where the lock or firing mechanism is mounted on such a plate (*see* Lock Plate). Dummy plates, or dummy side plates *(q.v.)* are sometimes used on box lock guns to give the impression of a side lock gun with hand-detachable locks.

SIDE PIN or SCREW a long screw that goes through the stock & fastens the locks of a side lock gun to frame & stock.

SIGHT a device or devices that aid in the aiming of a firearm. Rifles usually have two sights, the front sight at the muzzle end, & a rear sight which may be located on the barrel, the receiver, the action, or the tang *(q.v.)*. Shotguns usually carry a brass or ivory bead near the muzzle, may or may not have a second bead located about half-way down the barrel. Handguns usually have two sights, one near the muzzle which may resemble the front sight of a rifle, & a rear sight that may be fully adjustable for elevation *(q.v.)* & windage *(q.v.)*, or a non-adjustable one which may be simply a small groove machined in the slide *(q.v.)*

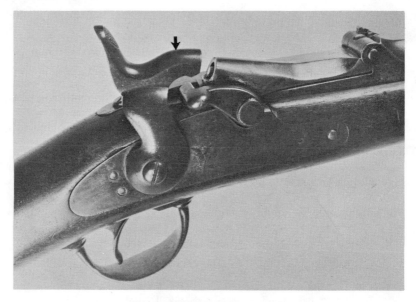

Sidehammer on the Springfield Trap Door 45-70.

of a semiautomatic pistol or in the top strap *(q.v.)* of a revolver. By aligning the rear sight, the front sight & the target, the projectile will hit the target, providing the gun is properly sighted-in *(see* Sighting-in).

SIGHT, ADJUSTABLE many rifles & handguns are equipped with rear sights that allow elevation & windage adjustments. By moving the rear sight up or down, left or right, often by means of a click *(q.v.),* the

At left is double action revolver with non-adjustable sights. At right, the fully adjustable rear sight of a 45 ACP match gun.

sight can be adjusted so that the projectile strikes at any desired point on the target *(see* Rule of Three; Sighting-in). Some firearms have a rear sight that is NON-ADJUSTABLE, thus making the gun unsuitable for precise long range shooting *(see* Kentucky Windage).

SIGHT, APERTURE a sight with a hole, often of variable diameter, that permits more accurate aiming.

Aperture rear sights are suitable for hunting & target shooting, but aperture front sights, in conjunction with a similar rear sight, are used only for match or target shooting. Aperture sights with iris discs, ground lenses, & variable inserts have been used on many target rifles, notably Schuetzen rifles *(q.v.). Also see:* Sight Disc; Sight Inserts; Sight, Peep; Sight, Rear; Sight, Tang; Sight, Vernier; Sights, Target.

SIGHT, BARLEYCORN a type of front sight that resembles an upside-down V.

SIGHT, BLADE *see* Sight, Front.

SIGHT, BUCKHORN a now nearly obsolete design for the rear sight of a rifle. The Buckhorn & the Semi-Buckhorn rear sights were developmental attempts to create a sight that could be readily picked up by the shooter's eye & that allowed fast alignment of front sight & target.

SIGHT DISC a special insert that can be used with peep sights *(see* Sight, Peep). The sight discs come with internally adjustable iris diaphragm, thus allowing the shooter to vary size of the aperture. One sight disc even has a provision for a prescription ground corrective lens.

SIGHT, EXPRESS a type of folding leaf sight, with several leaves, found almost exclusively on British double rifles chambered for Express cartridges *(see* Cartridge, Express). The leaves have varying V cuts, are fitted with springs for easy manipu-

225

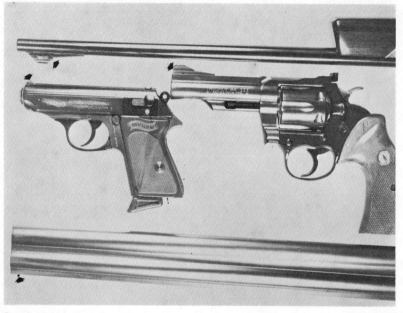

Top to bottom: Rifle front sight with hood removed, small front sight on Walther PPK semiautomatic pistol, large sight on Colt MKIII Trooper, and front bead sight on O/U shotgun.

lation. Several British gunmakers also offered night or moon sights for such guns. *Also see:* Sight, Leaf.

SIGHT EXTENSION　a device often added to semiautomatic target pistols to increase the sight radius *(q.v.).* The front sight is mounted on the sight extension which projects beyond the muzzle of the gun.

SIGHT, FOLDING　multiple leaf sights (*see* Sight, Express; Sight, Leaf) have spring-activated leaves which can be folded down to make any leaf of the sight available. Folding sights are arranged so that the leaf that is set for the closest range is nearest the eye, & this leaf is usually non-folding.

SIGHT, FRONT　formerly called

FORESIGHT, design depends on the gun, that is rifle, shotgun, handgun. The front BEAD of the shotgun is usually brass, a light colored metal or plastic bead. Ivory beads are becoming scarce. A number of special sights that replace the original factory bead are offered. Many of them are a bright red plastic that is readily picked up by the eye & in some of these sights, an optical plane has been added to catch the light in the sight for greater visibility. Handgun sights, especially on target guns, vary somewhat in thickness of the BLADE, are usually non-adjustable. Many different blade forms are seen. Front sights for rifles are usually mounted on a ramp *(q.v.).* The part of the front sight used to align eye, rear sight, & target is often a brass or gold bead that may contain a red or white plastic insert to help the eye pick up the sight. On target rifles, special front sights are used (*see* Sight, Globe Front).

SIGHT, GLOBE FRONT   a special front sight hooded to prevent the entry of light that disturbs accurate sighting. The globe front sight has easily interchanged inserts of various configurations. *Also see:* Sight Inserts.

SIGHT, HOODED   a fixed sight with a metal cover or hood often found on the front sight ramp of sporting rifles. Here, the hood serves to protect the sight from accidental knocks, as well as to give the sight greater optical definition by excluding light. Front sights on match rifles almost invariably are hooded (*see* Sight, Globe Front).

SIGHT INSERTS   thin metal inserts that fit into spring-activated slots in the globe front sight. Inserts are painted black for maximum visibility, come in many different designs, such as post, aperture, etc.

SIGHT, IRON   *see* Iron Sights.

SIGHT, LEAF   thin, rather small metal rear sight that carries in the top edge a cut that, in sighting, is aligned with the front sight & the target. This cut or SIGHT NOTCH varies a great deal in size & shape. Some leaf sights have a number of leaves, each leaf being calibrated for a given distance. *Also see:* Sight, Express; Sight, Folding; Iron Sights.

SIGHT, MIDDLE   on skeet & trap guns, the conventional front bead sight is often supplemented by a second, somewhat smaller bead located about mid-point on the barrel.

SIGHT, NYDAR   a sight, now almost obsolete, that employs a small mirror in conjunction with a reflecting surface on which a target image, such as a dot in a circle, is projected from the mirror. This sight does not offer any degree of magnification as does a scope. In use, the target image reflected from the mirror is super-imposed on the target the shooter is aiming at. The Nydar sight was popular with shotgunners for some time, later attained a degree of popularity with hunters who use a handgun, providing shooting was not over extended ranges.

SIGHT, OPEN   *see* Iron Sights; Sight, Leaf; Sight, Express.

SIGHT, OPTICAL   *see* Scope.

SIGHT, PAINE   a round or U notch rear sight with a bead front sight. Originated by Ira Paine, famed U.S. pistol shooter, the sight was long favored by competitive shooters, but has been replaced by the rectangular rear notch & the Patridge square blade front sight (*see* Sight, Patridge).

SIGHT, PATRIDGE   a front sight that has parallel sides, thus appears to be rectangular or square when fitted into the sight picture of the rectangular notch of the rear sight.

227

SIGHT, PEEP   a rear sight, often with an interchangeable aperture or peep insert, through which the front sight & the target are aligned. Peep sights are adjustable for windage

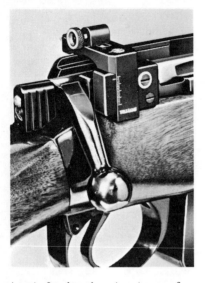

(q.v.) & elevation *(q.v.)*, are frequently used on target rifles & sometimes equipped with rubber eye pieces to exclude light rays which hamper the shooter in getting a good sight picture.

SIGHT PICTURE   optical picture obtained by a shooter after he has aligned the rear sight, the front sight & the target. When using an open sight, if a shooter places the front sight in the notch of the rear sight so that the entire front sight is visible, he draws a coarse bead. If only the top of the front sight or only a part of that sight is visible in the notch, he draws a fine bead.

SIGHT RADIUS   is the distance

between the front sight & the rear sight. The longer the sight radius, the easier & more accurate the sighting. Sight radius is especially important on competition handguns, & semi-automatic pistols are frequently equipped with a sight extension *(q.v.)* to obtain a greater sight raduis.

SIGHT RAMP   *see* Ramp.

SIGHT, REAR   is the sight nearest to the shooter's eye. A rear sight can be a simple open or iron sight *(q.v.)*, a leaf or express sight, a peep or aperture sight mounted on the receiver, a vernier aperture sight mounted on the tang *(q.v.)*. British long range target rifles have the rear sight mounted on the buttstock. Sights fastened on the cocking piece, bolt sleeve & other parts of the gun were popular, but only a few of the old target rifles are found with those easily damaged sights.

SIGHT, RECEIVER   any sight mounted on the receiver of a rifle or shotgun, usually a peep sight *(see* Sight, Peep).

SIGHT, SCOPE   *see* Scope.

SIGHT, TANG   an aperture sight *(see* Sight, Aperture) at the end of a short tang or sometimes a rod, & hinged so that it can be folded down to prevent possible damage to the sight. The tang sight is mounted to the rear of the receiver to bring it closer to the eye. Tang sights saw extensive use on long range target rifles & many of these were equipped with very accurate verniers for elevation & windage adjustments (*see* Sight, Vernier).

SIGHT, TANGENT   a rear sight, usually an open one, that is adjustable for elevation only. Found on some pistols, the tangent sight is also widely used on military rifles. The sight leaf is spring-activated, rides on two inclined bars & the sight rails are notched so that the leaf can be set for the desired elevation.

SIGHT, TUBE   a metal tube used, at one time, to house the front & rear sight on some target rifles. A tube sight, adjustable for elevation & windage, is now used by top-ranking target shooters in conjunction with I.S.U. *(q.v.)* sights.

SIGHT, VERNIER   a rear peep sight, often tang-mounted, that is adjustable for elevation by means of a highly accurate vernier. Windage adjustments are made in vernier-equipped front sights which often carry a spirit level to indicate possible cant *(q.v.)*.

SIGHTS, TARGET   a combination of globe front sight & peep rear sight on match rifles. Many of the I.S.U. *(q.v.)* matches are fired with such sights, often also called International sights.

SIGHTER   *see* Sighting Shot.

SIGHTING-IN   process of adjusting the sights, usually the rear one, or the elevation *(q.v.)* & windage *(q.v.)* adjustments of a scope, so that the bullet will hit a pre-determined point of aim on the target at a specific distance. Much of the trial & error method of sighting-in a rifle can be eliminated by the use of a collimator *(q.v.)*. Although this device is of some help in sighting-in a handgun, especially if the gun is equipped with a scope *(q.v.)*, the sighting-in of a handgun from an improvised rest *(q.v.)* is still the only way of setting the sight so that the gun shoots to the point of aim *(q.v.)*.

The rifle-style sights on shotguns designed for slug shooting must be adjusted by the trial & error method. Such guns are sometimes equipped with a scope, iron sight *(q.v.)* or peep sight (*see* Sight, Peep). Although the shotgun may have no adjustable sights, the gun should still be sighted-in. This should consist not only of patterning the gun with various shot sizes, but also of shooting tests that

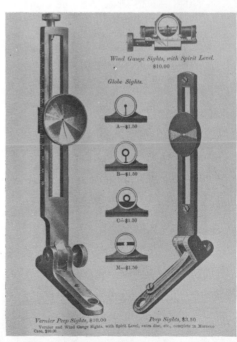

Vernier rear sights and front sights reproduced from a scarce catalog of the period. None of these sights are now commercially offered.

will indicate if the gun actually shoots to point of aim. In side-by-side & O/U guns, it is important to determine if both barrels place the shot pellets into the same area, or if one of the barrels places the shot high, low, left or right of the point of aim.

SIGHTING SHOT   or SIGHTER, one or more shots fired before firing for score in a competitive match. A sighting shot is also advisable for hunters if the rifle has been exposed to bad weather & possible warpage of the stock, or to extensive travel where the sights might have been knocked out of alignment or the scope jarred loose.

SIGNAL PIN   *see* Cartridge Indicator.

SILENCER   mechanical device that reduces or deadens the sound of a gun being discharged. Ownership or use of a silencer is illegal in the U.S. Despite popular belief, a semiautomatic pistol of a certain design will function with a silencer, but the usefulness of the device has been overrated in popular literature. The baffles in the silencer reduce gun noise, but a bullet travelling at supersonic speed will, by breaking the sound barrier after it leaves the muzzle, make a silencer less effective.

SINGLE ACTION   *see* Pistol, Single Action; Revolver, Single Action.

SINGLE SHOT   abbr. SS, is a firearm, either rifle, shotgun, or pistol, that does not have a magazine

(q.v.) or similar device & that is loaded with only one cartridge or shell. When the gun is discharged, the fired case is removed either by ejection *(q.v.)* or extraction *(q.v.)* & a new cartridge or shell is manually placed into the chamber of the

Left to right: BSA Martini Cadet now chambered for 357 Magnum, a Winchester High-Wall chambered for 6 mm/303 wildcat, and another High-Wall in now obsolete 219 Zipper.

gun. Historically, the single shot is the forerunner of the modern action designs. In recent years, interest in single shot rifles & handguns has increased & newly designed single shot rifles & handguns have become available. Among the better-known single shot actions *see:* Action, Aydt; Action, Ballard; Action, Dropping

Block; Action, Falling Block; Action, Farquharson; Action, Flobert Rolling Block; Action, Guedes-Castro; Action, Haenel-Aydt; Action, Martini; Action, Rising Block; Action, Rolling Block; Action, Sharps; Action, Trap Door.

SINGLE TRIGGER   *see* Trigger, Single.

SIXGUN, SIX SHOOTER   popular terms for any revolver *(q.v.).*

SIX O'CLOCK HOLD   the most commonly used sighting picture in target shooting. In handgun shooting, the top of the front sight is aligned with the six o'clock *(see* Clock System) position on the bullseye, the gun being sighted so that the point of bullet impact is in the bullseye. Most shooters only see the rear sight sharply defined, while front sight & target appear fuzzy to the majority of handgunners.

SIZING   the mechanical restoration of a cartridge case or shotshell hull to its previous size & approximate dimensions, or in the case of bullets, the swaging *(see* Swage) to the desired diameter. In handloading, brass cartridge cases are resized to restore them to their original dimensions. This process is known as full length sizing, is accomplished with a full length sizing die for the specific caliber. If the case will be fired over & over again in the same rifle, then excessive cold working *(q.v.)* of the brass can be prevented by neck-sizing only, thus extending case life *(q.v.). Also see:* Anneal; Neck-sizing.

Lubricator – Sizer by Lyman.

Shotshell hulls are resized full length at all times, the resizing including the brass head of the hull. Cast bullets, after cooling & inspection, are forced through a special tool that sizes the bullet to the exact diameter desired, forcing at the same time the lubricant into each grease groove *(q.v.)* of the bullet. This tool, the lubricator-sizer, is filled with a semi-solid lubricant, can be used for cast bullets of all sizes when the suitable die is installed in the tool.

SKEET   a shooting game that simulates bird shooting afield. Skeet had its origin in the U.S., is now a formal-

231

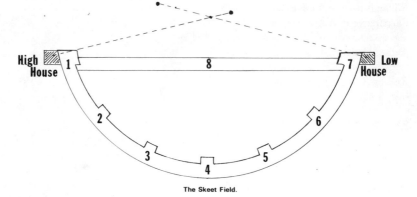

The Skeet Field.

ized claybird *(q.v.)* sport, under the auspices of the National Skeet Shooting Association. The skeet field has a HIGH HOUSE at the left side of the field, a LOW HOUSE at the right. Eight shooting stations are used & shooters call for the bird from the high house by shouting "Pull," for the low house birds the call is "Mark." A shooter starts at station #1 at the high house, taking the bird from the high house, then the bird from the low house. These two shots from each station, one from each house, continue until station #8 is reached. There, in the center position of the semi-circle of the skeet field, the shooter must break the high & low house birds, both incoming clays, before they cross overhead. In a regular round of skeet, that is 25 targets, the process is repeated with doubles *(q.v.)* from stations #1, 2, 6 & 7, with the birds being thrown from high & low house, making a total of 24 shots in all. The first "lost" bird in a round is repeated at once & is counted as the 25th shot. *Also see:* Lost.

SKEET CHOKE   *see* Choke, Skeet.

SKEET GUN   a shotgun, either autoloading, side-by-side, O/U, or pump action with the barrel or barrels equipped with a skeet choke *(see* Choke, Skeet). Skeet guns are usually equipped with a ventilated rib *(see* Rib, Ventilated), & skeet guns are offered in 12, 20, 28, & 410 ga.

SKELETON BUTTPLATE   *see* Buttplate, Skeleton.

SKELETON STOCK   a stock, often made from heavy or stiff wire or cast metal alloys, with the center of the stock removed so that weight is reduced, yet the advantage of a stock is retained. Now most frequently seen on military small arms & survival guns, the skeleton stock was at one time quite popular, even on long barreled handguns. *Also see:* Bicycle Rifle.

SKID MARKS   marks left on a bullet that did not accept the rifling of the barrel immediately after making contact with the rifling. Especially in revolvers, the bullet skids forward for a short distance before bullet rotation begins. Skid marks are

232

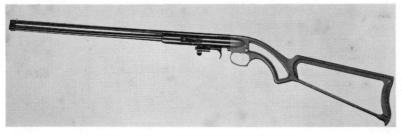

Skeleton stocks are most frequently seen on military arms.

shown by the marks of the lands *(q.v.)* running parallel until the regular, somewhat angling engraving marks (*see* Bullet Engraving) appear. Skid marks usually don't appear on pistol bullets since the bullet does not travel as long a distance before making contact with the rifling as does the revolver bullet.

SLACK   *see* Trigger, Double Pull.

SLAVE PIN   a small pin that aids in holding gun parts together during assembly. Slave pins, however, only help to align parts & do not remain in the gun once the assembly is completed & the regular pins have been seated.

SLEEVING   *see* Barrel Relining.

SLIDE   term with two meanings: (1) in semiautomatic pistols, the slide is the movable metal housing or sleeve that covers a part or the entire barrel as well as the uppermost cartridge in the magazine or the magazine follower if the magazine is empty, & the firing mechanism of the gun. The slide may contain the breechblock. Recoil moves the slide to the rear, spring action returns the slide to the forward or the "in bat-

tery" position. (2) in pump action guns (*see* Action, Pump) the action bars *(q.v.)* are sometimes referred to as slide.

SLIDE ACTION   *see* Action, Pump.

SLIDE STOP   a small lever at the side of the slide in some semiautomatic pistols that engages a notch in

Upper arrow indicates slide, lower arrow near trigger indicates slide stop.

the slide to hold the slide in a rearward position. In some pistols, the slide stop, when removed from the frame of the gun, also allows withdrawal of the slide, barrel, or both.

SLING   a leather or web strap fas-

233

tened most frequently on rifles, sometimes on European shotguns, to facilitate the carrying of the gun & also to aid in shooting.

SLING, CARRYING   a sling designed primarily for carrying a rifle or shotgun. This type of sling is usually not readily adjusted for length, is not very suitable for shooting except as a hasty sling (*see* Sling, Hasty).

SLING FROG   *see* Sling Hook.

SLING, HANDGUN   a new type of sling introduced with the increased interest in hunting with a handgun. Essentially a leather strap, sometimes padded where it goes around the shooter's neck, the sling ends in two loops. Depending on the design of the sling, the loops are placed either around the butt of the gun, or around the butt & one thumb. With both hands firmly grasping the gun, the arms are then raised to eye level, thus tightening the sling around

the neck. This gives the handgun a fair degree of support, allows better shot placement.

SLING, HASTY   any sling that can be used by the rifle shooter to obtain greater support for the gun. The sling is wound around the left arm of the right-handed shooter & sling tension aids in steadying the rifle.

SLING HOOK   also called FROG. Usually two such hooks are used to connect the loose ends of the sling. Hooks are readily moved to different positions along the length of the sling, thus allowing adjustment of the sling for carrying, shooting, & storing of gun with a tightened sling.

SLING KEEPER   the small movable leather loop that helps to hold two parts of the sling together.

SLING, LATIGO   patented sling that allows rapid adjustment for

Padded sling around shooter's neck, when pulled taut, gives handgun great steadiness, allows careful aiming, almost like a rifle.

234

The target sling.

carrying, shooting, & storing of gun with tight sling without the use of sling hooks.

SLING, MILITARY simple leather strap with hooks that can be adjusted for length. Once popular on hunting rifles, the military sling has been almost completely replaced by various easy-to-handle hunting slings such as the Latigo sling (*see* Sling, Latigo).

SLING RING *see* Saddle Ring.

SLING, SHOOTING leather or web strap that can be tightened readily for shooting so that it gives the rifle or shotgun a firmer support than could be attained without the use of the sling.

SLING SWIVELS *see* Swivels.

SLING, TARGET a special type of sling that is shorter than the usual carrying or shooting sling. In small-bore shooting, one end of the target sling is hooked into the hand stop *(q.v.)* swivel on the gun, the other end is hooked into the sling cuff that goes around the left upper arm of a right-handed shooter. With the left hand pressed against the hand stop—a target shooter's mitten *(q.v.)* is used —& pulling on the short sling against the tight cuff, excellent support is gained for the rifle in the prone, sitting & kneeling position. In the off-hand position, the hip rest *(q.v.)* is used.

SLING, WHELEN an adaptation of the U.S. military sling designed by Col. Townsend Whelen for carrying & shooting.

SLIP GUN single action revolver (*see* Revolver, Single Action) on

235

which the trigger has either been removed entirely or tied back against the rear of the trigger guard. This allegedly was a trick used by Western gunmen who either fanned the gun (*see* Fanning) or fired the gun by slip shooting, that is, pulling back the hammer & letting it fall, repeating the process as rapidly as possible until all cartridges in the cylinder had been fired.

SLIP SHOOTING   *see* Slip Gun.

SLOW FIRE MATCH   *see* Match.

SLOTTED JAG   *see* Jag; Cleaning.

SLUG   often loosely used to describe a heavy bullet, but more appropriately used in referring to a rifled slug *(q.v.)*.

SMALL ARMS   a term primarily used by the military, small arms include all weapons which can be carried on or by one man, fired with one or both hands. By military definition, this also includes machine guns.

SMALL ARMS AMMUNITION any small arms *(q.v.)* cartridge with a bullet that has a diameter up to & including 1″.

SMALLBORE   usually used in conjunction with 22 rimfire cartridges or guns, although smallbore also is used to describe any rifle caliber with a bore diameter of less than 0.25″. In addition, smallbore de-

scribes a shotgun gauge smaller than 16 ga. In England, any rifle bore smaller than 7 mm or .284″ is termed a smallbore, yet in Africa, big game hunters frequently consider any rifle with a bore diameter less than .375″ as small bore.

SMALL OF THE STOCK   *see* Stock, Small of the.

SMOKELESS POWDER   *see* Powder, Smokeless.

SMOOTHBORE   a firearm with a barrel that is smoothbored, that is has no rifling whatsoever. Smoothbore is often used to describe a shotgun.

SNAP CAPS   protective devices the size & shape of a shotshell or car-

tridge, often inserted into the chambers of double shotguns or rifles to prevent firing pin damage when snapping the triggers or dry firing. Snap caps are usually chrome or nickel plated, contain in the primer cup a spring-activated nylon plug that absorbs the shock of the falling firing pin.

SNAPHANCE also spelled SNAPHAUNCE, the type of firing mechanism found in the earliest forms of flintlock guns.

SNAP SHOT a shot fired without careful aiming or sighting, usually at a moving target.

SNUB-NOSED REVOLVER *see* Belly Gun.

SOFT POINT *see* Bullet, Soft Point.

SOLID *see* Bullet, Solid.

SOLID FRAME, any gun that cannot be taken apart readily, without complete mechanical disassembly, is considered to have a solid frame. Many shotguns are of the solid frame type, as are all currently produced U.S. rifles & many single shot rifles. *Also see:* Frame.

SOLID HEAD *see* Case Head Forms.

SOLID RIB *see* Rib, Solid.

S.O.R. *see* Speed of Rotation.

SOUTHGATE EJECTOR *see* Ejector, Southgate.

SP abbr. for soft point, *see* Bullet, Soft Point.

SPACER a shaped piece of plastic, wood, or rubber that is used under a forend tip, pistol grip cap, or a recoil pad. Spacers are primarily decorative, but under recoil pads one or more spacers can increase length of pull (*see* Stock Dimensions) if desired.

SPANNER the small crank that is used to put under tension the spring in wheel-lock guns.

SPEED ACTION *see* Lock Time.

SPEED LOCK, *see* Lock Time.

SPEED OF ROTATION abbr. S.O.R. Accuracy of a bullet during flight depends, to some degree, on its speed of rotation, expressed as rps (revolutions per second).

$$\text{SOR} = \frac{12}{\text{rate of twist}} \times \text{fps MV}$$

or divide rate of twist into 12, then multiply by muzzle velocity of bullet expressed in fps. Thin jacketed bullets driven at high velocities & therefore high S.O.R. often tend to disintegrate in flight. As velocity decreases along the bullet's trajectory, the speed of rotation also decreases. The forward movement of a bullet is slowed down faster by air resistance than is the bullet's speed of rotation.

SPENT BULLET *see* Bullet, Spent.

SPIN *see* Bullet Spin.

SPIN ENERGY is the kinetic energy of a spinning bullet in flight. The spin adds but little to the velocity of the bullet itself, about 12-14 fps for a 150 gr. .308" bullet.

SPITZER *see* Bullet, Spitzer.

237

SPLINTER FOREND *see* Beavertail Forend.

SPLIT RECEIVER BRIDGE *see* Receiver Bridge.

SPLIT CASE a fissure or crack in a cartridge case. Case splitting can be caused by excessive pressure, too much cold working of the brass, or the age of the brass. *Also see:* Case Head Separation; Case Rupture; Brass, Season Cracking of.

SPLIT NECK *see* Split Case.

SPOOL MAGAZINE *see* Magazine, Mannlicher.

SPORTERIZING the process of making certain changes on the exterior of a military rifle so that the gun becomes more suitable for sporting use. Sporterizing includes: discarding military trigger & installing an adjustable trigger; removing military sights, replacing them with a ramp front sight & sporting rear sight; or, if a scope is to be installed, altering the safety when the action is drilled & tapped for scope blocks;

altering the angle of the bolt handle so that it will clear the scope. In sporterizing a military rifle, the wooden hand guard is usually discarded, the military sling swivels are removed, the stock is reshaped & refinished, a recoil pad replaces the iron buttplate of the military stock. The military stock is often replaced completely by a custom stock. *Also see:* Conversion.

SPORTING GUNS a term often used to differentiate between military weapons, law enforcement weapons, & guns used for sporting purposes only.

SPOTTER term with two meanings: (1) in big bore & long range target shooting, the shooter in some matches has a spotter right behind the firing line. With the help of a spotting scope (*see* Scope, Spotting), the spotter informs the shooter as to the exact point of bullet impact on the target. (2) in big bore target shooting, the pit crew uses a spotter or marker *(q.v.)* to indicate where the bullet strikes the target. *Also see:* Maggie's Drawers.

Above, a military rifle; below, the same gun after sporterizing.

SPREAD, MAXIMUM the maximum distance between bullet holes on a target. *Also see:* Dispersion, Horizontal; Dispersion, Vertical; Group Measurement; Scoring Plug.

SPREADER LOAD *see* Brush Load.

SPRING every gun contains one or more springs. These are of two basic types, the flat or V spring & the helical or coil spring. The FLAT SPRING is found in box lock & side lock actions, also in some revolvers. The HELICAL or COIL SPRING is used in many current production revolvers, in firing pin mechanisms, etc.

SPRUE the opening in a bullet casting mold that permits entry of the molten metal. In bullet casting *(q.v.)*, the hot lead or lead alloy is poured into the thoroughly heated mold until the bullet cavity is completely filled & the hot metal overflows the cavity as well as the sprue.

SPRUE CUTTER the small metal guard on a bullet mold that moves, by means of a pivot pin, on the mold, covering to some extent the sprue. When the cast metal has cooled & hardened, the sprue cutter is knocked aside with a wooden mallet, thus shearing off the excess lead from the mold. This excess metal, also called sprue, is re-melted for the next casting session since it is pure lead rather than dross *(q.v.)*. *Also see:* Sprue; Bullet Casting.

SPUR, HAMMER *see* Hammer Spur.

Mold at left shows sprue cutter moved up, mold at right shows cutter in place with sprue right after casting.

SPUR TRIGGER *see* Trigger, Spur.

SQUIB LOAD a load, usually with a cast lead bullet, that contains a reduced powder charge. The bullet, if cast, may or may not carry a gas-check. Sometimes half-jacketed pistol bullets are used in squib loads. While some handloaders use rifle powders for squib loads, others have successfully used some of the pistol powders in these loads. The advantage in squib loads lies in the fact that the shooter can use his big bore hunting rifle for practice without danger of excessive barrel wear & throat erosion. *Also see:* Chamber Throat; Barrel Erosion.

SS abbr. for single shot *(q.v.)*.

S/S abbr. for side-by-side, *see* Shotgun, Double.

STABILIZER more commonly known as barrel weight or weights.

239

Many target grade handguns designed for competitive shooting come with detachable barrel weights to minimize muzzle jump *(q.v.),* thus reducing recovery time, that is the time it takes for the shooter to regain the desired sight picture.

STACK BARREL another term used to describe the over and under *(q.v.)* barrel arrangement.

STACKING ROD a short rod with a rounded end extending forward from the front barrel band on some military rifles. Used to stack military rifles by interlocking the stacking rods of several such arms.

STACKING SWIVEL a swivel that somewhat resembles a sling

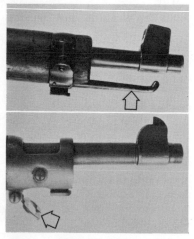

Stacking rod and swivel.

swivel, fastened onto the forward barrel band. Found on military rifles, the stacking swivel serves the same purpose as the stacking rod *(q.v.).*

STANDING BREECH *see* Breech, Standing.

STAR (*) a British military designation of model variations, such as MARK II*.

STAR CRIMP *see* Crimp.

STAR GAUGE type of gauge used to determine how accurately the rifling had been cut into a barrel. Star-gauged barrels were, at one time, highly desirable in the 03 Springfield. The star gauge has now been replaced by air gages.

STATION *see* Skeet; Trap.

STEADY PIN small projection at the end of the mainspring that fits into a corresponding hole or depression in the lock plate of a side lock action gun (*see* Action, Side Lock).

STENDEBACH IDEAL SLUG a shotgun slug made in Germany prior to WWII. The spin of the slug was considerable & the internal helical vanes gave the slug outstanding accuracy.

STIPPLING the roughening of a surface by making points or dots thereon. In firearms, stippling may be done on wood or metal to give the shooter a better grip on the gun & is often applied to the front & back strap of match handguns, especially the 45 ACP. Stippling is done by hand with a special punch, & because it is not in wide demand, it must be done by a custom pistolsmith who specializes in accuracy work.

Stipling.

STIRRUP (1) rod-like pin in some semiautomatic pistols such as the S&W Model 39 that is fastened at its upper end to the hammer, at the lower end serves to compress the mainspring. (2) in some tip-up revolvers (*see* Action, Top-break), closure & locking of the hinged frame is accomplished by means of a stirrup, such as seen on the Webley 455 Revolver.

STOCK the wooden, plastic or metal part of a long gun *(q.v.)* that contains or holds the barreled action & which enables the shooter to hold & aim the firearm. On handguns, the wooden or plastic grips are also called stocks (*see* Stock, Pistol). *Also see:* Buttstock; Cheekpiece; Comb; Forend; Forend Tip; Grip; Grip, Pistol; Grip, Straight; Heel; Monte Carlo; Toe of Butt.

STOCK, AFGHAN distinguished by the exaggerated curve of the buttstock & extremely narrow butt. Found on various muzzle-loading guns produced in Afghanistan, the stock designs vary a great deal in length, amount of curvature, etc. Similar stock shapes are encountered on early Arab guns, many of the stocks being decorated with brass studs & semi-precious stones.

STOCK BEDDING *see* Bedding; Inletting.

STOCK, BENCHREST a rifle stock designed for competitive benchrest shooting. The benchrest stock has a bore height comb, a wide forend with a flat bottom, a very straight stock, a large pistol grip, sometimes is equipped with a flat-bottom butt so that the rifle can recoil in a straight line on the rest *(q.v.)*. Benchrest *(q.v.)* stock must conform to NBRSA rules, & stock may have a thumbhole (*see* Stock, Thumbhole). Benchrest stocks

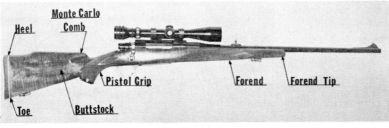

Stock nomenclature

have no swivels *(q.v.)*, seldom have checkering *(q.v.)*, often are made from laminated woods to prevent warpage (*see* Stock Warpage).

STOCK BLANK the rough-sawed piece of wood from which a stock for a rifle or shotgun is fashioned & shaped. Stock blanks are offered in many grades, from very fancy to plain, this indicating the direction of the wood grain, the degree of figure in the grain, etc. Stock blanks are available in a wide choice of woods, with American walnut & Claro walnut being the most popular, but any wood that is hard & tough enough can be used for a stock, including tropical woods, cherry, sycamore, etc.

STOCK BLANK, SEMI-INLETTED a stock that has been machine-shaped so that the forend *(q.v.)*, the pistol grip (*see* Grip, Pistol), & buttstock *(q.v.)* have already been formed, with only finishing or slight minor alterations being needed to complete the exterior work on the stock. The forend on the semi-inletted blank contains the barrel channel *(q.v.)*, & the stock has been inletted for the action. On the semi-inletted blank, the stockmaker or hobby stocker has only to complete the final inletting of action & barrel in addition to any external shaping of the stock to suit personal taste & requirements.

STOCK, CALIFORNIA a type of rifle stock design that originated with several California stockers. Excessive roll-over cheekpieces that

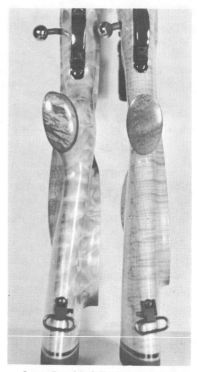

Extreme lines of the California stock are especially apparent on the stock at left, although roll-over cheekpiece at right is considerably over-sized.

actually extend over the edge of the comb, the extremely forward-swept pistol grip, the extra high comb that requires the cutting of a deep groove into the wood so that the bolt can be pulled back, the reducing of forend thickness & stock wrist (*see* Stock, Small of the), plus the use of very light colored woods & very thin tapered barrels, are typical. The utilitarian thumbhole (*see* Stock, Thumbhole) of the competition rifles also has been enlarged & streamlined on many of the California stocks.

STOCK CHECKERING *see* Checkering.

242

STOCK CRAWLER a rifle shooter who, while sighting-in *(q.v.)* or aiming, keeps moving his head forward on the stock. Stock crawling can be due to an improperly focused scope or too great a length of pull *(see* Stock Dimensions). Such a shooter can, by reducing the eye relief *(q.v.)* of a scope on a rifle with hefty recoil, be cut by the rim of the ocular lens housing.

STOCK DIMENSIONS a number of actual stock measurements are basic to any gun stock. Factory stocks on rifles & shotguns are designed for the "average" shooter & for the ultimate use of the gun (target shooting, hunting, skeet or trap, varmint shooting). Stock dimensions also depend, to some extent, on the caliber involved in the case of centerfire rifles. Stocks for trap guns are straighter than those for field & skeet guns to help absorb recoil & give the shooter a better sight picture. In general, fewer shotguns are custom stocked than are rifles since most shotgunners simply accommodate themselves to the shotgun stock, the claybird shooter being the exception.

More rifles are custom stocked since riflemen usually have their own ideas about stocks. Factory guns of the target variety have special stocks, that is, guns used only for prone shooting have stocks designed for that position, while guns for bench-rest shooting & off-hand matches have stocks suitable for these competitive shooting sports. Varmint rifles usually have high combs (*see* Comb) to accommodate the shooter's eye more readily to the higher mounted scope.

However, too little differentiation is made in factory stocks as far as recoil is concerned, the stock for a light caliber rifle such as the 270 Winchester usually having the same dimensions as the stock for a .30 caliber or bigger magnum rifle. In distributing recoil over the shooter's shoulder, the general rule is that the bigger the buttplate area, the more easily the recoil is absorbed. Similarly, the heavier the rifle, the less the recoil effect, but hunting rifles must be kept on the light side, in contrast to some target rifles, to make it possible for the hunter to carry his rifle all day. Thus, a scoped 270 can weigh as little as 7 lb., but a big bore British double rifle can weigh 10 or 11 lb., partly because the gun is seldom carried all day & too light a gun would make shooting a big bore rifle a highly unpleasant experience.

The height of the comb depends not only on the sight height, but also to some extent on the facial structure of the shooter as well as on the caliber

of the rifle. Straight stocks, or a comb that slopes forward slightly will help to reduce recoil effect on the shooter. Some stockmakers feel that LENGTH OF PULL, the distance from the center of the trigger to the center of the buttplate, is not nearly as important as comb thickness & cheekpiece shape. While length of pull is perhaps more important in shotgun stocks, it should certainly be considered more in making rifle stocks, especially if the gun to be stocked is in the magnum class. Too long a stock, even with enough comb & cheekpiece, will make the average shooter a stock crawler *(q.v.)*. *Also see:* Cast-off; Cast-on; Drop; Drop at Comb; Drop at Heel; Pitch.

STOCK DROP   *see* Drop.

STOCK, ENGLISH or STRAIGHT *see* Grip.

STOCK, EXTENSION   a wire or light metal frame, usually folding or collapsible, used extensively on military arms such as submachine guns & on some survival guns. The term is also used in error to indicate a holster stock *(q.v.)*.

STOCK FINISHING   *see* Finish.

STOCK, FULL LENGTH   a method of stocking where the gun stock extends from the buttplate to the muzzle. The full stocked Kentucky rifle *(q.v.)*, either flintlock or percussion, is now widely available in reproduction guns for hunting as well as target shooting. A full length stock was popular on European

military carbines, & the Mannlicher stock is now widely used in Europe as well as in the U.S. on sporting carbines, especially for mountain hunting & scabbard *(q.v.)* use.

STOCK, GLASSBEDDING OF *see* Glassbedding.

STOCK, HOLSTER   *see* Holster Stock.

STOCK, LAMINATED   the idea of using laminated wood, layers of two or more kinds of wood glued into a piece large enough to make a gunstock, originated during WWII in Germany when wood supplies dwindled to dangerously low levels. The

laminated stock has become popular in the U.S. for competition rifles & is offered on some factory stocks for hunting rifles, has the advantage that laminated wood seldom, if ever, is affected by warpage or shrinkage.

STOCK, MANNLICHER a type of full-length stock (*see* Stock, Full Length). Several bolt action sporting rifles are now offered with this type of stock.

STOCK, OFFSET a stock on which the entire buttstock is curved so that the shooter can fire the gun from the right shoulder while using his left eye, or vice versa, if the stock is shaped correctly. Not available on any factory guns, one stockmaker offers such a stock under the name "Cross-Over" stock.

STOCK PANEL slightly raised portion of the stock, usually found on German bolt action rifles as well as on some German bolt action shotguns. The panel extends usually the full length of the action, acts as decoration as well as a stock re-enforcement. Although the panel can be removed by sanding, it is not advisable since it does weaken the stock, especially on guns with heavy recoil & removal also lowers the value of the gun.

STOCK, PISTOL the wood, plastic or metal parts that make up that part of any handgun held in the shooter's hand while firing the gun. Semiautomatic pistol stocks are

sometimes referred to as panels, while those on revolvers are often called grips. Pistol stocks, like rifle stocks & shotgun stocks, are often designed for specific gun uses, such as target shooting, combat shooting, also for recoil reduction & concealment purposes.

STOCK, PISTOL GRIP *see* Grip; Grip, Pistol.

STOCK, RIFLE *see* Stock; Stock Dimensions; Stock, Full Length; Stock, Laminated; Stock, Mannlicher; Stock, Steel Bedding of; Stock, Target; Stock, Thumbhole; Stock, Two Piece; Stock Warpage. *Also see:* Bedding; Glassbedding; Skeleton Stock.

STOCK, SEMI-PISTOL GRIP *see* Grip, Semi-pistol.

STOCK, SHOTGUN factories offer only two basic shotgun stocks, the field or skeet stock & the trap stock. The latter usually has a straighter comb, that is less drop *(q.v.)*. Custom stocks are most frequently found on trap & skeet guns. The typical shotgun stock is a two piece stock (*see* Stock, Two Piece). *Also see*: Stock Dimensions.

Arrow points to stock panel. This is an almost exclusive feature of guns made in Germany.

STOCK, SKELETON   *see* Skeleton Stock.

STOCK, SMALL OF THE   also called WRIST. The part of the stock between the rearward end of the action & the comb, it is also the part of the stock that is grasped by the shooter's hand. The bottom part of the wrist may be straight (*see* Grip), or shaped to fit the hand (*see* Grip, Pistol; Grip, Semi-pistol).

STOCK, STEEL BEDDING OF a process similar to glassbedding (*q.v.*) in which steel is used. Some match rifles are steel bedded for extra accuracy, but the process has never found wide acceptance, either by shooters or custom stockers.

STOCK, STRAIGHT   stock without a pistol grip (*see* Grip, Straight).

STOCK, TARGET   a stock designed especially for some type of target shooting, either shotgun, handgun or rifle. In the latter class, a target stock can incorporate a hook plate (*q.v.*), a palm rest (*q.v.*), a hand stop (*q.v.*), & possibly a thumbhole (*see* Stock, Thumbhole). *Also see*: Stock; Stock Dimensions.

Shotgun stocks for trap & skeet guns, if custom made, are designed to fit the shooter's physical build & facial structure, such measurements sometimes being made with a try gun (*q.v.*). Such stocks may include a cheekpiece (*q.v.*), a Monte Carlo comb (*q.v.*), as well as thumbhole (*see* Stock, Thumbhole). *Also see*: Stock Dimensions; Stock, Shotgun.

Handgun target stocks are fashioned to the shooter's hand, are designed so that the gun recoils in a straight line & that the trigger finger makes the correct amount of contact with the trigger. The ball of the first digit of the trigger finger is considered the best means of exerting enough pressure on the trigger to fire the gun, without pulling the gun to one side or the other.

STOCK, THUMBHOLE   a stock with a contoured hole in the rear of the pistol grip that allows the shooter to insert his thumb through the stock. This allows better gun control, has been found of importance during competitive rifle matches. Thumbhole stocks are now also custom made for shotguns & sporting rifles, such as the bull pup rifle shown, in contrast to the free rifle with all of the desirable target shooting refinements.

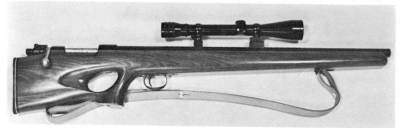

A 22-250 bullpup with over-sized thumbhole. Gun was made by L. H. Brown, Kalispell, Mont.

STOCK, TWO PIECE a stock consisting of the buttstock *(q.v.)*, & a separate forend *(q.v.)*, such as found on shotguns (double, O/U, pump & autoloader), on single shot & lever action rifles, pump & auto-loading rifles.

STOCK WARPAGE even sea-soned & kiln-dried wood will absorb moisture when exposed to rain or a high degree of humidity. Laminated stocks (*see* Stock, Laminated) are most resistant to warpage. Glass-bedding *(q.v.)* is another method of preventing warpage, as is sealing the barrel channel & all inletted areas against moisture with lacquer, var-nish, etc. A forend that has warped can actually force the barrel of a rifle out of the bedding to such an extent that it becomes impossible to hit a target at 100 yards. Free-floating *(q.v.)* or free-floating & then glass-bedding are the only sure ways to cure serious stock warpage.

STOCK WRIST *see* Stock, Small of the.

STOCKMAKER'S HAND SCREWS also called INLETTING SCREWS or headless guide screws. These extra-long screws are used by stockmakers during the inletting *(q.v.)* of an action, permit easier handling of trigger & magazine hous-ing by keeping these parts in align-ment with the receiver during fitting steps.

STOP any mechanical device that stops movement. *Also see:* Hand Stop; Bolt Stop; Slide Stop.

STOPPAGE in military usage, the failure of a gun, usually a machine gun, to function. Stoppage is usually due to faulty ammunition. *Also see:* Malfunction.

STOPPING POWER the ability of a given caliber with a specific bullet to stop a game animal in its tracks, especially a dangerous one that is charging. Stopping power depends on bullet diameter, energy of the bullet at the given range, & bullet weight.

STRAIGHT or straight run, a term indicating that a trap or skeet shooter broke all of the birds he fired at during a shoot.

STRAIGHT PULL *see* Action, Bolt.

STRAIN GAGE a relatively new system used for determining pressure levels in the chamber of a gun. Pres-sure exerted on the inside of the chamber walls momentarily affects the molecular structure of the steel. The strain gage, fastened to the out-side wall of the barrel or chamber,

Pressure barrel in special firing device shows how strain gage is attached to barrel.

picks up these variations which are amplified & then stored for interpolation in a cathode-ray oscilloscope. The strain gage system can be used on actual guns as well as on special pressure barrels, has the advantage that barrels need not be drilled as for the crusher gage *(q.v.)* system. *Also see:* Pressure Determination.

STRAIN SCREW   a small screw that bears against the bottom end of a leaf-type mainspring, holding that spring under tension & permitting adjustment of tension. Such a screw is encountered in some revolvers, a few rifles & shotguns. By backing the screw out a few turns, the tension is reduced, thus makes spring removal possible.

STRAP   another term for sling *(q.v.) Also see:* Backstrap; Front Strap.

STRIATION   *see* Bullet Engraving.

STRIKER   a short rod which is coil spring-activated & is housed either in a bolt *(q.v.)* or within the breechblock *(q.v.)*. It acts as a firing pin, but unlike a true firing pin *(q.v.)* which is activated by the hammer *(q.v.)* blow, the striker is released by the trigger. In some guns, the striker acts as a firing pin *(see* Firing Pin, Spring-activated), in others, the striker acts upon a separate firing pin, hence the term is often confused with a firing pin. To release the striker spring tension in some bolt action rifles, when dry firing *(q.v.)* is undesirable, close & lock the bolt

while maintaining pressure on the trigger. Some semiautomatic pistols, such as the British Webley & its U.S. copy, the Harrington & Richardson, also use the striker system.

STRIKING   *see* Barrel Striking.

STRING   a specific number of shots fired during one stage of a match. A string may consist of five or 10 shots, depending on the course being fired.

STRINGING   the horizontal or vertical dispersion *(q.v.)* of successive shots fired from a rifle at a target while using a rest. Such stringing is usually due to excessive forend tension *(q.v.)*.

STRINGING, SHOT   *see* Shot Stringing.

STRIPPING   a term with three meanings: (1) the taking-down of a firearm. Field stripping refers to the simple disassembly of a firearm for regular cleaning & maintenance. Usually accomplished without tools, some semiautomatic pistols are supplied with a universal tool. (2) the transfer of cartridges from the stripper clip *(see* Clip, Stripper) into a magazine of a firearm, or the removal of cartridges from a clip, such as the 45 ACP. (3) bullet stripping *(q.v.)*.

STRUT   *see* Hammer Strut.

STUB TWIST   another name for Damascus *(see* Barrel, Damascus).

STUD   a   projection,   usually

248

metal, that engages or holds another mating part, such as the studs engaging the QD swivels (*see* Swivel, QD).

SUBCALIBER   indefinite   term describing a small caliber (*see* Subcaliber Barrel.

SUBCALIBER BARREL   a small caliber barrel that is placed within the barrel of a gun, usually a rifle, to permit the firing of small caliber ammunition. These barrel adapters or auxiliary barrels have been used in training military recruits to give them practice with a regular size weapon. Barrel adapters are popular in Europe where they are often chambered for Schonzeitpatronen (*q.v.*). *Also see:* Barrel Insert.

SUBCALIBER GAUGE   in all-gauge claybird competitions, the 28 & 410 ga. are considered as sub gauges.

SUICIDE SPECIAL   mass-produced variety of inexpensive rimfire revolvers, usually equipped with a spur trigger (*see* Trigger, Spur). Guns carried many fancy names, are sometimes also called Saturday Night Specials. Many of these guns have attained collector status.

SUIGI FINISH   a method of darkening stock wood by scorching. This enhances the figure of the wood. *Also see*: Finish.

SULFUR CAST   *see* Chamber Cast.

SUPERPOSED   SHOTGUN   a

tradename for one make of over and under (*q.v.*) shotgun.

SUPPLEMENTAL   CHAMBER *see* Cartridge, Auxiliary.

SUSTAINED LEAD   *see* Lead.

SWAGE   a method of cold working (*q.v.*) & shaping metal, usually bullets, by means of a die or dies. All jacketed bullets are swaged, &

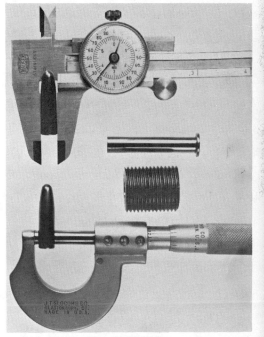

Vernier caliper (top shows original bullet diameter of .323". Ram of die is inserted in shellholder, die is threaded into top of press. After thoroughly lubricating bullet, it is swaged from .323 to .318 as indicated by micrometer below.

currently many of the factory wadcutter bullets (*see* Bullet, Wadcutter) are also swaged. Bullet swaging for the handloader is a relatively simple process, requiring a minimum of tools. Needed are: a heavy duty press, one set of swaging dies for each caliber & type of bullet, that is halfjacket pistol or full jacketed rifle bullet, suitable lead core wire (*see* Bullet Core), jackets & cups, plus a core cutter. Before buying swaging dies, the handloader should ascertain if the contemplated dies will fit his press. Although some dies will fit, they will not produce a satisfactory bullet.

Another form of swaging is the reduction of case head diameter by forcing the cartridge case through a suitable swaging die. Special swaging dies are also used to reduce bullet diameter. For instance, there are a good many of the German 8 mm rifles around which require a .318" bullet. Bullets of that size are hard to find, & firing .323" bullets in those barrels can be dangerous. However, a special swaging die effectively reduces bullet diameter from .323 to .318 without altering the ballistics properties of the bullet.

In commercial bullet making, lead wire for bullet cores is often swaged by pulling the wire through carefully calibrated holes in one or more steel plates.

SWAN DROPS   round lead pellets made in England during the 18th century & earlier. The swan drops, there were 15 to 1 oz. of lead, weighed 29 gr., measured .268" in diameter. As the name implies, the pellets were designed for hunting swans. Also made were goose drops & duck shot, both smaller than swan drops. On the ascending side were musket grape shot, small & large buck shot.

SWEDGING   erroneous for swage (*q.v.*) or swaging.

SWING   *see* Lead.

SWING THROUGH   *see* Lead.

SWING-OUT CYLINDER   *see* Cylinder, Swing-out.

SWIVEL BAND   metal strap around the forend of military rifles, holding the sling swivel (*see* Swivels), sometimes used as stacking swivel (*q.v.*).

SWIVEL RAMROD   a ramrod found on percussion handguns that

is fastened to the barrel or barrels by means of a swivel. When the ramrod is moved to the rear & seated in the ferrule, the swivel folds flat underneath the barrel.

SWIVELS   metallic loops, usually oval in shape, used to fasten a sling (*q.v.*) on a firearm. On hunting rifles, one swivel is fastened to the underneath part of the buttstock, the other is either set into the wood of the forend or onto a special swivel ring around the barrel itself. This latter system is found most frequently on high quality custom rifles & on some continental guns, rifles as well as shotguns. On match guns where a target sling with cuff is used (*see* Sling, Target), the forward swivel is wide to accept the sling hook *(q.v.)*, but no provisions are made to fasten a sling to the buttstock. On some target guns, the forward swivel is a part of the hand stop *(q.v.). Also see:* Lanyard.

SWIVELS, QUICK-DETACH-ABLE or QD   these sling swivels consist of two parts, a stud that is fitted into the wood of the buttstock & the forend in the same locations as the standard swivels *(q.v.)*, & a spring-activated swivel that locks into a hole in the stud.

T

TAKE-DOWN   *see* Stripping.

TANG   a term with two meanings. (1) an extension of the receiver that is inletted into the buttstock & which serves, in part, to hold the receiver & stock together. The tang on double shotguns (*see* Shotgun, Double), as well as on some rifles, often houses the safety (*see* Safety, Top-Tang). On the Schuetzen rifle *(q.v.)* & similar target rifles, the peep or vernier sight (*see* Sight, Peep; Sight, Vernier) was often fastened to the tang to bring the sight nearer the eye, thus making the sight picture *(q.v.)* sharper. (2) the metal bar or bars which permit elevating or lowering the rear sight (*see* Sight, Tang.)

TAPE PRIMER   *see* Primer, Tape.

TAPPED & DRILLED   incorrect phrasing for DRILLED & TAPPED, *see* Scope Bases.

TARAGE TABLE   a computed mathematical table that indicates, from the compression of the copper crusher (*see* Crusher Gage), the pressure the crusher was subjected to in the chamber of a pressure gun (*see* Pressure Determination). Tarage tables are also used to interpolate time of flight expressed in milliseconds into velocity expressed in fps or feet/per/second.

TARGET   for formal match shooting & sighting-in *(q.v.)*, a sheet of paper or cardboard, most often with concentric circles; the inner circle, usually black, being the bullseye *(q.v.)*. Various values are assigned to

252

Side bars on vernier and military sights are also known as tang.

Arrow points to tang of this Westley-Richards Farquharson action.

the concentric circles, the total numerical value of the bullet holes in the target being totalled up for the shooter's score (*see* Scoring Plug). *Also see:* Benchrest Target. Target designs vary with the intended use of the target, the configurations of the target often representing game animals or special geometric figures that permit a more accurate aligning of the sights with the target.

TARGET, BACKING   a strip of paper mounted behind the benchrest target. The backing target often consists of a roll of paper that is motor-driven, thus moving the backing target slowly behind the actual aiming target, allowing judges to determine how many shots were fired at a specific target. This is of importance in special matches to determine if another shooter accidentally fired at the wrong target.

TARGET BACKSTOP   a dirt bank or other artificial background on shooting ranges designed to stop

bullets from continuing their flight after hitting the target. On indoor ranges, the backstop usually is an angled steel plate from which bullets bounce off, either into a deep layer of sand or a water tank. On outdoor ranges, the backstop should consist of sand or dirt, often re-enforced with timbers or railroad ties, but care must be taken that the backstop does not contain rocks or other objects which could cause bullets to ricochet *(q.v.)*.

TARGET, BOBBING   also called TURNING TARGET, is one often seen on handgun ranges where the target surface is presented to the shooter for a limited time only. When permitted firing time has elapsed, the targets in the target frame *(q.v.)* are turned sideways, signalling the end of that particular stage of fire.

TARGET, BULLSEYE   *see* Bullseye. *Also see:* Target.

TARGET BUTTS   earthen parapet in front of target pit *(q.v.)*.

TARGET FRAME   can be a simple wooden frame on which a target is nailed or stapled, or a wire frame which may or may not be operated electrically.

TARGET HAMMER   *see* Hammer, Target.

TARGET PIT   found almost exclusively on big bore ranges, the pit is usually equipped with sliding target frames that allow the pit crew to mark one target while another one is hoisted up in the second target frame. Built for maximum safety, many pits have either telephones or two-way radio contact with the range officer. *Also see*: Marker; Maggie's Drawers.

TARGET, RUNNING DEER   a mechanized target frame carrying a deer, boar, fox or other game or varmint animal reproduction, which travels over a short distance of open firing area at varying speeds at a predetermined distance from the shooter. In formal matches, such as I.S.U. *(q.v.)* events, range, time for target travel, caliber, sights, etc. are carefully supervised. In informal running deer shoots, practice for hunters is the primary interest.

TARGET SHOOTER'S MITTEN a padded mitten, worn on the left hand of a right-handed shooter, so that sufficient pressure can be exerted on the hand stop *(q.v.)* to give maximum support to the rifle. *Also see*: Sling, Target.

TARGET, SILHOUETTE   target

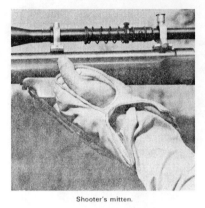

Shooter's mitten.

showing the outline of a man, widely used for military & police training.

TARGET, TIN HAT   British target that has the upper half of the bullseye & adjoining ring printed in black, the lower part being left white. Because of its design, this target is also called half-bullseye target.

T-BOLT   a patented design for a straight-pull action (*see* Action, Bolt).

TEATFIRE   *see* Cartridge, Teatfire.

TELESCOPE or TELESCOPIC SIGHT   *see* Scope.

TEMPERATURE OF IGNITION also called combustion point, the amount of heat required to ignite the outer layer of a substance to the point that the next layer of the substance will be ignited by the heat created by the burning of the first layer. In powder combustion, oxygen & heat must be present to sustain the process. Various powders have different combustion points, these

254

points depending on the chemical composition of the powder & its physical configuration. *Also see:* Combustion; Powder Burning Rate.

THIMBLE　　another name for ferrule *(q.v.)*.

THROAT　　*see* Chamber Throat.

THROAT PROTECTOR　　a small metal tube that fits into the chamber of a bolt action rifle after the bolt

has been removed. The use of this device is widespread among target shooters since the throat protector prevents any possible damage to the rifling by the cleaning rod by keeping the rod carefully centered in the bore.

THROUGH-LUMP　　a type of lump *(q.v.)* that is not connected to the barrels of a double shotgun until after it has been shaped in rough form. It is then brazed into place between the barrels & fitted by hand. *Also see:* Illustration of Flats.

THUMB CUT-OUT　　a machined cut-out on the left side of the Mauser Model 98 action so that there is space for the thumb as cartridges are

stripped from the charger clip *(see* Clip, Charger) into the magazine of the rifle. A corresponding cut is also found in the military stock. Since rifles built on the M98 action for sporting use are loaded without the clip, the cut-out is not important & copies of the action made for hunting rifles lack this feature.

THUMBHOLE STOCK　　*see* Stock, Thumbhole.

THUMB REST　　a protruding ledge on the left side of some handgun grips *(see* Grip) on which the shooter's thumb rests while firing.

Target grips usually have an extra large thumb rest to give the shooter greater control over gun movement.

THUMB SAFETY　　*see* Safety, Thumb.

TIMED FIRE　　a course of competitive shooting during which a shooter must fire a certain number of rounds during a given time interval.

TIME OF FLIGHT　　time elapsed for a projectile to cover a specific distance. For sporting arms, time of flight is usally given in milliseconds.

TIMING   *see* Cylinder Indexing.

TIPPING BULLET   *see* Bullet Wabble.

TIP-OFF MOUNT   *see* Scope Bases.

TIP TENSION   *see* Forend Tension.

TIP-UP REVOLVER   *see* Action, Hinged Frame; Action, Top-break; Frame.

TITFIRE   *see* Cartridge, Teatfire.

TOE   the lower edge of the butt *(q.v.)* on long guns. *Also see:* Stock; Illustration of stock nomenclature.

TOE, LONG   *see* Pitch.

TOE, SHORT   *see* Pitch.

TOGGLE JOINT   a mechanical system that joins two bars end to end, but not in line. When force is applied to the knee or joint, the two parts will be straightened out, each exerting force at the unjoined end. The Pistole Parabellum *(q.v.)* action is typical of the toggle joint system in use in firearms.

TOLERANCE   the permissible variations in dimensions occuring in the functioning parts of firearms, in cartridges, cartridge cases, bullets, etc. Most tolerances in firearms are in the order of $\pm$ 0.0001-0.0005″.

TONG TOOL   handloading tool that is not mounted on a bench, but held in the hands of the reloader. Such a tool is capable of performing all of the reloading operations of the loading presses, but is somewhat slower. Highly portable, this type of handloading tool is ideal for loading at the range & for beginners.

TOP-BREAK   *see* Action, Top-break.

TOP-BREAK REVOLVER   *see* Action, Hinged Frame; Action, Top-break; Frame.

TOP EXTENSION   *see* Extension Rib. *Also see:* Doll's Head.

TOP-LEVER   a centrally located lever on the top of the action which, when pushed to the right, unlocks the gun & permits the opening of the gun by pivoting the barrel or barrels downward. The top-lever is used on side-by-side shotguns, O/U shotguns, single barrel guns, as well as double rifles & combination guns. *Also see:* Action, Top-break.

TOP STRAP   the upper part of a revolver frame which often is either

slightly grooved, the groove serving as rear sight (*see* Sight, Rear), or which carries at its rearward end an adjustable sight (*see* Sight, Adjustable).

TORQUE a secondary recoil movement *(q.v.)* that appears in certain guns when they are fired. Torque is primarily a rotating or twisting motion, is encountered in heavy recoiling revolvers such as the 44 Magnum where, depending on grip shape & fit of hand to grip, the gun can almost twist out of the shooter's hand. Ultra light rifle barrels for high velocity calibers, especially if barrel taper is considerable & muzzle diameter is minimal, also produce torque. Here, the twist or torque is not as apparent, taking place in the direction opposite to the twist, that is a gun with right hand twist will torque to the left.

TOUCH HOLE in early guns, before the invention of the various lock or firing systems, a hole or vent at the rear of the firearm which connected from the outside of the barrel to the chamber of the gun containing the powder charge. A burning fuse or match, touched to the vent, fired the charge in the chamber. As the various ignition systems developed (*see* Ignition History), an external priming system replaced the fuse to ignite the main charge through the touch hole.

TRACER *see* Bullet, Tracer.

TRAJECTORY the curve of the path the bullet describes during its course of flight.

TRAJECTORY, FLAT a relative term used in conjunction with calibers which have only little bullet rise & drop from muzzle to target. All projectiles have some rise & fall, despite statements sometimes seen in gun literature.

TRAP the claybird *(q.v.)* game of trapshooting, also the mechanical device used for throwing the claybirds. Trapshooting at live birds, mostly pigeons, originated in England, was well established there by 1832 when the first live pigeon shooting club, the "High Hats," was founded near London. Usually the live pigeons were kept in a box with spring lid, were released by pulling a cord that opened the trap. Members of the High Hats are supposed to have placed a live pigeon under their tall hats, & when ready to shoot, lifted the hat, giving the bird a chance to escape. The hat would then be replaced & the shooter would fire at the bird. Another version of the High Hats states that the birds were kept under old discarded high hats to which a string was attached. When the shooter was ready, the cord was pulled, the hat was tipped over, & the bird flighted.

Today's trapshooting is vastly different. Instead of pigeons, claybirds are used. Five shooting positions or stations in a curve surround the trap house which contains the automatic trap. Each shooter fires at five birds from each station, each shooter in turn firing one shot. After each man has fired five times from his first station, he goes on to the next shooting post, this being repeated until every shooter has fired at a total of 25 birds.

257

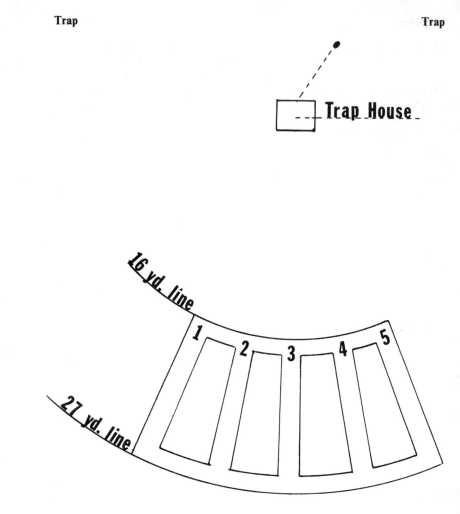

The stations are 16 yards from the trap, but handicap shooters, that is consistent high-scorers, may shoot from the 17 to the 27 yard line. Shooting doubles *(q.v.)* is another form of trap competition. The trap automatically changes the horizontal angle at which the clays are ejected. This alteration of angle, the change from station to station, changing of spring tension of the trap alters the flight pattern of the birds.

Sanctioned shoots are held under the auspices of the Amateur Trapshooting Association under strict rules & these events are registered shoots where the shooter establishes the classification in which he fires.

For practice, a number of smaller, highly portable traps are on the market, & these afford an excellent method for learning wingshooting. *Also see:* Trap Gun; Trap, Hand.

258

TRAP DOOR   *see* Action, Trap Door.

TRAP DOOR BUTTPLATE   a buttplate *(q.v.)*, usually steel or brass, with a small spring-closing lid covering a cavity in the butt. Often encountered on military rifles, the space was used to carry extra sights, cleaning equipment or other accessories, including one or two extra rounds of ammunition.

TRAP or TRIP GUN   *see* Set Gun.

TRAP GUN   a 12 ga. shotgun, usually with a full or improved-modified choke *(q.v.)* barrel or barrels, & a stock designed for trapshooting *(see* Stock, Shotgun). Trap guns usually carry a ventilated rib *(see* Rib, Ventilated), may be pump, semiautomatic, side-by-side, or O/U. Single shot guns are used only when doubles competition is not contemplated.

TRAP, HAND   a device that permits the launching of a claybird by hand. Based on strong springs, the hand trap makes it possible to throw a wide variety of flight patterns for practice shooting.

TRIGGER   usually a curved, sometimes grooved or serrated, metal bar that, when pulled rearward, releases its engagement on the sear *(q.v.)* or hammer *(q.v.)*, thus firing the gun.

TRIGGER, ADJUSTABLE   a trigger that is adjustable for trigger pull *(q.v.)*, thus allowing the shooter to adjust the trigger to a light, medium or heavy pull. Match triggers are not only adjustable for pull, but also for trigger creep *(q.v.)* & trigger overtravel *(q.v.)*. In some match rifles & pistols, the shooter can even change the position of the trigger to some degree to gain better trigger control.

TRIGGER BAR   a flat bar that, in some actions, transfers the trigger pressure to the sear.

TRIGGER CREEP   is the quite noticeable movement of the trigger in the time interval between taking up the slack in the trigger & the moment the firing mechanism of the gun is activated by the completed trigger pull. All conventional triggers have some slack, but in finely tuned triggers, such as set triggers *(see* Trigger, Set), this slack is not noticeable.

TRIGGER, CRISP   a trigger that releases the firing mechanism without a perceptible movement. Such a trigger is often referred to as being a clean breaking trigger. *Also see:* Trigger Creep.

TRIGGER, DOUBLE   this type of trigger most frequently encountered on side-by-side shotgun, double rifles, & O/U shotguns. In the side-by-side guns, the front trigger fires the right barrel, the rear trigger the left one. In O/U guns, the front trigger fires the upper barrel, the rear trigger the lower barrel. Some bolt action rifles appear to have double triggers, but these are double set triggers *(see* Trigger, Double Set).

TRIGGER, DOUBLE PULL also known as TWO STAGE trigger, MILITARY or TWO STAGE PULL trigger. This type of trigger has a very definite trigger SLACK, that is there is considerable movement of the trigger in a rearward direction before resistance is felt or before the gun fires. The reason for the double pull trigger is two-fold. Mechanically, this type of trigger is found almost exclusively in

bolt action rifles, primarily military ones, where the sear is located in the receiver & where mechanical tolerances, use & abuse, are greater than normal. The extra hump on the top of the military trigger is responsible for the two stage pull, but also makes possible the certainty of cocking that could not be achieved without it in the military rifle. The second reason for the two stage pull is one of training recruits as well as safety. The long trigger pull, with the considerable pull needed for final release of the sear, assures greater safety since accidental discharge through jarring is unlikely. Moreover, the long & delib-

erate pull is supposed to train recruits in careful aiming. On sporterized military rifles (*see* Sporterizing), the double pull is not desirable & most sporterized actions have either had the trigger reworked for a single stage pull, or had one of the commercial triggers installed.

TRIGGER, DOUBLE SET most commonly seen on match rifles & some European hunting rifles, the double set trigger consists of two individual triggers, the rear trigger setting the sear by means of one or more levers, the front trigger releasing the sear at the slightest touch. To fire such a gun, it is not essential to set the rear trigger first, but trigger pull of the front trigger, when not set by the rear trigger, usually has some creep (*see* Trigger Creep), & trigger pull *(q.v.)* is considerably heavier. *Also see:* Trigger, Hair; Trigger, Single Set.

TRIGGER, FOLDING or HINGED a trigger that folds forward & toward the frame of the gun. On some fine double guns with double triggers, the front trigger was so hinged to protect the trigger finger from recoil action

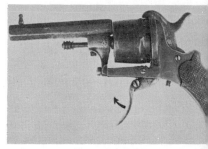

Trigger folds forward on this old Belgian pinfire revolver.

when pulling the rear trigger. The hinged trigger was also prevalent in revolvers, was used as late as 1929 on the 10.35 mm Italian service revolver.

TRIGGER GUARD   an oval, sometimes circular, band of metal, horn or plastic that is fastened fore & aft of the trigger on the under side of the stock, providing the trigger with some degree of protection from an accidental move that could discharge the firearm. *Also see:* Scroll Guard.

TRIGGER, HAIR   a non-specific term describing a trigger that requires only a very light trigger pull *(q.v.).*

TRIGGER, HINGED   *see* Trigger, Folding.

TRIGGER, INERTIA   a trigger system found in many side-by-side & O/U shotguns with a single selective trigger (*see* Trigger, Single Selective). In the inertia trigger the recoil force shifts the trigger action from one lock to the other, still cocked lock.

TRIGGER, MILITARY   *see* Trigger, Double Pull.

TRIGGER OVERTRAVEL   rearward movement of the trigger that continues after the hammer *(q.v.)* or sear *(q.v.)* is released. *Also see:* Trigger Stop.

TRIGGER PLATE   in box lock & side lock shotguns (*see* Action, Box Lock; Action, Side Lock), the bottom steel bar projecting rearward from the rear of the action which carries the triggers. In a transitional development between box lock & side lock actions, the entire lock *(q.v.)* system was carried on the trigger plate. Typical of the TRIGGER PLATE ACTION is the Blitz in Europe, the Dickson "round" action in England.

TRIGGER PULL   the amount of

Shown is a spring trigger pull scale; for match use a rod with specific weights attached is used. Before using, ascertain that the gun does not contain a live round, either in chamber or magazine.

force required to move the trigger sufficiently to the rear so that the gun fires. Trigger pull is expressed in pounds, & is strictly controlled in competitive shooting. The heavier the pull, the greater the likelihood of an accidental movement of the gun before the projectile leaves the barrel, thus spoiling the aim. While a light trigger pull is desirable, too light a pull is dangerous since the gun can be fired by a jar or bump. A trigger that releases the sear, hammer, or striker without prior perceptible hesitation (*see* Trigger, Double Pull) is said to have a crisp pull or to break cleanly. Such a trigger will not have any overtravel (*see* Trigger Overtravel), nor will there be any creep (*see* Trigger Creep).

TRIGGER PULL SCALE   a spring-activated or a weight-equipped scale that, when hooked around the trigger of a cocked but empty firearm, permits an accurate measurement of trigger pull. On some scales, pull is expressed in pounds, on match rifles pull is often measured in ounces.

TRIGGER PULL, TWO STAGE *see* Trigger, Double Pull.

TRIGGER, RELEASE   a special trigger that releases sear & sear spring tension after its rearward travel is completed & when it is returning to its original forward position. Most often installed on skeet & trap guns when shooter begins flinching (*q.v.*). The use of a release trigger requires special shooting techniques,

since the gun must continue to track the target so that the shot column will connect with the target. In use, the shooter, after seeing the target correctly, pulls the release trigger to the rear & releases it immediately. Upon release & subsequent forward travel, the sear is released & the gun fires. The shooter does not know when the gun will fire, thus cannot anticipate the gun's discharge, reducing the possibility of flinching.

TRIGGER, RING   a ring-shaped trigger found on some early revolver designs.

TRIGGER, SERRATED   parallel grooves on the face of the trigger, running the full length of the area of the trigger located outside the gun frame. The serrations are designed to give the trigger finger a non-slip surface.

TRIGGER, SET   a trigger, either single set (*see* Trigger, Single Set) or double set (*see* Trigger, Double Set) that, by means of levers or small bars, can be engaged with the sear so that a very light pull will release the trigger.

TRIGGER, SHEATH   a type of trigger found in early Colt revolvers & other guns where the trigger barely projects out of the grip frame on the gun, & where the trigger is not protected by a trigger guard *(q.v.)*.

TRIGGER SHOE   a small mechanical device that can be fastened to a trigger by means of setscrews so that the trigger surface is somewhat enlarged, thus giving the trigger finger a greater bearing surface plus an improved hold because of the serrations on the trigger shoe.

TRIGGER, SINGLE a type of trigger mechanism used in double barrel shotguns that, with each pull of the trigger, fires one barrel. The single trigger can be of two types: (1) SINGLE NON-SELECTIVE where the firing sequence of the two barrels is mechanically determined & where the shooter has no choice of which barrel is fired first. (2) SINGLE SELECTIVE where a selector, usually incorporated into the top-tang safety (*see* Safety, Top-tang), permits the shooter to choose the barrel he wishes to fire as he moves the safety forward from the safe to the fire position.

TRIGGER, SINGLE SET a trigger, usually found in target & custom rifles, that permits setting the trigger by means of levers or bars, thus engaging it with the sear so that a very light trigger pull *(q.v.)* fires the gun. The trigger is set by pushing it forward until the engagement is felt as well as heard in most such triggers, then firing is accomplished by moving the trigger rearward. Most of these triggers have a trigger pull that is measured in ounces. *Also see:* Trigger, Double Set; Trigger, Hair.

TRIGGER, SINGLE STAGE a trigger that has a smooth pull & breaks, or is released, crisply & cleanly, without overtravel. *Also see:*

Trigger Overtravel; Trigger Pull; Trigger, Double Pull.

TRIGGER SLACK *see* Trigger, Double Pull.

TRIGGER, SPUR a trigger mounting system that housed the trigger in an extension of the frame in some old guns. The trigger projected only slightly from the front of the extension or spur, & no trigger guard *(q.v.)* was used on these guns.

TRIGGER SQUEEZE in rifle & pistol shooting, the trigger pull should be a careful slow squeeze where pressure on the trigger is increased gradually. The fast yanking of a rifle or handgun trigger results in a trigger jerk which may move the gun enough so that the target is missed completely. In contrast, in shotgun shooting the trigger is not squeezed, but pulled or slapped, since the careful squeeze of the trigger is not needed.

TRIGGER, STIRRUP a type of trigger arrangement found in some semiautomatic pistols such as the Russian Tokarev. A stirrup-shaped trigger bar that connects trigger & sear is encountered in some pistols such as the Browning Model 1922.

Typical of the spur trigger era is this Remington derringer.

TRIGGER STOP device consisting of either a screw or flat bar, that prevents trigger overtravel *(q.v.)*. Adjustable screw-type trigger stops

are sometimes installed in match guns to permit just enough rearward trigger movement to discharge the gun.

TRIGGER, TARGET a serrated trigger, often extra wide, that is fully adjustable *(see* Trigger, Adjustable). Target triggers are free of trigger creep *(q.v.)*, seldom have trigger overtravel *(q.v.)*.

TRIGGER, THUMB a simple trigger system consisting of a button that projects from the tang *(q.v.)* & which is fired by depressing the button with the thumb. Now obsolete, the last U.S. rifle to carry a thumb trigger was a Winchester 22 RF single shot gun that lacked a safety device.

TRIGGER, TWIN-SINGLE a trigger system employed in some shotguns where the two triggers can either be used as the conventional double trigger *(see* Trigger, Double), or

where both or only one of the triggers acts as a single, non-selective trigger *(see* Trigger, Single Non-selective). The Brno-Wesson O/U is such a gun, the rear trigger firing the lower, then the upper barrel if used as a single trigger.

TRIGGER, TWO STAGE *see* Trigger, Double Pull.

TRIGGER WEIGHT *see* Trigger Pull Scale.

TRIGGER, WOODWARD three pull trigger which, similar to the inertia trigger *(see* Trigger, Inertia), shifts the trigger action from one lock to the other in double shotguns. In the British Woodward trigger, the middle or waste pull prevents the accidental firing of the other barrel during recoil.

TROMBONE ACTION *see* Action, Pump.

TROUND plastic-cased cartridges made for the never-released Dardick rifles & revolvers. *Also see:* Caseless Round.

TRUNCATED BULLET *see* Bullet, Truncated.

TRY GUN a side-by-side shotgun with a fully adjustable stock, usually made by one of the top-ranking British gunmakers. The stock can be altered for length of pull, drop at comb & heel, as well as cast & pitch. The adjustments are made by means of locking screws & bolts, the try gun being used to determine the exact stock measurements required for a custom shotgun stock.

TUBE   a term often used to describe a barrel, either rifled or smoothbored. *Also see:* Magazine, Tubular; Sight, Tube.

TUBE WASH   a gradual wearing away of the case mouth of paper or cardboard shotshell cases due to hot powder gases, & the passage of wads & shot. The enclosing of the shot column *(q.v.)* in a shot collar *(q.v.)* has done much to reduce shotshell case mouth wear, & tube wash is no longer an important consideration for the handloader.

TUBULAR MAGAZINE   *see* Magazine, Tubular.

TUMBLER   *see* English Gun Terms.

TUMBLING   a term with two meanings: (1) the end over end turning of a bullet in flight, resulting at the target in keyholing *(q.v.)*. (2) the mechanical process of cleaning loaded pistol & revolver ammunition by means of various abrasive substances such as ground corn cobs in some sort of rotating drum. This process is employed by ammunition makers as well as by custom loaders. Rifle ammunition should not be tumbled since the vigorous process of tumbling could produce sufficient contact between a bullet tip & the primer of another round, resulting in the detonation of that primer.

TURN-BOLT ACTION   *see* Action, Bolt.

TURRET   *see*   Scope, Internal Adjustment.

TWIST   rate at which the grooves of the rifling *(q.v.)* spiral inside the barrel. Twist is expressed as one complete turn of the rifling in a given number of inches, that is, a 1:12 twist barrel is one in which the grooves complete one turn in 12 inches of barrel, while in a 1:8 twist barrel, the grooves complete one turn in 8 inches of barrel. A fast twist is one where the number of inches required for a complete turn is relatively small, such as a 1:8 twist. A slow twist is one where a great number of inches is necessary for a complete spiral of the grooves, such as a barrel with a 1:24 twist. The rotation of the grooves may be either to the right or to the left, thus a right-hand or left-hand twist. The RATE OF TWIST necessary to stabilize a bullet in flight is based on bullet length in relation to its diameter as well as to its anticipated velocity. A long bullet travelling at high velocity requires a fast twist, while a shorter, heavier bullet travelling at a relatively low velocity requires a slow twist. PITCH is the angle of the rifling in relation to the bore axis.

TWIST BARREL   *see*   Barrel, Damascus.

TWIST, GAIN   the rifling *(q.v.)* that changes the rate of twist (*see* Twist) as it progresses from chamber to muzzle. Gain twist rifling may start at the chamber at a 1:14 rate, having at the muzzle a twist of 1:8. *Also see:* Pope Rifling.

265

U

UNDERBOLTS the metal bars in some top-break actions (*see* Action, Top-break) that engage the bites *(q.v.)* of the lumps *(q.v.)*, serving to lock *(q.v.)* or bolt the barrels to the action body, & that are actuated by the top-lever *(q.v.)*.

UNDERHAMMER type of gun in which the hammer or the entire firing mechanism is located below the barrel. Widely used in percussion rifles & single as well as multi barrel pistols, the underhammer ignition system survived for quite sometime,

The underhammer gun.

was even used in modified form with paper cartridges in the Norwegian Model 1842.

UNDER-LEVER   *see* Action, Under-lever.

UNDERLUGS   another term for lumps (*see* Lump).

UPSET FORGING   a method of producing the beginnings of modern barrels from steel rod. Upset forging shortens the original rod, thickens & strengthens the breech end of the barrel-to-be.

USED GUN STANDARDS   the National Rifle Association as well as collectors have established certain descriptive standards which are used throughout the U.S. to describe the condition of a firearm.

Perfect: In new or mint condition.

Excellent: Virtually new, little use, no external or internal damages except at muzzle & other sharp edges where some wear of the bluing may be visible.

Very Good: Only minor surface scratches or dents, no pitting or corrosion, gun is in perfect firing order.

Good: The firearm is in working order, but there is some wear on moving parts, pitting or corrosion will not hamper the functioning of the gun.

Fair: The firearm has seen service, may need replacement of worn parts, no rust but some pitting which, however, does not make the gun unsafe or inoperable.

Poor: Badly worn parts which require replacement before the gun can be fired. Often referred to as junker & sometimes sought after for such parts as stocks, trigger guards, etc.

V

VARIABLE SCOPE   *see* Scope, Variable Power.

VARMINT RIFLE   a rifle chambered for one of the varmint calibers such as 222 Remington, 222 Remington Magnum, 223 Remington, 224 Weatherby, 225 Winchester, 22/250 Remington, 6 mm Remington or 243 Winchester. The rifle may also be chambered for a wildcat cartridge (*see* Cartridge, Wildcat). Varmint calibers usually have a flat trajectory (*see* Trajectory, Flat), firing a light bullet at high velocity *(q.v.)*. Varmint rifles usually have high comb *(q.v.)* stocks designed for scope use, often have extra heavy barrels which may be free-floating *(q.v.)* or glassbedded (*see* Glassbedding), a smooth trigger pull *(q.v.)*. For long range varmint hunting, rifles are equipped either

Varmint rifles. Left to right: 22-250 heavy barrel gun with varmint stock, 222 with double set triggers, and 17/223 with variable scope mounted low over line of bore.

268

with a variable scope (*see* Scope, Variable Power) or with a varmint scope (*see* Scope, Target & Varmint).

VARMINTER   the 22/250 was one of the longest-lived wildcat cartridges (*see* Cartridge, Wildcat). The caliber was developed in the heyday of developmental ballistics by J.E. Gebby, G. L. Wotkyns, & J. Bushnell Smith. Gebby applied for & was granted the tradename Varminter for the cartridge which was based on the 250/3000 Savage case. In 1964 Remington Arms introduced rifles & ammunition, calling the cartridge the 22/250 Remington. Original Varminter wildcat cases vary widely in shoulder design. Remington's 55 gr. bullet is claimed to have a muzzle velocity (*see* Velocity, Muzzle) of 3760 fps.

VELOCITY   as used in the firearms field, indicates the speed of a projectile in flight. Velocity is expressed in feet/per/second or fps. While velocity can be measured, at least in theory, at any point along the projectile's trajectory, it is much simpler to determine the velocity somewhere close to the muzzle. With the known ballistics properties of the projectile & the measured velocity, the performance of the projectile anywhere along its path can be calculated. While shot (*q.v.*) flight behavior is of interest, its relatively limited range makes its ballistic behavior at 100, 200, or 300 yards academic.

The long range performance of bullets, primarily from rifles, & to some degree from handguns, can be determined on hand of ballistics tables. In the U.S., the Ingalls' tables (*q.v.*) are the standard means for calculating remaining velocity (*see* Velocity, Remaining) & trajectories. The British counterpart of the Ingalls' tables is the Hodsock tables. Velocity is determined by means of a chronograph (*q.v.*).

VELOCITY, ESTIMATED   fair degree of velocity estimation of projectiles is possible by means of the Boulenge chronograph, if the Newtonian law of falling bodies is used. However, this method is none too precise & if the Boulenge unit (*see* Chronograph) is used, it is possible to obtain a fairly accurate reading. Most velocity estimating done by handloaders is based on experience gained with other cartridges & bullets similar to the one under consideration.

Another method of estimating velocity of a given cartridge is possible if the accurate trajectory of that cartridge can be determined by actual shooting tests. If the trajectory of a cartridge with known velocity coincides with that of the cartridge with the unknown velocity, it is possible to obtain a fairly close velocity estimate, providing the bullet weight of both cartridges is identical.

VELOCITY, INSTRUMENTAL   the velocity of a projectile as determined by means of a chronograph (*q.v.*) at a specified point along the projectile's trajectory. If instrumental velocity of two cartridges is compared, the comparison is valid, only if identical bullet weights & shapes are considered & if the instrumental velocity was taken at identical distances from the muzzle or identical points along the two trajectories. *Also see:* Velocity, Muzzle.

VELOCITY, MUZZLE   the speed of a projectile at the muzzle *(q.v.)*. Because muzzle blast can affect the start screen of the chronograph *(q.v.)*, this screen is usually set up a measured distance away from the muzzle. Thus, the reading obtained from the interpolation of elapsed time of flight tables into velocity does not give true muzzle velocity, but the velocity of the projectile a given number of feet away from the muzzle. While density of air affects velocity, for all practical purposes, the Army Ordnance figure of 0.64 fps per foot distance from muzzle to the midpoint between the screens is sufficiently accurate.

If:

d = distance from muzzle to start screen
S = distance between screens
$D = d + 1/2S$
IV = instrumental velocity
C = air density factor Rho or 0.64 fps
then MV is:
$$D \times C + IV.$$
Thus, if d = 3 ft., S = 10 ft., then D = 8 ft., & if IV = 2700 fps, MV = 8 x 0.64 + 2700, or 2705.12 fps.

VELOCITY, REMAINING   the velocity of a projectile at any point of its trajectory.

VELOCITY, STRIKING   the velocity of a projectile at the point of impact. *Also see:* Velocity, Terminal.

VELOCITY, SUMMIT   the velocity of a projectile at its highest point along its trajectory.

VELOCITY, TERMINAL   in popular usage, is identical to what ballisticians call the striking velocity (*see* Velocity, Striking). In small arms ballistics, the terminal velocity is defined as being the constant speed of a projectile after air drag & gravitational pull have reached the point where the two forces cancel each other's effect on the projectile.

VENT   any opening or orifice, such as the one found in the nipple *(q.v.)* of percussion arms. Many rifle receivers have gas vents to permit gases to escape in case of excessive pressures. Bullet molds are sometimes vented, by means of shallow grooves, to permit casting of perfectly made bullets.

VENTILATED CHOKE   a type of variable choke (*see* Choke, Adjustable) that is equipped with a slotted sleeve that permits gas escape, thus reducing recoil to some extent. A ventilated choke works on the same principle as a muzzle brake *(q.v.)*. *Also see:* Compensator, Cutts.

VENTURI SHOULDER   cartridge case shoulder (*see* Case Shoulder) design originated by Ralph Waldo Miller. These wildcat cartridges (*see* Cartridge, Wildcat) were named Powell-Miller-Venturi-Freebored or PMVF *(q.v.)*, but the shoulder design cannot be considered as even one-half of the Venturi truncated cone system used for the measurement of gas pressures or the flow of liquids. The Miller shoulder was very flat with little shoulder angle & velocities for various necked-down magnums were claimed to be in the area of 6000 fps, with a drop of only 8″ over 300 yards. In the large belted magnum cases, barrel wear was extreme & the so-called Venturi shoulder case design never became popular. Some writers have claimed that the current Weatherby cases have somewhat modified Miller or Venturi shoulders, but the Weatherby shoulder is generally considered as a radius shoulder *(q.v.).*

VERNIER CALIPER   a straight-line caliper or measuring device equipped with a vernier that allows the taking of precise measurements in length, width, thickness & depth within the limitations of the caliper itself. Most vernier calipers permit reading of 0.0001″. The standard

vernier caliper requires a certain amount of skill to obtain accurate readings & has been replaced to some degree by the dial caliper which uses a dial rather than the sliding vernier scale.

VERNIER SIGHT   *see* Sight, Vernier.

VERTEX   the highest point in a bullet's trajectory *(q.v.).*

VERTICAL JUMP   *see* Muzzle Jump.

VERY PISTOL   a single shot pistol designed to discharge a signalling aerial flare, which may or may not be equipped with a parachute. Invented by Lt. Edward Wilson Very, U.S.N., the flare pistol was quickly adopted by all countries, with many writers giving an English inventor credit for the device, probably be-

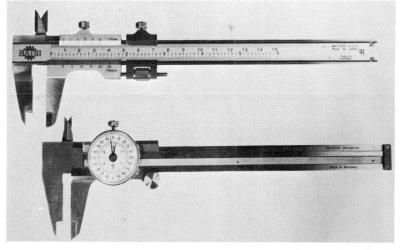

Vernier caliper at top requires careful reading of vernier scale, one at bottom permits easy reading on dial.

cause Webley was a major producer of flare guns during WWI. The name Very is now popularly & wrongly applied to any flare or signalling gun.

VIBRATION   *see* Barrel Vibration.

VIERLING   *see* Combination Guns.

VIERLINGSPATRONE   the Austrian name given the 22 Winchester Centerfire cartridge. Although the cartridge was discontinued in the U.S., it still enjoys some limited popularity on the continent where many combination guns *(q.v.)* are chambered for it. Originally a black powder cartridge, it became the forerunner of the 22 Hornet which is now virtually obsolete.

At left, the 22 Winchester Centerfire cartridge, still popular in Europe, from which was later developed the 22 Hornet which is now almost obsolete in the U. S.

V-RING   the inner circle within the 8″ black bull on the military A target, where the bull has the value of 5.

V-SPRING   *see* Spring.

W

WABBLE *see* Bullet Wabble.

WAC PISTOL not a military small arm, but the name given the French **MAB** semiautomatic pistol sold in the U.S. by the Winfield Arms Co.

WAD a felt, paper, cardboard or plastic disk that is used in a shotshell

Two plastic wads with shot collars flank a simple shot collar.

(q.v.). Wad design & material varies with the intended use of the wad, the ultimate use of the shell, as well as the gauge *(q.v.).*

WAD, BASE a compressed filler found at the head of the shotshell where it aids in holding the case material, paper or plastic, in place, & also supports the thin brass head & sidewall. The base wad is permanently installed in the shotshell hull & helps to keep the powder near the flash hole. Base wads differ in size, thickness, form & composition.

WAD, CARD a thin cardboard wad, sometimes waxed & of different sizes, placed over the shot charge to prevent lead pellets from spilling out of the shell in case the crimp *(q.v.)* opened. With the widespread use of plastic hulls, the card wad has been nearly obsoleted. Also sometimes used as a spacer wad (*see* Wad, Spacer).

WAD, FILLER   *see* Wad, Spacer.

WAD, OVER-POWDER   or OP WAD, a felt, paper, cardboard or plastic wad placed over the powder charge, thus separating powder & shot pellets. The shotshell loading press has a rod-type rammer that seats the OP wad, often with a predetermined amount of pressure (*see* Wad Pressure). The increasing use of plastic wads, often in conjunction with a shot collar *(q.v.),* & the improved obturate *(q.v.)* properties has altered wad designs, usage, & wad pressure requirements considerably.

WAD, OVER-SHOT   a thin wad placed over the top of the shot charge to help in sealing the shell. *Also see:* Wad, Card.

WAD PRESSURE   when felt & cardboard wads were used as OP wads (*see* Wad, Over-powder), the pressure exerted on the OP wads was essential to give the powder the correct amount of compression for maximum ballistic performance of the shell. The plastic shot cups, often incorporating the wad, do not require wad pressure, but do necessitate a charge reduction if load data for other than plastic wads are used. Since the plastic shot cups provide a greater gas seal in the barrel than other wads, pressure from the burning powder is also greater, therefore charge reduction is necessary.

WAD, SPACER   a now virtually obsolete wad, usually felt or similar material, placed on top of the OP wad (*see* Wad, Over-powder) & used to fill the hull so that the total inside height of the components was of the correct height to permit a proper closure crimp. Also known as FILLER WAD.

WAD, TOP   same as the over-shot wad, but not required for the star crimp (*see* Crimp) or plastic hulls. *Also see:* Wad, Over-shot; Wad, Card.

WADCUTTER   *see* Bullet, Wadcutter.

WALKING BARREL   a barrel that has had to be straightened & which, when heated due to firing, will bend again, thus changing its zero, also enlarging group *(q.v.)* size.

WARPAGE   *see* Stock Warpage.

WATER TABLE   *see* English Gun Terms.

WAVE THEORY   actually a simple physical process that occurs within the cartridge case as the powder burns. The molecules within a container of any gas are in constant motion, bouncing off each other as well as off the inside walls of the container. The motion of the gas molecules is constant for any specific temperature level of the gas. This kinetic theory of gases has been proved time & again. When the gases are heated, the motion of the molecules increases, & the thermodynamic equilibrium is changed—not only does the velocity & direction of the gas molecules change, but the gas also heats the colder inside walls of the container, in this instance, the cartridge case. The motion of the heated gas molecules is often blamed for numerous happenings, such as brass flowage, pressure & velocity variations between identical loads, etc.

The air column in the barrel is being rapidly pushed out of the barrel by the moving bullet. This process not only heats the air (or gas) molecules, but a certain amount of compression of the gas also occurs. When the mass of gas is finally pushed out the muzzle, the constricting walls of the barrel suddenly cease to hamper molecular gas movement, while at the same time the exterior temperature exerts its effects on the heated gas molecules. This wave of air leaving the muzzle of the gun, ahead of the projectile, has been studied photographically, constitutes the beginning of the noise created by firing a gun & appears to be related to some degree to muzzle jump *(q.v.)*.

WAX BULLET   *see* Bullet, Wax.

WCF   abbr. for Winchester Center Fire.

WEB   a term with two meanings: (1) the wall thickness of a tubular propellant powder. The web, or wall thickness, of a powder affects its ballistics properties such as burning rate (*see* Powder Burning Rate) & temperature of ignition *(q.v.)*.

(2) the thickness of brass in a cartridge case in the solid portion between the bottom of the primer pocket *(q.v.)* & the interior of the case.

WEBLEY-FOSBERRY REVOLV-ER   *see* Revolver, Automatic.

WHEEL-LOCK   a very early ignition *(q.v.)* system that used iron

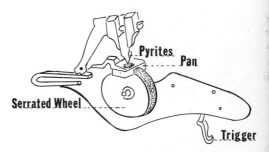

pyrites which were struck by the edge of a serrated wheel that had been put under spring tension. Pressing the trigger release the wheel so that it revolved, the sparks from the pyrite igniting the priming charge in the pan *(q.v.)*, this burning charge then igniting the powder charge in the chamber.

WHITWORTH THREAD   standard form of screw thread used in Great Britain, hence also on English guns.

WILDCAT CARTRIDGE   *see* Cartridge, Wildcat.

WILLIAMS BULLET   *see* Bullet, Williams.

WIND CLOCK   *see* Clock System.

WIND DEFLECTION also called WIND DRIFT or WINDAGE, affects all projectiles to some degree. Deflection is especially critical in target shooting, but light high velocity bullets used for varmint hunting are also prone to wind deflection, especially when wind direction & velocity varies in hilly country. If the wind comes from the shooter's right or 3 o'clock (*see* Clock System), the rifleman must hold into the wind, or to the right of the point of aim *(q.v.)* so that the wind deflection will push the bullet toward point of aim. Understanding wind movements & compensating for them is a hard-learned skill, often known as wind doping *(q.v.)*. *Also see:* Deflection; Holding-off; Kentucky Windage; Mirage.

WIND DIRECTION *see* Wind Flag.

WIND DOPING the ability to calculate wind deflection & its effect on a projectile. For competitive shooting, Didion's formula can be used. To calculate deflection or D,

$$D = W_Z (T\text{-}T_V)$$

where

D   = Bullet displacement in feet
W_Z = Cross wind velocity in fps
T   = Time of flight
T_V = Bullet vacuum flight time, usually stated as $\dfrac{X}{V}$ or range in ft divided by MV in fps

Wind doping is a matter of experience, & many good rifleman have the ability to dope wind to such an extent

that the formula is not needed. *Also see*: Wind Deflection.

WIND DRIFT *see* Wind Deflection.

WIND FLAG small flags on target ranges that show the shooter from which DIRECTION wind is blowing. Depending on range & shooting distance, wind flags may be located anywhere between shooter & target. Wind flags also help the experienced shooter to dope wind, often help in estimating wind velocity.

WIND GAGE a device that, when exposed to any air movement, indicates the velocity of the wind.

Wind gage.

WINDAGE a term with two meanings: (1) sometimes used to describe wind deflection *(q.v.)*. (2) the horizontal movement of any type of sight *(q.v.)*. *Also see*: Windage Adjustment; Elevation; Elevation Adjustment; Scope, Internal Adjustment; Sighting-in.

WINDAGE ADJUSTMENT on receiver sights & scopes, is accomplished by means of a micrometer screw or knob that is marked not only with the direction of the movement but also with divisions, sometimes clicks *(q.v.)*, which indicate the amount of lateral or horizontal movement of the point of impact *(q.v.)* on the 100 yard target with each movement or turn of the knob or screw.

WINDAGE IN BLACK POWDER SMOOTHBORES is the difference between the measured diameter of the cast lead ball & the bore diameter. This space, or windage, makes loading easier, especially if there is a build-up of black powder fouling *(q.v.)*.

WINDAGE KENTUCKY *see* Kentucky Windage.

WINDAGE RULES as issued by the U.S. Army for target shooting with the M1906 rifle & M2 ammunition, uses a simple formula to calcualte windage correction in Minute of Angle *(q.v.)*.

$$WC = \frac{W_V \times R}{10}$$

where:

WC = windage correction in MOA

W_V = wind velocity across the range

R = the range in yards

Assuming a 10 mph wind & a 200 yard range, $WC = \dfrac{10 \times 200}{10} = 2$ MOA, or 4″ at 200 yards. *Also see*: Wind Doping.

WINDER MUSKET a 22 rimfire single shot, lever action rifle, made by Winchester at the suggestion of Col. Winder for civilian & military target shooting. Manufacture of the gun was discontinued in 1920.

WING SAFETY *see* Safety, Wing.

WITNESS MARK a small line, sometimes called index mark *(q.v.)*,

The two arrows point at the two marks known as witness marks which must coincide as shown for proper alignment of sights and headspace.

one each on action & barrel of some guns. The marks must line up when the barrel is fully turned into the action so that the sights are aligned.

WOBBLE   in a semiautomatic pistol, means that the barrel does not lock up tightly in exactly the same position from shot to shot.

WOBBLE, BULLET   *see* Bullet Wabble.

WOODWORTH CRADLE   a modification of the Mann V rest (*see* Rest) that permits firing of a completely assembled rifle.

WORM   a corkscrew-like device that can be attached to or is permanently fastened to the ramrod or cleaning rod of muzzle-loading guns. By turning the worm into the ball, patch or charge, it is possible to pull the unfired components from the gun.

WOTKYNS-MORSE BULLET *see* Bullet, Wotkyns-Morse.

WRF   abbr. for Winchester Rim Fire.

WRIST   *see* Stock, Small of the.

WUNDHAMMER SWELL or BULGE   a slight enlargement of the pistol grip on bolt action rifles. Originated by the gunsmith of the same name, the Wundhammer swell

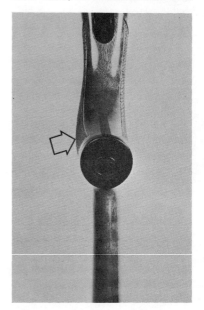

affords the shooter a better hold on the pistol grip with the swell filling the palm. If the swell is adequate & fits the hand properly, the hand will naturally return to the identical position each time. This stock feature is especially helpful in off-hand shooting.

X

X-RING on the NRA smallbore target, the X-ring is the inner 1″ diameter circle within the 2″ bull or bullseye. X-ring sizes vary with the target, & the number of X-rings scored by a shooter can decide the outcome of a match. The higher the number of shots within the X-ring, the higher the score. Targets on which the highest score is 5 have a V-ring *(q.v.)* serving the same purpose.

Y

YAW a bullet movement which occurs when a bullet has a poor ballistic shape or is fired at the improper velocity. In yaw, the bullet nose rotates around the line of trajectory so that the central axis of the bullet in flight is at an angle to the trajectory.

YOKE *see* Crane.

Z

ZERO   that sight setting of a rifle or handgun that, at a specific distance with a specific load, will place the bullets into the center of a target, providing there is no wind or other factors to influence the trajectory of the projectile.

ZERO DEFLECTION   a sight that is adjusted in such a manner that the line of sight & axis of the gun are parallel.

ZERO SHOT   shot fired to verify that the zero setting of the sight has not been altered or changed.

ZEROING IN   process of adjusting the sights of a rifle, handgun, or slug-shooting shotgun with rifle sights or scope, so that the projectiles will hit the target at a specific range at point of aim, taking into account the curved trajectory of the projectile.

Thus, if a 200 yard shot is anticipated, it is possible to sight-in a gun to zero at that range, yet the zeroing or sighting-in *(q.v.)* can be done on a 100 yard range by means of the trajectory tables offered by most ammunition makers. If a 30-06 rifle is to be sighted to print dead on at 200 yards with the 180 gr. bullet, the sights should be adjusted so that the group prints 2.5″ high at 100 yards, that is 2.5″ above the exact point of aim. This will place the same bullet dead on at 200 yards. At 300 yards, the bullet will be 10.5″ low, & at 400 yards, the bullet will strike the target 32.5″ below point of aim. *Also see:* Point of Aim; Elevation

Adjustment; Windage Adjustment; Trajectory.

ZINC FOULING   a zinc residue in a rifled barrel may occur if undersized zinc alloy bullets are fired. Zinc alloys are harder than the usual lead alloys, hence bullets should be no more than .001-.002″ larger than bore diameter *(q.v.)*. Severe lead fouling has been successfully removed by firing several zinc alloy bullets. Bullets equipped with zinc gas-checks *(q.v.)* or washers leave very little or no fouling in the bore.

ZIMMERSTUETZEN   a small-bore German single shot rifle, usually chambered for a 4 mm rimfire cartridge. The cartridge contains no propellant charge, only a priming compound, & these indoor target rifles may either be of the breech-loading type or may be loaded from the muzzle with a special loading device on the barrel.

BIBLIOGRAPHY

ACKLEY, P. O., Handbook for Shooters & Reloaders, 2 Vols., Salt Lake City, Utah, 1962.

ACKLEY, P. O., Home Gun Care & Repair, Stackpole, Harrisburg, Pa., 1969.

ALBAUGH, W. A. III, and SIMMONS, E. N., Confederate Arms, Stackpole, Harrisburg, Pa., 1957.

ALBAUGH, W. A. III, BENET H., JR., and SIMMONS, E. N., Confederate Handguns, Riling & Lentz, Philadelphia, Pa., 1963.

ANGELUCCI, A., Catalogo Della Ameria Reale Di Torino, Ameria Reale di Torino, Italy, 1967.

ANONYMOUS, Facts about Telescopic Sights, Bausch & Lomb Optical Co., Rochester, N.Y., 1956.

———Textbook of Small Arms 1929, Holland Press, London England, 1961.

———U. S. Army Special Forces Foreign Weapons Handbook, U. S. Army John F. Kennedy Center for Special Warfare, Ft. Bragg, N.C., 1967.

ARNOLD, R., Automatic and Repeating Shotguns, A. S. Barnes, N.Y.C., 1962.

ASKINS, CHARLES (Sr.), Game Bird Shooting, Macmillan Co., N.Y.C.,1931.

———Rifles & Rifle Shooting, Macmillan Co., N.Y.C. 1912.

BADY, D. B., Colt Automatic Pistols 1896-1955, Borden Publishing Co., Los Angeles, Cal., 1963.

BAKER, C., Modern Gunsmithing, Small Arms Technical Publishing Co., Plantersville, S. C., 1933. (2nd Ed.)

BARNES, F. C., Cartridges of the World, Gun Digest Co., Chicago, Ill., 1969. (2nd Ed.)

BEARSE, R., Centerfire American Rifle Cartridges 1892-1963, A. S. Barnes & Co., S. Brunswick, N.J., 1966.

BEVIS, J. R., DONOVAN, J. A., Modern Rifle, Vol. 1, Practical Exterior Ballistics, Butte, Mont., 1917.

BLACKMORE, H. L., British Military Firearms 1650-1850, Herbert Jenkins, London, 1961.

BOCK, G., & WEIGEL, W., Handbuch der Faustfeuerwaffen, J. Neumann-Neudamm, Mesungen, Germany, 1965.

BOGARDUS, A. H., Field, Cover, and Trap Shooting, J. B. Ford & Co., N.Y.C., 1874.

BREATHED, J. W., Jr., SCHROEDER, J. J., Jr., System Mauser, Handgun Press, Chicago, Ill., 1967.

BROWNELL, F. R., Gunsmith Kinks, F. Brownell & Son, Montezuma, Iowa, 1969.

BROWNING, J., and GENTRY, C., John M. Browning American Gunmaker, Doubleday & Co., Garden City, N.Y., 1964.

BURRARD, G., The Modern Shotgun, A. S. Barnes, N.Y.C., 1961.

————Notes on Sporting Rifles, Edward Arnold, London, 1958.

CASWELL, J., Sporting Rifles and Rifle Shooting, D. Appleton & Co., N.Y.C., 1920.

CHAPEL, C. E., Field, Skeet and Trapshooting, Funk & Wagnalls, N.Y.C., 1962.

————U. S. Martial and Semi-Martial Single-Shot Pistols, Coward-McCann, Inc., N.Y.C., 1962. (1st Ed.)

CORNER, J., Theory of the Interior Ballistics of Guns, John Wiley & Sons, Inc., N.Y.C., 1950.

CROSSMAN, E.C., The Book of the Springfield, Small Arms Technical Publishing Co., Georgetown, S.C., 1951.

CUMMINGS, C. S. 2nd, Everyday Ballistics, Stackpole & Heck, Harrisburg, Pa., 1950.

DATIG, F. A., Cartridges for Collectors, Vol. 1, Borden Publishing Co., L. A., Cal., 1956.

————Cartridges for Collectors, Vol. 2, Fadco Publishing Co., Beverly Hills, Cal., 1958.

————Cartridges for Collectors, Vol. 3, Borden Publishing Co., L.A., Cal. 1967.

————(Ed.), DWM Cartridges 1896-1956, Fadco Publishing Co., Beverly Hills, Cal., 1962.

————The Luger Pistol, Borden Publishing Co., L. A., Cal., 1962.

de HAAS, F., Single Shot Rifles and Actions, Gun Digest Co., Chicago, Ill., 1969.

DOWELL, W. C., The Webley Story, Skyrac Press Ltd., Leeds, England, 1962.

DUNLAP, J., American, British & Continental Pepperbox Firearms, H. J. Dunlap, Los Altos, Cal., 1964.

DUNLAP, ROY F., Gunsmithing, Stackpole, Harrisburg, Pa., 1963.

EDWARDS, W. B., Civil War Guns, Stackpole, Harrisburg, Pa., 1962.

ERIKSEN, E., Danske Orgelespingolen, Norlundes Bogtrykkeri, Kopenhagen, Denmark, 1945.

ERLMEIER, H. A., and BRANDT, J. H., Handbuch der Pistolen und Revolver Patronen, Erlmeier Verlag, Wiesbaden, Germany, 1967.

FRAZER, WM. D. (Major), American Pistol Shooting, E. P. Dutton & Co., Inc., N.Y.C., 1929.

GARWOOD, G. T. (GOUGH THOMAS), Gough Thomas' Gun Book, Adam & Charles Black, London, 1969.

GEORGE, J. N., English Guns and Rifles, Stackpole, Harrisburg, Pa., 1947.

———English Pistols & Revolvers, Arco Publishing Co., N.Y.C., 1962.

GLENDENNING, I., British Pistols and Guns 1640-1840, Cassell & Co., Ltd., London, England, 1951.

GLUCKMAN, A., Identifying Old U. S. Muskets, Rifles & Carbines, Stackpole, Harrisburg, Pa., 1965.

GOULD, A. C., Modern American Pistols & Revolvers, Samworth, Plantersville, S. C., 1946.

———Modern American Rifles, Samworth, Plantersville, S. C., 1946.

GRANT, J. J., Boys' Single-Shot Rifles, Wm. Morrow & Co., N.Y.C., 1967.

———More Single-Shot Rifles, Wm. Morrow & Co., N.Y.C., 1959.

———Single-Shot Rifles, Wm. Morrow & Co., N.Y.C., 1947.

GREENER, W. W., The Gun and Its Development, Cassell & Co., London, England, 1884. (2nd Ed.)

———The Gun and Its Development, Bonanza Books, N.Y.C., 1967. (9th, Reprint)

HACKLEY, F. W., WOODIN, W. H., and SCRANTON, E. L., History of Modern U. S. Military Small Arms Ammunition, Macmillan Co., N.Y.C., 1967.

HATCH, A., Remington Arms in American History, Rinehart & Co., N.Y.C., 1956.

HATCHER, J. S., Hatcher's Notebook, Telegraph Press, Harrisburg, Pa., 1957.

———Pistols and Revolvers, Small Arms Technical Publishing Co., Marshallton, Dela., 1927.

———Textbook of Pistols and Revolvers, Small Arms Technical Publishing Co., Plantersville, S.C., 1935.

HAVEN, C. T., and BELDEN, F. A., A History of the Colt Revolver, Wm. Morrow & Co., N.Y.C., 1940.

HIMMELWRIGHT, A.L.A., Pistol and Revolver Shooting, Outing Publishing Co., N.Y.C., 1915.

———The Pistol and Revolver, Remington Arms-Union Metallic Cartridge Co., N.Y.C., 1908.

HOWE, J. V., The Modern Gunsmith, Funk & Wagnalls, N.Y.C., 1934.

HOWE, W., Professional Gunsmithing, Small Arms Technical Publishing Co., Plantersville, S.C., 1946.

INGALLS, J. M., Exterior Ballistics in the Plane of Fire, Van Nostrand, N.Y.C., 1886.

JOHNSON, M. M. and HAVEN, C. T., Automatic Arms, Wm. Morrow & Co., N.Y.C., 1941.

JONES, H. E., Luger Variations, Torrance, Cal., 1959.

KARR, C. L., Jr., KARR, C. R., Remington Handguns, Stackpole, Harrisburg, Pa., 1960.

285

KEITH, E., Big Game Rifles and Cartridges, Small Arms Technical Publishing Co., Plantersville, S.C., 1936.

——Rifles for Large Game, Standard Publications, Inc., Huntington, W. Va., 1946.

——Sixgun Cartridges and Loads, Small Arms Technical Publishing Co., Onslow Co., N.C., 1936.

——Sixguns, Stackpole, Harrisburg, Pa., 1961.

KOLLER, L. R., Shots at Whitetail, Little, Brown & Co., Boston, Mass., 1948.

LANDIS, C. S., Twenty-Two Caliber Varmint Rifles, Small Arms Technical Publishing Co., Georgetown, S.C., 1947.

——Woodchucks and Woodchuck Rifles, Greenberg, N.Y.C., 1951.

LAVIN, J. D., A History of Spanish Firearms, Arco Publishing Company, N.Y.C., 1965.

LEWIS, B. R., Small Arms & Ammunition in the U. S. Service, Smithsonian Institution, Washington, D.C., 1960.

LOGAN, H. C., Cartridges, Stackpole, Harrisburg, Pa., 1952.

——Underhammer Guns, Stackpole, Harrisburg, Pa., 1960.

LORD, F. A., Civil War Collector's Encyclopedia, Stackpole, Harrisburg, Pa., 1963.

LOWRY, E. D., Exterior Ballistics of Small Arms Projectiles, Olin Mathieson Chemical Corp., New Haven, Conn., 1965.

LOWRY, E. D., Interior Ballistics, Doubleday & Co., Inc., 1968.

MacFARLAND, H. E., Gunsmithing Simplified, Combat Forces Press, Washington, D.C., 1953.

——Introduction to Modern Gunsmithing, Stackpole, Harrisburg, Pa., 1965.

MADIS, G., The Winchester Book, Taylor Publishing Co., Dallas, Texas, 1961.

MAHRHOLDT, R., Waffen-Lexicon, F. C. Mayer, Munchen, Germany, 1957.

MANN, F. W., The Bullet's Flight, Ray Riling, Philadelphia, Pa., 1965.

MATHEWS, J. H., Firearms Identification, U. of Wisc. Press, Madison, Wisc., 1962. (2 Vols.)

MATTERN, J. R., Handloading Ammunition, Small Arms Technical Publishing Co., Marshallton, Dela., 1926.

McCAWLEY, E. S., Jr., Shotguns and Shooting, Van Nostrand, Princeton, N.J., 1965.

MOORE, W., Guns, The Development of Firearms, Air Guns and Cartridges, Grosset & Dunlap, N.Y.C., 1963.

MOULTON, F. R., Methods in Exterior Ballistics, Dover Publications, Inc., N.Y.C., 1962.

MUSGRAVE, D. D., and NELSON, T. B., The World' Assault Rifles and Automatic Carbines, T.B.N. Enterprises, Alexandria, Va., 1967.

NARAMORE, EARL, Principles and Practice of Loading Ammunition, Small Arms Technical Publishing Co., Georgetown, S.C., 1954.

NEAL, R. J., and JINKS, R. G., Smith and Wesson 1857-1945, A. S. Barnes, N.Y.C., 1966.

NELSON, T. B., and LOCKHOVEN, H. B., The World's Submachine Guns, International Small Arms Publishers, Cologne, Germany, 1963.

NESS, F. C., Practical Dope on the Big Bores, Stackpole & Heck, Harrisburg, Pa., 1948.

——Practical Dope on the .22, Stackpole, Harrisburg, Pa., 1955.

NEUMAN, G. D., The History of Weapons of the American Revolution, Harper & Row, N.Y.C., 1967.

NEWELL, D. A., Gunstock Finishing and Care, Stackpole, Harrisburg, Pa., 1966.

NONTE, G. C., Jr., The Home Guide to Cartridge Conversions, Stackpole, Harrisburg, Pa., 1967. (2nd Ed.)

NUTTER, W. E., Manhattan Firearms, Stackpole, Harrisburg, Pa., 1958.

OLSON, L. E., Mauser Bolt Rifles, Fadco Publishing Co., Beverly Hills, Cal., 1957.

OMMUNDSEN, H. and ROBINSON, H. H., Rifles and Ammunition, Waverley Book Co., London, England, 1915.

PARSONS, J. E., Smith & Wesson Revolvers, Wm. Morrow & Co., N.Y.C., 1957.

POLLARD, H. B. C., Automatic Pistols, WE, Old Greenwich, Conn., 1920.

REYNOLDS, E. G. B., The Lee-Enfield Rifle, Arco Publishing Co., N.Y.C., 1962.

RICHARDSON, P. W., Exterior Ballistics and Miscellaneous Notes, Published for private circulation, 1918.

RILING, R., Guns and Shooting, Greenberg, N.Y.C., 1951.

——The Powder Flask Book, Robt. Halter, New Hope, Pa., 1953.

ROBERTS, N., and WATERS, KEN, The Breech-Loading Single-Shot Match Rifle, Van Nostrand, Princeton, N.J., 1967.

ROBERTS, N. H., The Muzzle-Loading Cap Lock Rifle, Stackpole, Harrisburg, Pa., 1952.

SCHMIDT, R., Die Handfeuerwaffen (2 Vols.), Akademische Druck u. Verlagsanstalt, Graz, Austria, 1968.

SCHMUDERER-MARETSCH, M., Jagd-Und Sport-Waffenkunde, Paul Parey, Berlin, Germany, 1928.

SERVEN, J. E., Colt Firearms 1836-1960, Serven Books, Santa Ana, Cal., 1960.

SHARPE, P. B., Complete Guide to Handloading, Funk & Wagnalls Co., N.Y.C., 1953.

——The Rifle in America, Funk & Wagnalls Co., N.Y.C., 1958.

SIMMONS, R. F., Wildcat Cartridges, Wm. Morrow & Co., N.Y.C., 1947.

SMITH, W.H.B. with BELLAH, K., Book of Pistols and Revolvers, Stackpole, Harrisburg, Pa., 1965.

SMITH, W.H.B., with SMITH, J. E., Small Arms of the World, Stackpole, Harrisburg, Pa., 1966.

SMITH, W.H.B., The Book of Rifles, Stackpole, Harrisburg, Pa., 1963.

STEINDLER, R. A., Modern ABC of Guns, Stackpole, Harrisburg, Pa., 1965.
———Reloader's Guide, Stoeger Arms Corp., S. Hackensack, N.J., 1968. (2nd Ed.)
STERN, D. K., 10 Shots Quick, Globe Press, San Jose, Cal., 1967.
STOECKEL, J. F. (STØCKEL) Vols. 1 & 2. Haandskydevaabens Bedommelse (A Consideration of Gunmakers), Norlundes Bogtrykkeri, Kopenhaven, Dan., 1964.
SUYDAM, C. R., The American Cartridge, G. R. Lawrence, Santa Ana, Cal., 1960.
SWANSON, E., Automatic Pistols, Wesmore Book Co., Weehawken, N.J., 1955.
TAYLERSON, A. W. F., ANDREWS, R. A. N., FRITH, J., The Revolver 1818-1865, Crown Publishers, Inc., N.Y.C., 1968.
TAYLERSON, A. W. F., The Revolver 1865-1888, Crown Publishers, Inc., N.Y.C., 1966.
TAYLOR, J., African Rifles and Cartridges, Stackpole, Harrisburg, Pa., 1948.
THIERBACH, M., Die Geschichtliche Entwicklung der Handfeuerwaffen, Akademische Druck u. Verlagsanstalt, Graz, Austria, 1965.
THOMAS, GOUGH (PSEUD.), Shotguns and Cartridges, Percival Marshall & Co., London, England, 1963.
THOMAS, H. H., The Story of Allen and Wheelock Firearms, H. H. Thomas, Lexington, Ky., 1965.
VICKERY, W. F., Advanced Gunsmithing, Small Arms Technical Publishing Co., Georgetown, S.C., 1955.
WAHL, P., & TOPPEL, D., The Gatling Gun, Arco Publishing Co., N.Y.C., 1965.
WALLACK, L. R., The Anatomy of Firearms, Simon & Schuster, N.Y.C., 1965.
WATROUS, G. R. (Ed. Hall, T.E., and Kuhlhoff, P.), The History of Winchester Firearms 1866-1966, Winchester-Western Press, N.Y.C., 1966.
WHELEN, TOWNSEND, Small Arms Design & Ballistics, Small Arms Technical Publishing Co., Georgetown, S.C., 1945.
———The American Rifle, Century Co., N.Y.C., 1920.
———The Hunting Rifle, Stackpole & Heck, Harrisburg, Pa., 1940.
———Ed., The Ultimate in Rifle Precision, Stackpole, Harrisburg, Pa., 1958.
———Why Not Load Your Own?, Combat Forces Press, Washington, D.C., 1957.
WHITE, H. P. and MUNHALL, B. D., Cartridge Headstamp Guide, H. P. White Laboratory, Bel Air, Md., 1963.
———Centerfire Metric Pistol and Revolver Cartridges, Infantry Journal Press, Washington, D.C., 1948.
WHITE, H. P., MUNHALL, B. D. and BEARSE, R., Pistol and Revolver Cartridges, A. S. Barnes & Co., N.Y.C., 1967.
WINANT, L., Early Percussion Firearms, Wm. Morrow & Co., N.Y.C., 1959.